SPIRIT WARRIORS

SPIRIT WARRIORS

*Exorcism for the
Ekklesia*

L. T. MASSEY, PHD

Silver Dove Broadcasting

COPYRIGHT

Bible Quotations from King James & New King James Versions
ISBN 978-0-926392-02-1

Silver Dove Broadcasting Ministries
33 Archer Way - Dahlonega, Georgia 30533 USA
Website: https://www.SpiritWarriors.us
Email: SpiritWarriors@windstream.net

Cover Photo ©2018. NASA/ESAM *La Carina Nébula*, NGC3372. Livio and the Hubble 20th Anniversary Team. One of the Milky Way's premier star factories is *La Carina Nebula* which came to life about three million years ago when stars first ignited in a cloud of molecular hydrogen. In this view, jets of gas erupt from infant stars emerging from their birthplaces. All rights reserved.

PUBLICATIONS

*"Therefore, every scribe instructed concerning the
kingdom of heaven is like a householder who brings
out of his treasure, things new and old."*
~ Matthew 13:52

Massey, Laurel T., *The GUIDE: Becoming a Spirit Warrior & Intercessor* (2022), Morris Publishing USA.

Massey, Laurel T., *Spirit Warriors ~ Exorcism for the Ekklesia.* ePUB (2023) Silver Dove Broadcasting.

Massey, Laurel T., *El Unico Verdadero, Dios mas Alto.* (2022) Silver Dove Broadcasting. USA

Massey, Laurel T., *The One True, Most High God* (2005, 2023). Silver Dove Broadcasting. USA

Hughes, Laurel T., *Issues of Conscience ~ Journals on the Science & Sale of Life.* (2000) Bridge-Logos Publisher.

Hughes, Laurel T., *El Alimento Perfecto ~ Enciclopedia de la Mujer Cristiana, Toma 2* (1994), Morris Press, USA.

Hughes, Laurel T., *Combat Manual ~ Prayer Counseling for Deliverance.* (1988) English & Hindi, Word Vision Publishers

Slade, Laurel G., 175 *Consejos Para Reuniones de Mujeres.* (1979) Barcelona, Spain, Editorial CLIE.

Slade, Laurel G., *El Alimento Perfecto Toma 1* (1977), Bogotá, Colombia. Worldwide Evangelism Crusade - La Buena Semilla.

Chaplain Kurt and Laurel Massey serve Jesus with bible-based training materials, website resources, radio broadcasting and serving believers in the chapel community of Ekklesia 30533 of North Georgia. Contact them for speaking, conferences, and on-site training. WEB: www.SpiritWarriors.US contains a library of free podcasts, materials and online ordering.

The CHRISTIAN WARRIOR Series

By Dr. L.T. Massey

> "Enemy-occupied territory---that is what this world is. Christianity is the story of how the rightful king has landed, you might say landed in disguise, and is calling us to take part in a great campaign of sabotage." - C.S. Lewis (1960), *Mere Christianity*

Writing a book series for mature believers in Christ Jesus, is an ambitious task. There are a few upcoming books to be written. The last four titles are an endeavor to complete in a future no one can hold to surely. This is my faith list that the Lord God will grant the strength of body and spirit in collaboration with Him, by a sound mind with the tenacity to finish well.

Perhaps there will be more, or perhaps not.

No matter with books and the telling of stories.

But regarding life, we do know that all lives matter to the Redeemer who made the way possible and eternal. Heaven is filled with only the ones who made Jesus Christ matter to them. Hell is filled with only the ones who never chose Jesus Christ to matter with them. The world is filled with people who need to know the difference and the Christian Warrior's assignment is to tell it plainly and often.

BOOK 1. Spirit Warriors ~ Exorcism for the Ekklesia (Oct., 2021). This is the first in the Christian Warrior Series set forth as a practical guide to the deliverance of evil spirits that harass and possess. Its truths establish a warrior servant class for Jesus Christ's Kingdom for right now, amid the chaotic global events of the End Times and multiple false narratives. It is available in the ePUB format. The book has 340 pages, 6"x9", coil bound when ordered from the author at her website and perfect bound when ordered from Internet providers. Second reprint (July, 2023). ISBN 978-0-926392-02-1.

BOOK 2. The GUIDE ~ Becoming a Spirit Warrior & Intercessor (June, 2022). This second book in the Christian Warrior Series is the step-by-step working guide for developing believers to walk in their gifts and calling as deliverance chaplains. It uses *Spirit Warriors – Exorcism for the Ekklesia* as its textbook for individual or group learning.

Step-by-step leadership principles guides new and seasoned group leaders from pre-planning to completing the eight-week interactive study course that finishes with a Certification launching men and women into ministry. The format is 8.5"x11" with a 170 page count in a coil-bound workbook when ordered from the author's website. ISBN 978-0-926392-03-8.

BOOK 3. Spirit Warrior's Advanced Strategies -The Craft of Expelling EVIL. (Sep. 2023). Christian Warriors with some deliverance experience will appreciate this updated version of the classic first book. In it are new materials, stories, alien encounters, the giants, and exact methods for combating evil—not just facing off with low-level demons.

World empires are vying for position as billionaires, bored with having just money, conspire to control all under their cloaks of evil. A special section will emphasize the world web of the elite (their term) Free Masons This book has 325 pages in perfect bound and ePUB. ISBN 978-0-926392-09-0.

BOOK 4 Revelation Warriors ~ The Code of Sevens (2024). This third book in the series begins in the first chapter of *The Revelation of Jesus Christ* and marches through the events of the end moments of Church utilization up to the biblical moment Christ returns for His faithful bride (Revelation 14). This Day of the Lord will be the climax to the sounding of the seventh trumpet as He said. It joyfully reveals the multiple Sevens of God. Revelation Warriors are born-again believers who will experience the last apostate church age, watch the opening of Seven Seals, and hear the Seven Trumpets blown.

Are you prepared for the mass psychosis of the Antichrist, the realistic AI robotic technology that deludes the entire world, the deceptive holograms of psychosis, super warfare avatars, alien invasion hoaxes, unmasking gender dysphoria, embracing the iconic 666 tattoo to survive life, seeing the False Prophet propagandize his media to establish a one-world religious structure that will sadly witness millions perish? Then there's Israel. ISBN 978-0-926392-07-6.

BOOK 5: Millennium Warriors ~ 1,000 Years with the King. Book 5 is a researched view of the last eight chapters of the revealed prophecies by Jesus Christ, completing the study of *The Revelation.* It explains the order of events to those left on Earth during the last perilous years of the greatest impact of Tribulation with the unleashing of God's wrath of retribution.

These new believers will have seen Messiah arrive to take back His saints but did not believe in Him before that event. Most of the world was left behind in shock and despair and revival broke out. These few--mostly Jews--will firmly believe in their Messiah and redeemed by faith, conscripted into serving as Tribulation Warriors for the Gospel of Christ.

Exciting clusters of *The Code of Sevens* keep going until the termination of *The Revelation* when everyone shouts: MARANATHA! Even so, come quickly Lord Jesus! These profoundly saved warriors will live through the remaining seven bowl judgments emptied against Antichrist and the False Prophet, when Satan is finally bound in supernatural chains by the powerful Apollyon of the Bottomless Pit.

Readers will learn of the fates of the dark angels, the world-class warriors gathered at Armageddon, and how Jesus Christ, as witnessed by His army, takes them all down. Judgment Day has come. The sentencing of the unsaved is made. The rewards are granted for all overcomers who will enter the visible Kingdom Age to reign with King Jesus at this last return to dwell in His own, one-world government for the next 1,000 years.

BOOK 6. Kingdom Warriors: Running Hard & Finishing Well. This book in the series shows the valuable biblical phases of maturing in Christ. It takes us from the status of totally lost to celebrating the holy assignments of living for Christ as a bride-partner. Right now, before everything hits the fan, no matter at what time the spiritual journey has begun, readers will master Christ's principles for blessed and triumphant living.

Do you understand what is valuable to the Father for the here and now for the faithful? Who will become the obedient, the tip of the spear, the faithful unto death to gain their eternal rewards? *Kingdom Warriors* reveals the vibrant Christ-follower who, moment-by-moment, is tuned to God's voice in daily living plus able to capture the two dozen 'Mysteries of the Kingdom' that Jesus explained in detail, so critical to be called a child of His own.

BOOK 7. Daily Intel for Warriors. Take time with 366 daily soakings in the presence of the Holy Spirit. You will fine-tune your spirit to understand the stories of triumph and failure following the directions of the Lord for you personally. As to intercessors--petitions, supplications, thanksgivings, and deeply felt groaning will reach the throne room of Heaven that thunders back results to earth. *Daily Intel for Warriors* will refill the tattered soul. you will experience a spiritual 'fireside chat' that sees, hears, and feels the turbulence outside but has become fearless inside. Even the Generals rest and refocus at each season of life and this devotional will rejoice in that personal passage.

DEDICATION

"Therefore, every scribe instructed
concerning the kingdom of heaven is like a householder
who brings out of his treasure things new and old."
Matthew 13:52

This work is dedicated to You, my Lord Jesus Christ—who is Everything to me—Redeemer, Way-maker, Spirit Warrior, Ever Faithful One, Lover, Universe Creator, The One True, Most High God, and my very best Friend.

Deep affection for making life memorable goes to the love of my life, the exceptional Kurt W. Massey with a grateful heart for our marriage, intimate friendship, the joy and laughter we share, and the radio ministry we produce as the two *Bible Voices for Today* heard in Canada, Israel, East Africa, the United States, and beyond.

Special love to my precious mother Genevieve and outstanding father, Alton Tarris who showed me what a godly father is, so I could embrace my heavenly Father for my lifetime and eternal journey.

A grateful dedication to Rose Clary a visionary, and to Judith Rainey, close friend, pro-life warrior, and radio co-broadcaster. This is given to all of you new and experienced Spirit Warriors: may we have wonderful and miraculous stories to tell one another with all the saints who have paved the way before us, with their unique exploits that the Lord Jesus has done on the battlefields of the centuries.

Dahlonega, Georgia
September 2021

XII - DEDICATION

CONTENTS

FOREWORD

"Teaching the Coming Kingdom of God
and the Republic for Which We Stand"
- Professor Toto Vaughn

Dr. Laurel Massey has perceived by the Spirit of God, the pinpointed need for this hour. Many think that our current problems are political, societal, or ecclesiastical but nothing could be further from the truth: they are spiritual.

Until we as a people truly understand what is written in this book, we will continue to wind back up at the beginning of the same circles that we are running in. I wish to thank the author for her tireless work in bringing the real truth to the forefront. Only when we understand the principles laid out in this writing, can we effectively deal with society's many plagues of addictions and mental torments.

In a time when fear is ravishing the land of America and the nations of the world, the information contained in this writing will bring calm to those troubled seas of your mind. Herein, in these pages, lies the keys to the abyss of misunderstanding and misapplied focus and prayers. These truths will forever pull back the curtains for you, so you can see clearly and understand perfectly.

Bishop Shane Vaughn, Th.D.
~ a.k.a. 'Professor Toto'
First Harvest Ministries
Waveland, Mississippi

PREFACE

"The promise of God is that we will have internal rivers
of water flowing into everlasting life.[1] *To live at an*
oasis in the desert is the very symbol of power.
Everyone must come to those who have access to life-giving water.
Everything lives where the river flows.
~ Graham Cooke

Welcome to the world of the unseen and supernatural of the Living Yahweh, Creator of all!

The writing of this book was compiled with the wisdom of the Holy One by insights gained through practical exorcism experiences since 1972 on a South American field of service. It was inspired by the fresh, deeper truths gleaned in a scholarly dedication to biblical accuracy, and by acutely listening to the voice of the Holy Spirit over decades of study and journal entries.[2]

Spirit Warriors was intentionally composed as a strategic guide for Christian believers and doers to biblically handle the directives of Jesus Christ's Great Commission[3] that sets at liberty those captivated and captured by Satan. Its purposes are both to learn the believer's authority in exorcism and to implement the Holy One's gifts to do so.[4]

We begin with our best and perfect Mentor, Jesus Christ's own call to this ministry, and with the very prophecy given thousands of years before His advent in Bethlehem. He fulfilled His Messianic calling described by the prophet Isaiah.[5] It is this citation that is brought to the crowd's remembrance in the gospels of Mark and Luke[6] when Jesus begins to publicly serve His Father and enlighten all who would pause to listen.

You will notice a group of Readings listed at the end of the book. These Readings address specific issues that may be interesting in expanding your knowledge in the supernatural realm of the ekklesia (New Testament-based local churches).

One is the story of Corrie ten Boon and how forgiveness for the most terrible criminal of Nazi Germany, freed her. Along that theme, Reading 5 discusses the principle of binding and loosing in context of how and why Jesus taught it. It surprised me and might surprise you to see how this principle has been misused, avoided, or neglected in deliverance for decades.

While the world looks for demonic paranormal connections, Spirit Warriors clarify the godly supernatural dimension of our living King as our Source of authority, power, and gifting to push back the gates of Hell for those asking for help (Seekers). It 'pulls back the curtain' of deception and destruction while providing God's solutions and purposes.

Finally, the Appendices are concentrated definitions and outlines for practical reference and application during deliverance sessions. For instance, *Appendix A* contains *The Declaration of Faith* to be recited at each Seeker's first session. Salvation is the most critical deliverance possible and fully addressed then.

It nullifies the sting of death and for that reason, we must understand it and able to communicate exactly just what biblical salvation is and what it is not. As *The Confession of Faith* is repeated by the Seeker publicly to the team, it confirms and declares their salvation commitment to Jesus Christ. What the demons hear is a declaration of war and they are on the wrong side.

Sinners can be (and many are) demon possessed. Christians cannot be possessed by the devil. We are possessed, owned, bought, and paid for by the blood of Jesus Christ.

Christians can however, be demonized, harassed, tormented, made to feel guilty, falsely accused, and consistently abused like a thorn in their side, by evil beings they have complete control over, if they only knew it. This body of information will help you know it and how to expel them from self and others.

At the conclusion of most chapters is a bit of space left over. Why waste that blank paper? This is a place for you to express your thoughts and make notes for personal application of how the Holy Spirit is impressing or challenging you. Consider using what you learn to encourage other believers to step forward as Spirit Warriors.

[1] John 7:38. Graham Cooke quote from *"Keys to Brilliant Focus – The Power of Wisdom to Reclaim Your Identity"* (2012), Book 3.

[2] King James and New King James bible versions and Strong's Exhaustive Concordance of the Bible complied by James Strong, STD, LLD, along with dictionaries of the original Hebrew Old Testament and the Greek New Testament.

[3] Mark 16:15-18; Matthew 28:18-20; Luke 24:44-49.

[4] 1 Corinthians 12:1-11.

[5] Isaiah 61:1, "To proclaim liberty to the captives, and the opening of the prison to those who are bound."

[6] Mark 16:14-18, along with the promise of the Holy Spirit in Luke 24:46-49 to implement that commission to preach the full gospel (*Sozo*).

INTRODUCTION

The Critical Need for Spirit Warriors

"Character comes before equipping;
Obedience to His voice will hold the anointing;
Gifts are supernatural flashes from the Holy One to
Convince death-encrusted pagans that
The Christ—Redeemer Jesus—
Is their sole way out of death's capture
Into the health of Liberty and Light.
Spirit Warriors can help get them there." L. T. Massey

We have entered a time warp that was created when Jesus Christ stepped off His throne and was handed the scroll of the endings to unravel of church time.[1] Seven impenetrable seals fastened these timed events on the curled scroll of the ages. This was *the little book*[2] the prophet Daniel held in his mind as images of fantastic phantoms raced before him, throwing him into the dust. Unimaginable and indiscernible visions came at the last of his life that stunned him to silence for days.

Truly, he had no vocabulary to work with. Thankfully, he only had a foretaste of the violent, the bizarre, the technological, the horrific actors and cataclysmic events demons would inspire and raging humans would implement.

Much more was built on just cracking open Daniel's *little book* by Jesus' closest human friend, John, when he was mysteriously sent to a prison island in old age while the other disciples became martyrs for their Lord. John, the bishop of Jerusalem's church was instructed to write, *"The Revelation of Jesus Christ, which God gave Him to show His servants—things which must shortly take place. And He sent and signified it by His angel to His servant John who bore witness to the word of God, and to the testimony of Jesus Christ, to all things that he saw."*[3]

My, oh my, oh my.

When we were in 2021, it seemed to be the very threshold of the final days' disclosures with reeling from the shakeup of just the Second Seal's opening![4] The First Seal slid past those Watchers when the, yet unknown Antichrist, quietly rode his misrepresented white horse of peace[5] onto world scenes that eerily were looking like the days of Noah. Antichrist has been busy for decades setting up coalitions of the very influential, extremely wealthy, brilliantly minded, media geniuses, the military war hungry, the technology savvy, and the politically well-positioned all-wicked ones. He has an elaborate Satanically planned future for us.

Antichrist[6] and those with him, are lusting for the top of the world position that Jesus will make certain they will end at the bottom of the world. This man will be exposed as Antichrist on exactly the day and way Jesus Christ told us[7] so those of us who are watching, will truly recognize him just as he is well known in the spirit world.

The infusion of Satan himself into the Antichrist causes the world power coalition to make him supreme world leader (for one hour) that is a throne, power to carry it out, and their positional authority,[8] all to be used as a puppet (just as Satan infused Judas Iscariot, Caligula, Hitler, Stalin, Mao, Margaret Sanger, Karl Marx, and many, many others) to do his bidding. He was trespassing inside their minds.

Moving forward, the entire world is at the precipice of anxiety created by Christ's releasing of the Second Seal as, *"Another horse, a fiery red, went out. And it was granted to the one who sat on it to take peace from the earth, and that people should kill one another; and there was given to him a great* sword."[9]

"People killing people" is not necessarily a conflict using military personnel and materiel (this will come later during the bowl judgments of Revelation 16). It can mean to simply create a voluntary and/or

mandated bio-terrorism, untested medical experimental drugs erroneously called a 'vaccine' when it does not fill that science, to injure and kill millions globally *("a great sword")*.

This is well underway. In the next event of the Third Seal, think of the domination of exclusive central bank digital control, manipulation of sources of food, water, and basic survival.[10] This makes global control possible! Antichrist will have all this power with the consent of the world's elites for several years, maybe before he is even recognized as such.

It is history by now, but we have contemporaneously lived through the blanketing stratosphere of unreasonable global fear, with governments collapsing, church buildings and ministries folding up by the hundreds of thousands with the reality that some would never reopen. Did it perpetrate the persecution in all places mastered by the principality of fear and its cohorts of anxiety, suicide, and death by poison? As if this masquerade was all it took to cease worshiping our God! But it was.

Early days, you remember, many followed untested opinions and rules. Nations dried up. Many died, yes, but at the average rate of death for the annual standard influenza, despite using those cruelly imposed protocol precautions. Soon, we were overrun by corruption when the Bill of Rights and other liberties were kicked to the curb...until some brave legal souls pushed back with Constitutional lawsuits and won them.

By 2021, only the most daring Christ-centered ministries that could hear from God and stepped forward to stay open, remain unmasked, continue to sing, and embrace, brought social sanity. As we know now, it takes some time for real push-back (strong faith to persevere) to circulate cases through the sludge of legal swamps to make its way to Lady Justice.

Good news! North of the border in Canada (July 2021), one citizen[11] brought a lawsuit to stop the masking that made multiple thousands of children and asthmatics ill; the distancing, lock downs, the closed schools, and businesses, and so forth, and won their freedoms back with a court question that proved unanswerable by the government and Big Pharma: "Did you isolate the Covid-19 virus?" "Can you prove it exists?" And they could not. Because as valid virologists have told the world for months, Covid-19 proved to be a mild cousin to the common cold and is indistinguishable. It does not exist as a novel virus.

The real weapon would prove to be the fake 'vaccine' jab, not a virus concoction used as an excuse to get the jab. This plan-epidemic was an international deception where their supposed cure was worse than what was fabricated in a lab.

Undoubtedly it takes our resistance to injustice to maintain liberties. When the bullies take your valuables, you get them back or suffer loss. It only took one courageous citizen using the authority of the Canadian Constitution, to win. Spirit Warriors have far greater authority from the God of the universe to strongly resist the demonic trespassers and captors until there is no place left for them among us.

Why do we need Spirit Warriors today?

The nation's resulting cultural vacuum was immediately filled by a well-paid rebellious thuggery, philosophically prepped to wreak Marxist havoc. We watched their processes unfold by their total disregard of the law, going straight to the streets in violence, looting, criminality, the unhindered removal of historic statuary, with burning, assault, and wantonly killing innocent bystanders and business owners trying to protect their property after law enforcement was neutralized by local governing authorities to 'defund the violence.'

They defunded their own protection.

Police officers were then targeted to kill, many times with the blessing of extremely liberal gubernatorial and state political hacks overrunning major cities. A sucking sound was heard as residents of California, Illinois, New York, Seattle, Oregon, Minnesota, Wisconsin, and other liberal areas vacated to low/no tax, safer states. *Black Lives Matter* (BLM) was painted across Wall Street's elite pavements, plastered in isolated ghettos, and blazed its path across television screens as the new mantra. The organization would fade within two years as corruption in the multi-millions among its leaders was exposed. Wait for it.

"RIOT! You Gotta Love Us!" They insisted in the streets.

With that shutdown came a heavy upswing in suicide, divorce, child and elder abuse, unemployment, criminality, lack of common necessities, and media blackouts on common sense. Abortion facilities, bars and liquor stores, gambling casinos, all were immune to lock downs but churches were not. Oh wait, a presidential election was coming up! Don't let those Christians get together to discuss what was really going on and stop it.

Interestingly, this Neo-Marxist movement used a superficial pretext to incite violence against supposed racism that coupled with the COVID-19 fears as a volatile cocktail for national takeover. But truth will come out. Black conservative Christian radio host Abraham Hamilton, III,[12] established the connection between trained and funded Marxists and witchcraft practices within the top leadership of these groups. They came on the streets for violence and to "speak to the spirits of the dead"[13] to receive power and keep the charade up on behalf of the more powerful, world dominating elite with their consuming Agenda-30. There is no doubt that the root behind that organization is rebellion and witchcraft.

How do we Spirit Warriors see through all this political and social clutter that is just beginning? This is the real world and Seekers are often confused, deceived, anxious, victims, and sometimes desperate enough to volunteer for experimental untested, and proven deadly inoculations.

Now they stand before you as Seekers of hope for some relief.

How do you prepare for this in your life and in the lives of others? By going deeper. We see the prophetic one-world government of the Antichrist on the horizon. Powerful nations standing in the way must be neutralized and cannibalized first, shutting down Christians as the first line of watchmen on the wall by fueling fear-mongering over anything godly that previously worked in society.

By late 2020, President Donald J. Trump and Secretary of State began brokering Middle East peace and open trade treaties between centuries-long enemies. This had never been accomplished in world history, but God said it was time. Islamic nations were timidly coming to the White House table to sit with Israel, bringing nominations for the Nobel Peace Prize in their wake. Extraordinary. End times. But it did not last long enough with the rumored illegal election overthrow of 2020. Israel again was left without backup.

Spirit Warriors are needed in all places!

> *"For rebellion is as the sin of witchcraft and stubbornness is as iniquity and idolatry."*[14]

To God, these twin sins are equal in nature and outcome. Rebellion is a craft that is planned, educated, organized by deception, and violently implemented publicly. It has two faces: the face of witchcraft (occult) and the face of stubbornness (the 'my way' spirit). It is an occult religion publicly calling on unnatural spirits to validate the objectives worked toward through traded-for demon power to succeed for them. God calls that iniquity and idolatry: the taking of strange gods.

Rebellion is first evident in the soul then acted out in the body. Rebellion against God's natural and stated ways is equal to demonic witchcraft, stubbornness, and love of evil. These deeply offending sins usurp the human spirit to subdue and cower in the master power of this age, Fear. When eventually it is acted out by the soul and body, an unresistant trail of destruction right to Apollyon, is cut toward death.

Rebellion is an evil twist on the invention of novel (never seen before) approaches to do evil. For a few examples, take bio-terrorism where invented diseases are released worldwide, the unseen drone bombings of civilians, the use of women and children as human shields; shooting uninvolved people asleep in their beds, and taking out cops parked in patrol cars. Then there are the hijackings of political parties and church denominations, the use of supposed racism and white guilt as sparks to ignite rebellion as done in 1917 Russia. This is a craft at work!

The list of needs seems endless. There is still open slavery in African nations by mostly Muslims, while in Communist China, enforced prison and work camp extermination of Christians are put together to harvest organs. We hear of physical and psychological torture and walk past marketed chemical abortion pills in big box stores purchased by over-the-counter sales that hides sex slavery for pimps. The well-educated and wealthy use medical license to make gender selections of the unborn to obtain their favored traits, killing the rest not on their list. And, the deception of transgenderism is taking its toll from military to Hollywood.

Do we need Spirit Warriors to bring deliverance today?

The list of horrific sin snares goes on. Think of the exposed medical cannibalism of human baby parts 'for scientific research;'[15] the buying and selling of children and adults as sex slaves (pizza-gate, sex pleasure islands for the ultra wealthy and royal), or planned famines, wars, pestilences, and assassinations for political and material gain. Other evil schemes go with conceiving children just to sell for profit or use to offer in Satanic worship by the spirit of Moloch. The list of twisted evils is endless now, and we haven't even mentioned the proliferation of electronic deceptions and greed traps that are billion-dollar industries.

Murder, euthanasia, and suicide are aggressive death-acts grieving Father God as the Giver of those lives. Committing these abominable iniquities, in effect declares, "*I will* take my own life or another's life *when I want to*, not how or when God ordains its end. This soul position attempts to set one on the level of God's sovereignty. It says, "I want power over life and death like a god and will commit genocide to get it". It is pure blasphemy. Learn to recognize these areas in Seekers as they talk about their bondage and death choices so their alternatives to life will be understood.

During that most fateful tilt year of 2020, we watched the streets of many nations fall under the false flag of a concocted novel bio-weapon virus touted as causing "an extremely deadly pandemic."[16] It did.

It took a claw's swipe at shaky governments, long dead and luke-warm churches, thriving business operations and children happily going to school. Societies crumbled under a manipulated degree of social control by calling up the principality of fear to the point that officials elected or hired to protect our inalienable rights, discovered how to easily manipulate freedoms from trusting citizens.

Battle Cry! We need Spirit Warriors!

The Name and Blood of Jesus saves, delivers, and heals the body, soul, and spirit. The supernatural DNA of Jesus Christ is covered in Chapter 1. What we focus on is utilizing the name of Jesus Christ as our authority to expel demonic powers, and the power of that authority given to us by the shed lifeblood of Jesus.

Personal salvation debarred us from the clutches of the dark kingdom. The blood of Jesus *"...conveyed us who believe, into the kingdom of the Son of His love...through His blood"*. In the Spirit dimension, this is spirit-translation from one kingdom (the dark one of Satan) into the kingdom of Light that Jesus Christ owns, runs, empowers, and is responsible to His Father for. Let Paul explain it biblically and eternally: *"He has delivered us from the power of darkness and conveyed us into the kingdom of the Son of His love, in whom we have redemption."*

When a Spirit Warrior commands and demands the removal of evil, he and she calls out their authority to do so by invoking the perfect death of Christ's life blood that makes it achievable. This is how seasoned Spirit Warriors like Derek Prince can remain utterly calm and simply speak the demons out of detainees and self-deliverance functions. No shouting, no wild gestures, no desperation as if you don't believe it yourself, but speaking normally because the blood of Jesus has already purchased the power. We must speak it into verbal existence for that place and time.

Dr. Prince will take an hour or more with Seekers going through the steps of confession, forgiveness of others and self, repentance, and release of the idols. Through this method, demons are stripped of power. That is the operational part. Deliverance after these steps is almost automatic invoking the name and blood sacrifice of Jesus Christ (as your permission), is well known in demonic experiences going back centuries.

And, where did we land as we enter these extraordinary times of tribulations without a strong, supernaturally charged Ekklesia leading us out of the devilish chaos?

Jesus was stubbornly and righteously strong-willed in handling religious bigots of His day. He resisted their mediocre humanity corrupted by willing ignorance, their power grabbing, and demonic fears. He set to order their satanic deceptions and reactions for any who would listen, and dispensed their legalism by verbalized Truth. Crushing!

We have that exact technique at our disposal to employ. But it takes faith in Christ's promises and the courage to advance. One other element it takes is the activation of Spirit Warriors in every location where the Word of God is preached, taught, defended, extended, and loved.

NOTE. As Spirit Warriors, we recognize and must disclose that the team is not qualified as medical, mental health, psychological, or counseling experts. Make this disclaimer at the beginning of all sessions and explain it in writing, with signed acknowledgement of Seekers if needed. For teams that have handout literature, write this statement in it clearly. The team is a voluntary unit and not paid for ministering. Participation for exorcism is by voluntary consent of Seekers and ministers.

Jesus told us to, *"Watch and pray, lest you enter into temptation. The spirit indeed is willing but the flesh is weak."*[17] We watch local and world events closely. Then, we ask how to specifically pray so warfare in the heavenlies is initiated.

When we saw 230 American Christian missionaries in an non-negotiated pull out of our troops in Afghanistan beheaded and hundreds in Iraq killed, we are watching the news. USA Today (Aug. 16, 2021), "United States pulls out of Afghanistan and its fall to Taliban terrorists with no plan to evacuate Americans with 10,000-20,000 left in danger to get out as best possible."

We look at the bible and date ourselves to the opening of the Seals of Revelation 6. With this, we are equipped to effectively pray against those dreadful events and perhaps help in some way. Linda McCollum, an ardent intercessor, asked God how she should pray, and He replied, "Pray that they hide and scatter." This was the first step. Be looking for more.

Welcome to the war.

---

[1] Revelation 6, the Seven Seals of God opened by Christ alone.

[2] Daniel, chapter 12

[3] Revelation 1:1-2

[4] Revelation 6:3-4

[5] Revelation 6:1-2

[6] Tim Cohen, "The Antichrist and a Cup of Tea" book and website https://prophecyhouse.com.

[7] Matthew 24:14-15

[8] Revelation 17:11-18

[9] Revelation 6:3-4. Taking the jab of 'covid-19 vaccine', though possibly life threatening, is not the mark of the beast but could be one-half of what is required to make the actual mark of Antichrist function (a tattoo using Bill Gate's patented *Luciferase* ink technology that can electronically communicate with the graphite oxide in the jab, creating unique identifications and data retrieval). Receiving the mark is an act of worship to the Antichrist and a personal choice to believe in him (Revelation 13:14-18). This is not true of only receiving an inoculation. Study this out for yourselves.

[10] Revelation 6:5-6

[11] www.RedVoiceMedia.com. August 6, 2021 on, The Stew Peters Show podcast interviewing Patrick King.

[12] The Hamilton Corner; www.youtube.com/watch?v=xGJSEoirF90.

[13] Oduifa of Uruba people, West Africa is an occult, ancestor worshiping religion where the dead are inquired of to give guidance and provide unnatural power to the "protesters" of BLM (some who may or may not be aware of this connection), asking the demons by witchcraft to drive their acts to higher levels of evil. Check www.MidwestOutreach.org.

[14] 1 Samuel 15:23; Jude 11-13; www.youtube.com/watch?v=xGJSEoirF903.

[15] US Government grants millions to the University of Pittsburgh to handle pre-born organs for profit and research (August 2021).

[16] As of August, 2021, a documented 9000+ have died by taking untested vaccine concoctions of mega-pharmacological with hundreds of thousands injured and permanently harmed. World statistics are even more outrageous, yet the poison is not pulled off market except in several countries that caught on to casualties early and were not involved in the political agenda to keep the hoax going. When only a handful died from the Swine Flu vaccine, it was immediately removed from the market...but that was a different world then. Unexpected was the hundreds of prime young athletes Sudden Adult Death.

[17] Matthew 26:41.

| 1 |

Spirit Warriors On Call

"When demons are outside, resist them.
When they are inside, expel them."
~ Vlad Savchuk

Four Purposes for Deliverance from Evil

There are four concentrations of information in this *Exorcism Guide* as a practical approach for the biblical deliverance of those people captured and harassed by the supernatural forces of evil. It cannot answer all the questions you will have, for you will learn by involvement against these forces on the front lines of demonic activity.

We found some answers and wrote them here, but not all because the warring conflict of the kingdoms act at full force and are often moveable by your level of knowledge and faith. Times are certainly vastly different now than they were in the pre-electronic age, when I was first involved in a South American country for nine years as a young and totally inexperienced medical missionary. But the demons respond the same then as now; they just have some different names.

The first reason for this ministry is to facilitate deliverance for unsaved Seekers who are bound by the captivity of the devil in all ways. It also recognizes that believers who have made wrong and ungodly choices, are seeking repentance and a clean restart.

You will soon realize that this practical manual on expelling demons covers the many aspects of first recognizing the state of salvation—or not. That is the supreme goal. Next, it outlines the unique way freedom is made possible by Christ's blood covenant followed by the Seeker's voluntary allegiance to believe in and follow Jesus Christ all the way. Once in the kingdom, amazing gifts and miracles are available as Christ becomes the Director of lives.

Going deeper, born again, Holy Spirit-filled believers can determine if they are fitted for, and called to learn and practice the deliverance ministry. If you want to explore this ministry, become trained, or simply want to intercede for the need, then here are some preliminary questions for you to ponder:

- Are you already involved with a burden for intercessory prayer for others? How frequent is that ministry engaged?
- Are you certain of, or are you seeking a position in the Kingdom commission of Mark 16:17?
- If a Seeker approached you, can you determine if they have a personal belief and trust in Jesus Christ to redeem them, or will you become the evangelist right then, explaining the simple Gospel?
- Can you function as part of a team under authority?
- Looking at Jesus' ministry, what biblical strategies address the next steps of deliverance after salvation?

The most striking act of salvation–the human spirit rebirth—first seizes a Spirit Warrior from the total depravity of unbelief with its natural eternal consequences. This fact is the primary way to understand how the blocked or opened spiritual access to successful supernatural solutions occurs.

Second regarding seeking believers, you will learn that ministry as an exorcism deliverance team is God's ongoing method for spiritual breakthrough, renewal, course corrections, and the closing of sin portals; as well as, how to escape from the onslaught of the demonic trying to gain reentry.

In this ministry, Spirit Warriors provide to believers the security in Christ of a safe place for honest repentance as the way back to holiness and a righteous relationship with Jesus Christ that he or she forfeited through carnal choices that now are molesting their soul area. With unsaved Seekers, Spirit Warriors provide the most needed missing piece of presenting the Savior and healing.

Third, as a personally Christ-following Spirit Warrior, you will learn to use the powerful manifestations of the Holy Spirit with the authority given by Jesus Christ to exorcist evil spirits and do much more healing as He gives expression to the team.

Exorcism is a service ministry to the unsaved but likewise, one for backslid believers who must make public repentance and reversals (as witnessed by the team) in order to slam shut the doors they opened, and begin functioning in the kingdom as healthy sane participants where they are destined to serve.

We first begin with our best and perfect Mentor, Jesus Christ's own call to this ministry, with the very prophecy given hundreds of years before His first advent at Bethlehem. He fulfilled His Messianic calling described by the prophet Isaiah. It is this citation that is brought to the crowd's remembrance in the Gospel of Luke when Jesus begins to serve His Father

Sozo: The Promises of Full Salvation

Let's begin with a study of some key words that will help extend our understanding of what salvation contains. When you look at the declaration of Jesus Christ describing His destiny[1] and purpose for an Earth visit, this is what we see:

The Spirit of the Lord is upon Me;

Because He hath anointed Me

To preach the gospel to the poor;

He hath sent Me to heal the brokenhearted,

To preach deliverance to the captives,

And recovering of sight to the blind,

To set at liberty them that are bruised,

To preach the acceptable year of the LORD."

Look carefully at the progression in this passage that begins with The Holy Spirit of God, the Spirit's anointing (divine choice) then follows with "the how" it was to happen—by preaching. What was preached?

The Good News that the poor (and we are all destitute of divinity) are targeted for is: (1) salvation. Next comes (2) healing of the broken soul, (3) deliverance for demonized captives, and (4) the opening to God's insight. Finally, the outright (5) gift of liberty is made to become the people He created us to be, and (6) live in peace. Wow, all that accomplished with the word, *sozo*.

Sozo. Root word of *Deliverer, Deliverance, to Deliver* as found in the *King James (KJV)* and the *New King James (NKJV)* bibles. There are about 1700 biblical citations denoting the words: *to deliver, deliverance, deliverer*[2], along with like-related words.

Deliverance. (Strong's[3] #859 NT) - *freedom, pardon, deliverance, forgiveness, liberty, remission.* Noah Webster cites:[4] "Release from captivity, slavery, oppression, or any restraint; rescue from danger or from any evil."

Set at Liberty. (Strong's #1657-1659 NT) - *a condition of unrestrained pleasure; e.g., as a citizen and not as a slave, whether as freeborn or liberated; to be exempt from mortal liability; to deliver and set free to choose.* Noah Webster: "Freedom from restraint; applicable to the body, the will or mind…when not checked or controlled."

Freedom. "A state of exemption from the power or control of another; liberty; exemption from slavery, servitude, or confinement. Freedom is personal, civil, political, and religious". Approaching each situation, supernatural deliverance removes the evil input that contributes to a person's problems so he or she can dispense with the unnatural attachment of a demonic spirit corrupting their soul, as acted out in the body. Then, it effectively reverses damage.

Of primary consideration again, is first receiving or confirming Christ's gift of salvation to remove one from the power of Satan's domain and be translated into Jesus Christ's domain. Our spiritual residence is everything.

The Supernatural DNA of Jesus Christ

We go to Scripture to understand the effective Holy Spirit-led and Father God-led ministry of Jesus Christ. He is our sole model and inspiration that extends our faith for God's results that are His will and for our life's commission. It is vital to understand how our Lord interacted and intervened in the dimension between human freedom and demonic slavery.

Christ's whole life's ministry on earth was completed in Acts 2:1 that could only occur after His obedient life, death, supernatural resurrection, and His securing the keys of death and hell's gate. The power of these keys (divine authority to open and close in the spirit world) was conveyed to His promised supernatural Successor, the Holy Spirit. At this point, His earth assignments were finished. Christ provided, by Himself, conquest over Satan's ability to dominate the human species and that transpired through His *sozo* blood sacrifice.

Jesus Christ brought the revival to the nation of Israel and further, to the rest of the world of faith-filled Gentiles, too, after 480[+] years of God's operational silence. Centuries into the future, two godly Jewish couples would be angelically approached at the exact moments in time that would be *the call* to continue God's plan through two Jewish baby boys: John the Baptizer and his cousin, Jesus of Nazareth.

We pick up on the young adult rabbi, Jesus' vocational office, knowing it as the fulfillment of Old Covenant writings. He began learning and taking this role at twelve when he chose to withdraw from his earthly-only identity to, *"...be about My Father's business".*[5] This was the first signal of revival to come.

The methodical way Christ achieved revival during His appointed season, points us to what revival looks like for our own generation. All true God-initiated revivals begin with the brooding Holy Spirit who initiates the anointing that Jesus Christ lived out. In our flawed human way, the journey begins with intensive seeking of God *for Himself* that precipitates the screaming need for repentance and personal cleansing to align with the new Truth.

Deliverance from the disqualifications of approaching His holiness in an unholy corrupted condition will result in personally and eagerly relinquishing our willfulness, rebellion, pride, and carnality (the old man). We see this ravenous hunger for God as a pattern, time and again in the many historic revivals that stemmed from the original event of the first baptism of and in, the Holy Spirit implemented at Pentecost.

Simply put, it takes seeing our inadequate condition for spiritual intimacy and then renouncing all contaminants of self- and demon-devised encumbrances to enter Truth. With this enlightenment, Seekers are shown the relationship between a saved and unsaved condition as the starting point.

Sometimes they come to be released from a lack of peace and torment while, what they essentially hunger for, is the Lord Jesus Himself. This transition can only take place automatically at salvation. However, for those who have wandered the prodigal ways after tasting the Lord by salvation, it begins with a deep repentance that will not return them to corrupt living again by God's mercy.

[1] Jesus Christ in Luke 4:18-19.

[2] Deuteronomy 17-19; Leviticus 26:6-13; Psalm 34:17-19; Deuteronomy 28:47-48; Isaiah 59:1-2; 1 Samuel 17:47 (The battle is the Lord's); Judges 2:2-3; Joel 2:32; Joshua 23:10; 24:12; Proverbs 11:21; John 8:44-49; Galatians 5:1; 2 Corinthians 1:10; 3:18; and 1 John 3:7-9.

[3] Dr. James Strong (1822-1894). American Methodist theologian and scholarly writing with John McClintock. *"The Exhaustive Concordance of the Bible"* KJV (published 1890).

[4] *American Dictionary of the English Language*, Noah Webster, 1828.

[5] Luke 2:49.

| 2 |

An Inside-the-Kingdom View

"Is death the last stop?
No, it is the awakening." ~ Scott

The Life Blood Testament of Christ

It is critical for Spirit Warriors to deeply understand why Jesus Christ gave His divine life's blood as an eternal personal testament to obedience to the Father. That required Him to relinquish His human body of only three decades of age, as He was violently assailed with multiple attempts on His life. I wonder just how long He could have lived healing the desperately disadvantaged seeking a personal God, if the religious sector had left Him alone to His ministry.

But that took death to the body, a decision made in the Holy Councils of heaven before Earth was considered. He knew all He would be in for including the Father's glance away as centuries of human sin were piled on Him and divinely reckoned with. This is His testament of blood.

Covenants lie between two or more entities. No one must die for it to take place. For example, marriage is a God-covenant of lifelong promises made between a man and woman. When death occurs to one of the holders of that covenant, its legal bindings are severed to that spouse. God made a covenant of promises with Abraham concerning his posterity. Both were living when God offered His covenant to Abraham who had to receive it by faith, to be valid.

In comparison to a *testament,* the expressed will of the maker is only effective after he or she is deceased. Then is can be enacted.[1] Jesus Christ made no covenants while living, but He did make a testament[2] that was new and far reaching by dying at Calvary. In the original King James version, the translators never used the concept of covenant when quoting Jesus' work. It was a testament of Christ's will.

Further evidence shows that upon death, Christ was wrapped and laid in a stone locked chamber for three days. That condition brought the requisite supernatural aspect of release by His victorious resurrection that was apprehended from Death's claims.

From the beginning of the supernatural implantation of Christ into Mary's womb, He represented and fully demonstrated the miraculous Spiritual nature early on and throughout His lifetime. It never ceased. This separation from life into the assault on Death testified to His deity. It is this blood testament authorization His Spirit Warriors possess.

Back on Earth fifty days after the resurrection to life again on the Jewish holy day of Pentecost,[3] the Holy Spirit passionately rushed into the perfect situation with the powerful promises Jesus made to complete His work through us. This was the situation at the birth of the Ekklesia:

It has been 50 days since Jesus Christ ascended in glory and grieving continued but so did expectation. There was a gathering of expectant believers who knew Jesus intimately. They assembled in prayer and waited for the Promise of being in one accord of purpose; they saw the tongues of fire and experienced the Spirit's flame touch each of them, individually. As they pursued Him in corporate prayer, joy rose in praise and each began to vocalize unlearned languages. Each man and woman yielded to the Holy Spirit's direction for infilling to endow them with heavenly utterances of worship and warfare to come.

That day, the Holy Spirit brought His FIRE in the form of flaming tongue-shapes that linked each person to Himself with a dynamic anointing for His purpose that would never leave them. They knew they were spiritually called, their spirits inflamed, and sealed for service. Signs followed as verification.

In this first revival, the exhibition of the Holy Spirit of Fire was evident to its recipients and astonished pagans outside. The result of this sign was visualized by witnesses describing them as a drunken group! Understandable, since they had never seen anything like this in history to explain the phenomenon of exuberant joy and liberty. Drunkenness was the closest reason the unsaved could relate to, and they wanted this baptism of fire for themselves. Faith flowed.

The baptism of the Holy Spirit was vocalized through a multitude of known and unknown languages as all preaching is the good news of Jesus Christ's now, fully operational kingdom. The first fruits of the Church (Ekklesia universal) became evident when about 3,000 of the unsaved hungrily received the gospel and then immediately followed Christ in water baptism[4] as public testimony of their decision.

The culmination of revivals erupts into the physical multiplication of ekklesias, local cores of similarly touched people who fellowship together in a biblically governing system of worship. The enlivened groups increased into many areas through the natural process of planting home-bases to be first discipled by apostles like the married couple of Priscilla and Aquila, Titus, Timothy, Phillip, Apollos, Peter, Barnabas, Paul and many unknown others that will stretch across generations beyond the original ones Jesus named "apostles".

With maturity in the faith, evangelists, pastors, prophets, and teachers were developed and established in faraway locations to spread and keep the Gospel alive. This happened beginning with the gift of evangelism coupled with the correcting prophetic in operation. By establishing tested and committed oversight elders, teachers of God's

Word were developed to disciple new and maturing believers according to the apostles' doctrine.

In other words, the revival morphed functionally as it multiplied because the leadership at Jerusalem did not insist on confining it to their one location. Jesus' kingdom was never limited to the Jerusalem-based leadership since all the offices of Jesus Christ had to naturally expand. Millions were to come from every tongue, tribe, and nation with no man-fabricated boundaries of division by gender, race, nation, or age limitations.

The Old Covenant was retired. It had been fulfilled by Jesus Christ to make way for the new wine of the Church Ages, built on its solid, but crumbling foundation.

The Deliverance Ministry of Christ

It is most interesting and vital to see how our Lord ministered deliverance, salvation, and healing during His short walk on earth. Notice that He healed ALL who came to Him of WHATEVER problem, no matter how strong or violent the demons were. In some places where He ministered, people's faith was stronger and He could do more.

This meant that although the gift of healing within Jesus never changed or "lost power," the faith level of those with whom He worked with was subject to their own allowed level of belief. In some places, the Son of God Himself could not deliver or give healing because they simply were not ready to receive.

Yet, Jesus Christ is the all-powerful Son of God, God Himself, and a strong deliverer in the day of trouble to those who turn to Him.[5] Let's begin with His own call to this ministry with the very prophecy He fulfilled taken from Isaiah 61:

> "The Spirit of the Lord is upon me because He hath anointed me to preach the gospel to the poor; He hath sent Me to heal the brokenhearted, to preach DELIVERANCE to the captives, and recovering of sight to the blind, SET AT LIBERTY them that are bruised."[6]

For example, here are the Greek word meanings in this verse: *"And Jesus went about all Galilee teaching in their synagogues, and preaching the gospel of the kingdom, and healing all manner of SICKNESS"*

Nosos/Noseo - to have a diseased appetite, to hanker after and crave a sickness; to dote upon malady, disability, disease, infirmity as if clutching to oneself an evil thing), *"and all manner of DISEASE"*

Malakian – a softness or weakness to diseases, *"...among the people. And His fame went throughout all Syria and they brought unto Him all sick (frail, impotent) people that were taken with diverse DISEASES* (held in the custody of, or is a prisoner of a physical trouble), *and torments..."*

Basanismos/Kakos (Greek) - to maltreat, torture, make evil affected, vex, hurt, harm, pain, toil, toss), *"...those which were possessed with devils and those which were lunatic, and He healed them ALL."* [7]

NOTE: The Holy Spirit of God *is the power* for deliverance. He does not transfer it to His servants: He emits His power through His servants for the benefit of Seekers. After one is cleansed of demonic influence and vexation, the Kingdom of God—which is righteousness, peace, and joy in the Holy Spirit—has come upon you.[8]

Jesus promised[9] that his followers would do the same works and even greater works than those He did. Believers who hear His voice and follow His teachings these two thousand years after the resurrection, continue to have this same promise and commission. The baptism in the Holy Spirit with its gifts, callings, miracles, signs, and wonders is for today, too!

These are living and obvious ways God uses to proclaim the full Gospel to all who want to be whole right now. He directly commissioned 70 disciples to heal and cast out demons[10] with direct authority to wreak havoc in the evil spirit realm that was not done before. But first, we are going to get a closer look at the enemy's movements against humans that Jesus recognized and successfully countered as we are commissioned to do, likewise.

Jesus' ministry[11] clearly confirms that He healed ALL who came to Him of WHATEVER their condition of spirit, soul, and body. It mattered not how strong or violent the opposition. In some places where He went, people's faith and belief in Him were stronger to receive healing so He accomplished more. Their gates of belief were opened and the gates of fear shut.

This was possible by degrees although the fullness of healing within Jesus never changed or lost power. On the human side, personal belief to receive salvation, healing, and deliverance depended on those with whom He made Himself available for miracles. That is true with us today. If someone does not believe Jesus heals anymore or, at least won't heal them personally, they will receive the fruit of doubt they confess.

Each person is subject to their own allowed levels of belief or disbelief in Christ in any of His capacities of Redeemer, Healer, Deliverer, God Himself, and all other dimensions of divinity. When one fully believes, they are satisfied and have no need to ask for more than to grow in their faith. Specifically, we see that Christ healed:

- The blind and dumb (sightless and speechless)[12]
- Epileptic spirits[13]
- Unclean spirits (mentally and sexually perverted)[14]
- Spirit of infirmity (diseases and soul weakness)[15]
- Chronic mental and physical illness when a league of many demons stay long-time causing disability.

It is singular to realize that those with faith in Jesus can request and receive deliverance for another person. They stand in faith on their behalf. See the story of the Gentile mother in Matthew 15:22-28. What do you think was the exception made by Jesus to heal her daughter and why is this technique so significant for us today?

Exorcism Authority for Kingdom Servants

The outreach of the Holy Spirit's gifts went into operation at Pentecost and have functionally stayed in operation when He was not ignored or subdued by unbelief. The gifts kept in operation for hundreds of years despite opposition to full-gospel adherents—the "Pentecostals".

Fast forward to this time now. We see that various revivals have been documented in church history. Those periodic revivals all blossomed into local gatherings (often with persecution). One of the latest of which was the worldwide Charismatic Revival of the late 1960s into the mid-1970s. Thousands of non-denominational churches all over the world were birthed out of that one, filled by the Holy Spirit who reproduced the peace and joy as His personality filtered through God's willing believers.

I was serving as a medical missionary in Colombia, South America in that decade and this revival was massively sweeping through the nation and the Roman Catholic church with thousands saved, filled with the Spirit with speaking in tongues, getting healing, deliverance, with many signs that left no doubt as to its authenticity.

In Colombia, South America in 1973 when I served as a medical missionary, the 40 years of persecution of Evangelicals by Roman Catholics (via government sanctions) was called, *"La Violencia"* and abruptly stopped when many people heard the unvarnished gospel and were saved. We learned exorcism first hand with the afflicted lining up outside our doors to our second story apartment, standing in the street late into the night waiting their turns for relief.

Four of us were raw recruits to deliverance without any training but the authority of God's word! This is when we learned that demons know all languages and our demands made in English were answered exactly as asked in Spanish. We used the Spanish-to-English dictionary a lot, being new to the language. So, please do not dread becoming a Spirit Warrior with no experience. The key is a discerning spirit of the team.

Historically, all revivals create unique worship music as was true in this revival. Wonderful worship is still being played and sung today from the charismatic era. Great missionary efforts were launched. Nations were changed. The excitement of revival only lasts a few years at most. It is only a kick start for discipleship and maturing warriors into kingdom building in new places. When the purpose of revival is lost sight of, the impact is lessened and people are stuck expecting years of excitement instead of years of foundational work.

This Charismatic Revival swept the world as traditional churches found and appropriated the Holy Spirit's gifts. The powers of darkness took significant exposure, losses, and setbacks. The kingdom of darkness struck back with a renewal of the human-fabricated doctrine of Cessation, so as the years progressed, with it came the expected onslaught of unbelief that our God still worked and moved in His natural supernatural Personality way beyond the first church apostles to today.

This is one of the excuses they give for not bowing humbly and receiving whatever God offers as a method of building His kingdom, no matter what it appears to be to the cold-hearted. And with this dampening of the Holy Spirit movement headed by whole denominations, deadness returns and digs in with pride producing lukewarm churches.

Graciously, we still have many thousands of Spirit-filled churches and individuals that were established which were built upon previous revivals of the Spirit like the Azusa Street phenomenon in Los Angeles, California more than a half decade earlier. As we know, there is strategic reasons for all revivals: to expand the Kingdom of Jesus Christ and grow new believers into mature gatherings equipped to do damage to Babylon without our walls.

Recently, a diabolical planned epidemic (COVID) with advice from so-called experts who are vaccine shareholders, bombarded the world to fear, to distance, eliminate physical contact, don mandatory face coverings that are totally useless against microbes, and do physical and mental damage to children especially.

Voluntary or forced isolation, limitation of worshipers with a halt on worship (no singing or chanting), the insistence of these liberties restored if vaccinated by non-Constitutional threats, have shuffled up the lukewarm church again with some courageous exceptions that do expose it as evil. Others folded in the fear of the devil. You will meet Seekers who were damaged by this secular forced surrender. So, where are we now, on the Jesus Christ's Kingdom side of things? It is again time for the next Awakening that will come through persecution? Or, will it take the opening of all the Seals of Revelation to be released by Christ and then the more serious, seven Trumpets sounding to spark a great final revival and harvest of souls?

In the next chapter, we explore the dynamics of exorcism and how people get into the byways of destruction.

[1] Matthew 27:25; Luke 22:20, King James Version says *testament*, not covenant. Study Hebrews 9-11, especially noting Hebrews 9:16-17 as the concepts Paul taught.

[2] Hebrews 9:16-17

[3] Acts 1:12-14; Acts 2:1-4

[4] Acts 2:40-47

[5] Luke 4:40-41, Matthew 8:16, Mark 1:32-33

[6] Luke 4:18; Mark 16:9

[7] Matthew 4:23-24

[8] Romans 14:17. Other Scriptures: blind and dumb spirits (Matthew 12:22-24, Luke 9:14-15); epileptic spirits (Mark 9:17-29, Luke 9:37-43); unclean spirits (Mark 1:23-27, Luke 11:24-26); the children of God have deliverance (Matthew 15:22-28); the spirit of infirmity (Luke 13:10-13; legion of many demons remaining a long time (Luke 8:26-32).

[9] John 14:12

[10] Luke 10:1-17

[11] Matthew 12:22

[12] Matthew 12:22-24 and Luke 9:14-15

[13] Mark 9:17-29; Luke 9:37-43

[14] Mark 1:23-27 and Luke 11:24-26

[15] Luke 13:10-13; Luke 8:26-32

| 3 |

The Underpinnings of Spiritual Chaos

"I remember the story of the old man who said on his deathbed that he had had a lot of trouble in his life, most of which had never happened." Winston Churchill

The Core of Spiritual Problems

Christians have asked, "Where do all my problems come from? No matter what I do to follow God, strange things happen to divert me from being on top. It seems I just get further into debt or the children get sick, or something happens in my business that is totally unforeseen. I just can't figure out what is wrong!"

This is a good beginning question. Its answer lies in tracing the problem root to one or more of the following reasons why believers are plagued by demonic influence, cursed living, or family disaster. Many spiritual problems are the result of:

1. Not knowing God's WAYS or WILL.
2. Not knowing, believing, or trusting God's CHARACTER.
3. Not allowing Jesus Christ's LORDSHIP in every area of your life.

4. Not being willing to HEAR or OBEY the voice of God.

5. Not LOVING God with your whole being.

If with God's promised help you do not overcome the temptations of life, the sins of your self-nature, or the wiles of the devil, you will be overcome by whatever you fail to overcome. To whatever you give the preeminence and priority to, will be the exact thing that will dominate your life.

The positive side is to put God first, leading you into His blessings. However, if those priorities are out of God's will, they become idols that will erect a spiritual lordship within your spirit gradually allowing Satan access to steal your freedom in Christ.

Any problem a Christian cannot overcome by either prayer and fasting, repentance and forgiveness, the avid study of God's Word, or by spiritual discipline, is most likely due to an outside hindering force not natural to them. These characteristics show an evil spirit(s) in operation which is allowed power through the setting up of personal idols.

Demonic spirits deceive believers by placing within them unbelief that robs faith for prayer. Thus, deception will spiritually blind them to the true cause of their problem. Spiritual, outside hindrances cause true blindness in the human spirit to see Jesus Christ as the cure for all their ailments, problems, oppression, possessions, lack of fleshly control, and mental disturbances. All they see is disaster and are finally mentally overpowered.

Often this uncomfortable state escalates into anxiety or panic, causing the blinded believer to seek answers for their problems from world philosophies instead of looking to God alone. These people, now harassed in their spirits, souls and/or bodies, may, become extremely angry at God or others for "what they are going through". When these thoughts turn to unresolved bitterness and compulsive hatred, it will keep them from establishing a loving, open relationship with God in order to find true peace, meaning, and purpose to life. All this is traceable to a lying spirit.

Satan of course, is pleased at his own helpfulness in the disastrous, opportunity-wasted events in a believer's life and continues to ever bind and blind his victims for eventual dysfunction. When over time an unresolved issue develops, a lack of trust in God, a root of bitterness moves in and will only move out by acknowledgement, repentance, and deliverance.

There are about 1700 places in the Bible denoting 'deliver', 'deliverance,' 'deliverer,' and the like. Deliverance from evil spirits removes the supernatural part of a person's problem. After that, people can then deal with any natural sin attachments to the soul and flesh. There are several scriptures[1] that confirm this including this one:

> "You must actively obey Him in everything He commands. Only then will you be doing what is right and good in the Lord's eyes. If you obey Him, all will go well for you, and you will be able to go in and possess the good land which the Lord promised your ancestors. You will also be able to throw out ALL the enemies living in your land as the Lord agreed to help you."

Exorcism is Confidential

There is no need or scriptural basis for a Spirit Warrior to share anything seen or heard in a private session with anyone outside the ministry team. If outside relatives or others in the congregation ask for particulars, firmly admonish them not even to ask you. A simple, "I'm sorry, that's between them and the Lord", should do it. We value the Seeker and would not purposely cause them to stumble over a lack of confidence in their efforts to leave the past behind them. Be very strict about this form of gossip. Once deliverance is a part of the ekklesia fellowship and you remain hidden in the ministry, these situations will not come up.

Spiritual warfare can be highly exhilarating as victory after victory is won. Spirit Warriors must be careful to realize that whatever great breakthroughs happen belong to the Seeker's testimony—not to yours.

Personal testimony comes from wanting to share what God is doing with and in them.

Or, they may choose to never share. Respect their privacy and realize that the Spirit Warrior is but a hidden servant of God, His vessel that the water of the Word passes through on its way to healing. It is amazing to realize that you will not remember much of what happens anyway. Leave it to the Lord.

Experience and maturity in the use of this ministry will serve to precaution those called to never seek demons under every pew. They are not there. God will give you ministry through your pastor who is able to see what the Lord is doing in the whole church or in agreement with other team members.

People who seek demonic encounters without being in order and protected will find themselves open to deception and ministering out of season. This self-serving behavior will bring discouragement and take the power of God from you. Rather, wait on the Lord. You will be used as He sees fit and as you are prepared. This is part of being a humble and submissive servant, one sensitive to God's timing and His love for them.

The Dynamics of Exorcism

The New Testament exorcism of low-level demons by Jesus and His disciples before the Cross-death of Christ, established the divine authority He submitted to that clearly marked Him as Yahweh God's Son. He was not equal with others in His day who had some limited ability in using evil sources of power to cast out or subdue demons. These were the sorcerers and seers who made a living at it. No, the hallmark of Christ's ministry was the total deliverance every time of ALL who came to Him. His Source was divine and permanent.

Christ's ministry never failed. Every word He spoke was sent to do a job and did it consistently. Deliverance was used as a tool for healing people and pointing them toward the Calvary experience to come. The health and freedom it brought was a foretaste of the richness and depth of what salvation truly would accomplish for those who sought Him throughout the church age.

Even today, casting out the power of Satan from a life provides a basic, clean foundation from which to build the Christian way of living. This is pure salvation given by the Father to each person who chooses to take it as a gift from Him. In later years after Calvary where the blood of Christ purchased the authority over Satan, sin, death, and the world, He ascended to the right-hand throne of the Father where He continues to intercede for us.

Exorcism is and has been traditionally practiced by Christ's ministers under His authority down through the centuries in and by His Church. It is used to either bring the unsaved to Christ or as cleansing to His children. The deliverance ministry, remains relevant and beneficial today for each child of God to:

1. Take a full position with God and His Christ.
2. Be healed in spirit, soul, and body.
3. Testify to the power of God which is alive and practical to this generation.
4. Move into prosperity and blessings of God unhindered.
5. Serve as a means for gaining a lost world to Christ especially in mission and outreach work.

This should give you a fair beginning understanding of the doctrinal positions of the bible for ministry and for assisting Seekers to know how the deviation happened that allowed interference. Much of deliverance in our modern era involves discipleship because we do not want delivered ones failing from lack of knowledge of God and His ways.

Next, we see the power base of Spirit Warriors and how to acquire the Holy Spirit's supernatural resources in conquering Death, the Grave, and Hell. These are entities, not only positions of final and eternal consequence.

[1] Deuteronomy 6:17-19 (LIV); Leviticus 26:6-13; Galatians 5:1; Psalm 34:19; Exodus 14:13; Deuteronomy 28:47-48; Isaiah 59:1-2; 1 Samuel 17:47 (the battle is the Lord's); Judges 2:2-3; Joel 2:32; John 8:49; Joshua 23:10, 24:12; 2 Corinthians 3:18; Proverbs 11:21; 1 John 3:8

| 4 |

Exorcism is a Kingdom Distinctive

"...pray the LORD of the harvest to send out laborers into
His harvest. Go your way; behold
I send you out as lambs among wolves."
~ Jesus in Luke 10:3

The Baptisms of the Holy Spirit

We live in a world of predators. Our Seekers live in here, too, but are not armed to dismember the wolves. You might not be armed yourself. You will discover that in this Guide. Just as there are swordsmen who are quite skilled to kill in battle, there are others who merely hold a sword and play at it. Let's find out.

Deliverance is a very serious grace and the Seeker must be made aware of the scriptural order of a child of God. They should be in good faith with the Lord on the things He has told him or her to do (be saved/be baptized) before partaking of this ministry.

Please take time at this preliminary stage to be assured in your own mind that those you pray with are fully strengthened and in obedience

BEFORE deliverance. These basic steps are imperative to their spiritual position AFTER deliverance in order to maintain the holy ground newly won based on their position of the beloved.

The third recommended preliminary action to deliverance is to (3) seek and receive by faith the Baptism in the Holy Spirit. There are scriptures cited concerning this experience. The Baptism in the Holy Spirit may be prayed for with the counseling team before or after deliverance. Be led of the Lord. It is a spiritual transaction that causes the Seeker to be open to the Holy Spirit by a new flowing of his or her human spirit with God's own Communication network.

It is important to understand that one does not receive the Holy Spirit when praying to receive the Baptism of the Holy Spirit. The Holy Spirit is given only once at the time of salvation. All the gifts of the Spirit are given when He comes into you at salvation for, He is always in full possession of them and when He is indwelling you, the gifts are already deposited. All believers are gifted with the Holy One at salvation: it is not a separate grace. But you must unlock the treasury and herein are some keys.

Let this be clear that by adding that receiving the Baptism of the Holy Spirit brings an acute awareness and receptive heart (mind) to Him to work as He sees fit in each believer. It is God's business to send whatever gift(s) He gives. The Baptism in the Holy Spirit is refreshing to the human spirit to see and use the gifts already given. This may happen at the time of salvation, deliverance, during worship, water baptism, or anytime the Lord desires. It is taken by faith.

Being filled with the Holy Spirit of God is a highly joyous experience with some people speaking in other tongues. Others do not speak in tongues and it is not, by any means, a necessary occurrence. By active FAITH, you receive baptism(s) in the Holy Spirit—not by emotional (soul) or demand gift manifestation.[1]

It is helpful to realize and instruct the Seeker that in the finished work of Jesus Christ at Calvary when His incorruptible blood was obediently given[2] that these specific works and other, more numerous ones, were completed and paid for on behalf of all people. It is up to each one to believe for them. Jesus provided to us:

- Salvation from the consequences of natural sin and its curses.
- Salvation from death as a final Enemy-curse.
- Deliverance from the domination of sin, self, the world, Satan and all his minions.
- Healing happens in spirit, soul, body *"...by His stripes we were healed"* –and not by anything else,[3] so we may have a God-blessed life now.
- The imparting of the gifts of the Holy Spirit for ministry through the Baptisms of the Holy Spirit;[4] and,
- The opening of spiritual fellowship with the Creator of the universes and that is in them.

Salvation, deliverance, water baptism, and Holy Spirit baptism must each be appropriated (taken as your own) to become active in your life. If the Seeker has not experienced salvation or water baptism then you must first help them seek and receive these two basic steps. This is a significantly important step in assisting them to find and obey Christ in two fundamental areas of discipleship.

At the close of a deliverance session, the counseling team should petition the Holy Spirit to minister as Healer and to fill and flow into all those places where the evil one was discharged. Be sure to terminate all sessions with a healing prayer, with joy, and the positive confession of God's unfailing love.

It should be a strong concern of the Spirit Warrior that those prayed for become a committed member of a local church body where they can come under the discipline and blessing of the Word of God. It is here that added strength for continuing in the Christian walk under a shelter of spiritual protection and covering are available for on-going help and growth.

Some of you, who are reading this, will find a need for deliverance but may not have access to other Christians with whom to pray. Please do not undertake deliverance by yourself without the full protection of being saved and water baptized. Yet, even so, the Word of God given here will be quickened to the open heart for the Holy Spirit to minister directly to you. If you feel you need assistance for heavier deliverance or to share your experiences, contact us through our website contact page[5] to let us help you find someone in your State.

It cannot be stressed enough the necessity of the team and Seekers being fully protected before submitting for the battle of deliverance. Jesus tells us[6] that a person who gets incomplete, unprotected deliverance will be worse off by seven times with once expelled evil spirits re-entering what they think of as their house. The team must be in scriptural order before seeking deliverance for others. An unoccupied house is a person's soul that is not inhabited by the Holy Spirit of God and is open to evil influence.

The following text box confession helps to focus and review these key events in the Seeker's life. It becomes a good resource should demons come to accuse them later with temptations that were once conquered. If the exact dates cannot be remembered, of course God knows them.

If your Seeker has any doubts on his or her heart that these events did not occur, encourage them to believe and accept the Lord Jesus Christ as Savior in front of you, right now. If they have not obeyed in water baptism, suggest a local ekklesia where they may receive it as a testimony of His grace.

Please complete these questions before engaging in this ministry. You might want to have these printed up so the Seeker can take with them. Also, before continuing to pray with them, explain the text. The Spirit Warrior team may want to print this and give it to Seekers to keep as a memorial of their position in Christ.

Ministering Deliverance by God's Love

Ideally, this ministry comes out of a church body set up for deliverance that will process Seeker requests as they arise. There is an orderly way of handling sessions so that prayer ministers are not rushed by the Seeker, or are too hasty to minister before the safe guards are in place.

Be certain that the Seeker will be alright until those in charge are finding the will of God for the appropriate Spirit Warrior team, the place to minister, or for any spiritual preparations needed before and during ministry. Satan and the flesh compel and propel: the Holy Spirit however, is patient and timely, never pushy. He is a Gentle Spirit and does not rush in where He is not bidden from a sincere heart.

While Seekers are waiting for appointments, suggest that they might fast food intake if medically able, turn off television, videos, and unnecessary telephone conversations for a few days. They should pray and seek the Lord to identify what is bothering them—by name—by making a list for the team when they meet.

You might want to create an online checklist form they can print off and fill out at home with no identifying data (e.g., name, date of birth, anything personal should not be on the form!). Just list categories of areas they might identify as their situation. See *Appendix E, The Battalions of Spirit Powers* to help form your list as a beginning point for their upcoming session.

In helping to form teams for the ministry session, there are some basic commonsense considerations. For instance, intercessory prayer warriors can be alerted to begin the battle in the spirit and get discernment. For this reason and for self-protection ensuring that Satan has no place to ensnare and sidetrack the session. More detail on this is covered in Chapter 14, *Ministering Deliverance in Love.*

Satan's Great Evil Commission

A demonic spirit alone, or joined with those within a cadre of like-spirits to work in union, have primary objectives. We might see those objectives for existing completing their evil destinies. Mainly, demonic objectives work to destroy the peace and harmony of any possible or present connection a person has or will have with Father-God, with Jesus the Son, and with His Holy Spirit. They are very skilled at techniques to accomplish division, having observed human nature for thousands of years in all circumstances and through warring skirmishes with God's angels.[7]

With this overarching objective, familiar demons set up to work it out with small victories and drastic failures. They begin to introduce as much temptation to the human nature to trespass against the Lord's will that makes them live in anguish, guilt, shame, grief, misfortune, curse, privation, disease, separation anxiety, fears, and confusion, as far and long as possible.

These are distractions are generated to prevent us from solving our lost state by seeking and finding God. The unsaved of the world live in these conditions of gravity to varying degrees, depending on the false gods ruling in them and in their centuries-directed declining cultures.

But likewise, demonic spirits deploy the same tactics into the lives of believers (as permitted) to try to dissolve unity with the Father. This is what is going on when believers neglect personal study of God's word by choosing to ignore truth and stopping their communication with the Holy Spirit.[8]

Gradually, this sidetrack will abandon their kingdom purpose by refocusing their energy elsewhere. Often, it is an electronic fascination that robs people of reality and the real picture with the flashy false narratives found there.

Soon, they grow into a new belief system that parallels the worldview of secular culture. This can only demote our God-view. Some call this backsliding, an old-fashioned term for cooling off one's ardor for Jesus Christ by substitution of self-interests. Yes, all generations knew about leaving the Lord's ways to wandering in the devil's ways. When that path narrows too much and the fellowship of God is yearned for, help is sought.

Now, in this first half of the new 21st century, a esoteric mix of evil has arisen as the one world globalists work in union to take the world by conquest. It deals in street violence, racism that does not exist, fraudulent electioneering, political radicalism, vaccine confusion, gender dysphoria, culture kill (once traditionally godly), and outright legalized insanity.

Add to that the extraordinary advances in weaponry, bio- and cyber-terrorism, Big Tech communications control, Big Pharma, and Big Business swallowing up the liberties of individualism. A lot to pray against as newly assigned demons show their toady faces as different characters.

Satan commissions his demonic emissaries of evil to just be themselves! That means, to fully express their nature to seduce, entice to sin, confuse issues, to employ The Lie,[9] to display themselves however possible, and drive us toward destruction. The successful end of those efforts can only come by assisting the devil in his work to pervert all that is good, humanly ordained. Their natural goal is to enticingly lead the whole world astray from God,[10] one person, one family, and one nation at a time.

When not inhabiting humans, Satan and his demonic scabs must wander through isolated places with no conduit to show off their ways, a real obstacle to their objectives. Have you ever deeply pondered why Jesus Christ was sent by the Holy Spirit into a deserted wilderness for 40 days? Who was waiting there, relishing his unique opportunity to test Christ's relationship with His Father? Satan, of course. He was out there among the wild animals, with bad and good angels, proudly facing off for a fight with his Maker.[11]

God incarnate was standing in a God-dependent position of a total fast, in the measly shadow of a once gorgeous angel whom He created and threw out of heaven, millennia ago. But now, Jesus-man was in an entirely different posture, clothed in humanity's inadequacies, deciding to use the only weapons humans had in these face-offs with the satanic.

Besides the stress of fasting that taxed His human frame to its limits, was the soul pressure of disregarding the fragility of human limitations, naked of the solutions His sacrifice on Calvary would offer, in the future. What did He do?ave you

In all those 40 days, we have no record of what lengths Jesus Christ was pushed to endure the assaults against body, soul, and spirit from

His human position, but He overcame every temptation to turn against His Father. He used what we still have: The Name of the Father, prayer and fasting, and vocally declaring the Word of God to the extent that satanic forces must flee in defeat.

This same battle is here for each of us until we get home when Father promotes us. Until then, the victorious Christian learns to fight back in the power of the Holy Spirit, in the authority of the Name of Jesus Christ, dressed in the armor (over the soul) that He provided. He is our design, our Hope. Our victory.

Do you see the pattern for warfare? Fasting, prayer, Holy Spirit power, declaring God's word, casting demons out? Do you get the dichotomies of Evil and Yahweh in conflict for the human souls of all generations from Eden to Eternity?[12]

Can you get a sense of how He authorizes Spirit Warriors to wage war against evil spirit warriors, ready to release captured ones right at the tip of the frontier of death?[13] This does not happen without penetration into the very stronghold of the dark kingdom, shrouded behind thick secrecy and sorcery that we are uncovering.

Then the clear call arises from the throne room: "Expose their deeds of evil![14] Take forth the Light of My Truth so a human choice can be made by faith in belief for Me! Release the captives!"

What Opens the Doors to Demonic Oppression?

Attacks Against the Human Spirit. Attacks against the body can be formidable, but attacks against the inner man will keep one down longer than the body might stay alive. Accordingly, this is where we put the guards in place at the most vulnerable areas (opened doors of invitation) so we are not open to outside assault.

Without the protection of the relationship with Jesus Christ through being born-again and empowered, we will be like others who have no such protections from the possessors of destruction.

Portals are grand entrances. Attacks against the body can be formidable, but attacks against the inner man will keep one down longer than the body might stay alive. Accordingly, this is where we put the guards in place at the most vulnerable doors or portals, so we are not available to outside assault. Without the protection of the relationship with Jesus Christ through being born-again and empowered, we will be like others who have no such protections from the possessors of destruction.

The most common manifestations indicating the presence and activities of demons are found in the two foundational instinctual areas of the body: the five senses and physical organs, and secondly, in the soul as the seat of our emotions, will, imagination, and mind-intellect.

Apart from those in the human spirit as the sacred gate connecting us with the Holy Spirit in intimate communication, the spirit cannot be corrupted for it is an impenetrable possession of Christ bought at salvation. The spirit is marked by the Holy Spirit's right then as God's own. With that function covered, our soul then, is basically in command of our decision-making when it receives inputs from our body and direction by the spirit. Do we wait and listen? Do we choose the Lord's way or quickly do what feels good?

Demonic expressions in oppressed people utilize the body and soul areas in several variations. Some of these will be immediately obvious and aggressive while others are scarcely notable. Indicators may only be revealed by the operation of the gifts of the Spirit in the Spirit Warrior, or by a discerning prophet or intercessor who is able to make an identity call.

Attacks Against the Human Body. Included here, are brief compilations of these expressions as a partial exposure to their varied attack forms on the physical body first, then against the soul next. In deliverance sessions, stay alert to these bouts as having been observed first-hand during exorcism sessions.

These can be seen, sensed, or expected as manifestations of demonic influence. Many are especially evident when the evil spirits have been stirred up by the Name and in the power of Jesus Christ. They may react in ways through the body of the person by confrontation.

It is possible that some of their movements will become threatened against the Seeker or Spirit Warrior as a frantic redirection of the pressure coming against them. But be assured that nothing Satanic can stand against or harm the children of God who are utterly trusting in Him for safety.

It is always wise to get a medical opinion first when there might be chemical imbalances in the body or brain physicality causing clinical symptoms. Everything is not of a spiritual nature! Some destructive habits may have been opened allowing access to the demonic but others may be a result of the consequences of carnal choices and not demonic at all. A good example of this is self-starvation (anorexia and bulimia) that progresses to debilitation and possible death.

When the Seeker's choices to sin have become chronic and thus idolatrous, their constant summoning of the demonic into that very particular sin area brings with it, gross spirit interference. This is especially evident when the 'sin habit' turns into an addiction that cannot be broken without God's help such as, multiple courses of drug rehab that just doesn't cut it. Here are some manifestations of the body:

- Unusual restless talkativeness. Muttering, yawning, flailing of arms, legs, or head; taking a fetal position to whimper, to beg or threaten, and pleading not to be exposed or expelled.
- Glazed and dull eyes or overly bright and protruding gazes. The inability to focus naturally or keep their eyes open when spoken to (demons are trying to hide); eyes that snap open with anger or hatred; weeping and pleading to remain "in their home".
- Froth at the mouth, fetid breath, and over-salivating. Sometimes there is vomiting, burping, gassing, blasphemous language, threats of death or harm, begging to be left alone.
- Seeker has the inability to speak God's names. Jesus Christ, God the Father, Yahweh (or any of His names), Holy Spirit, or the cross of Christ when asking Seekers to pray in assisting with their own deliverance. This must be broken.
- Palpitations and body marks. Unnaturally accelerated or slowed heartbeat, flushed skin, welts, bruises suddenly appear; bites and scratch marks appear without touching them. NOTE: if there is

ever a question of health danger, stop the session. This area is rare, but possible. Never tolerate harm of any kind.

- Shunning, recoiling from, or fighting against the power of the Holy Spirit. This is body language in Seekers made against those who are questioning the demons; cowering in a corner or on the chair, getting under coverings (remove shawls, scarves, neckties, masks, hats). At times we have allowed the Seeker to remove their wigs from itching, or movement in the scalp, and sharp pinprick pains.

- Unusual coldness in the extremities or in the room. This indicates the presence of evil; hair or skin bumps rising involuntarily with a sense in their human spirit, sudden fear or unrest and disorder. NOTE: Ask the Seeker what they are feeling at the time and address that. Ask if they want to continue.

- Demons have admitted to causing mental and physical infirmities.[15] These "spirits of infirmity" can travel in gangs of disease clusters. Spirits may threaten the Seeker or Spirit Warrior with insanity, infection, heart disease, fear of influenza microbes, cancers, tumors, ulcers, arthritis, paralysis, deafness, blindness, insomnia, epilepsy, and anything they fear might happen. In deliverance sessions we have witnessed instant catatonia (extreme unmovable body positions) and tales of spirit rape in both males and females.

NOTE: Don't give heed to idle demonic threats that bring on fear. When they begin to threaten you or the Seeker, ask their name and expel the demonic deceivers that facilitate their assigned powers. Those specific responses of their intimidation and lies will be terminated so you can move on to the next.

Attacks Against the Human Soul. Again, this is not an exhaustive list of possibilities. Names keep changing with the twisting of popular culture, technology, and an ever-growing range of perversions.

So always depend on the Holy Spirit to discern the nature of evil so presented in sessions.

- Persistent or recurrent destructive emotions and attitudes. Theses can dominate a person even contrary to his or her own will resulting in resentment, fears, hatred, conceit, pride, envy, jealousy, self-pity, tension, self-destructive acts, suicide, revenge, impatience, rejection of others, meanness--a bullying attitude or actions; abusive rage, out of control wrath, a lack of conscience and compassion to inflict harm on one's children, self, and others.
- The staunch position of unforgiveness which is *the decision not to forgive—by giving up one's right to punish or wound the abuser* is never allowed to persist. Unforgiveness will stop deliverance making the Seeker's decision to forgive, aloud by names, is the only way to break through.
- Moods which are unreasonable or sudden with extreme fluctuations. If the Seeker has been receptive to oppression that has progressed into depression or experiences a rising of high euphoria often seen in bipolar disorders (schizophrenia). Be certain to explain that we are not medical doctors or mental health experts. All we can do is recognize some signs of opened portals that have taken certain directions.
- One is to ask if there has been a chronic or abusive use of alcohol, use of all recreational and some prescription drugs; addiction to acid and rock music that opens the door to swinging, controlling moods. People often exhibit a double-minded confusion and loss of their self-identity anchor. This creates a home for perplexity, irrationality, and mental unrest.
- Various forms of religious error. Bondage and submission to unscriptural religious systems, cults, doctrines of demons, world culture ideologies, political extremism that becomes a religion and all types of materials and psychological idolatry including false worship, name-and-claim, prosperity-only, polygamy,

Mormonism, Mary Queen-of-Heaven Worship, justification for non-biblical soul relationships, and many attractions to error. NOTE: This subarea can be quite long especially from pagan cultures. They must be turned over with discipleship to follow up in the word of God.

- Resorting to charms and luck. Fortune telling, attending seances to contact the dead, daily or occasional astrology readings (not to be confused with astronomy that is God's creative work). Seeking information from mediums, soothsayers, palm/hand readers, and believing in cultic idols and symbols; mindless with the repetition of prayer beads, mantras, magic sayings, and contacting dead saints that may sound religious.

NOTE: There are many representations of 'Jesus' in world religions but, there is only One, authentic Lord Jesus Christ the only Son of God as fully revealed in the Judaeo-Christian bible. Some demons go by the names of Jesus, Moses, Messiah, Guru, Master, and so forth, to impress and capture religious listeners.

- Enslaving personal habits. The abuse of any substance such as sex enhancing hormones, nicotine, addictive patches, vaping, chewing tobacco, marijuana, CBD; sugar and food gluttony or compulsions of bulimia and anorexia to be overly thin to control the body; scab picking, cutting, tattooing, body piercings, mutilation of genitals, abortion as birth control; lottery and gambling compulsions, and risking one's physical life for thrills. Perpetrating and participating in sex slavery or child depredation are totally demonic. There is a legal matter to consider in such cases.
- Mind Control Practices. Here is a list to start the narrative: addictive and uncontrollable video gaming, social media binging in all its forms, constant consultation with Internet trends or surfing, pornography that affects both children and adults. Also included are, the psychological manipulation of others, adhering to media-induced mind-control in the forms of brain-washing,

thinking exercises disguised as meditation, mind-reading; hypnotism techniques, subliminal suggestions, encouragement to perform extreme body fixations, "psychiatry as the answer," mind channeling the dead, or using spirit guides. The Brain is only two percent of the physical body yet it coordinates all the physical functions of the body; whereas the soul directs the thoughts processed in the brain area. You may discover that the Seeker is the perpetrator instead of the victim. This too, calls for repentance and a breaking away from 'false holy spirits'.

- Unclean language. Blasphemy (attributing to Satan what is of God); cursing, vulgar language, swearing including the use of 'Oh My God' (OMG) as a casual toss off phrase taking the Lord's name in vain; mockery, exaggeration, dirty joking, gossip, idle and empty talk; a compulsion to constantly talk or dish out verbal abuse; creating and spreading disinformation, deceptive language, double-speak, and lies.

- 2. Unmanageable perversions. Sexual partnerships in place of marriage union of one man with one-woman, gender dysphoria, false sexual orientations; e.g., bisexuality, transgenderism, pedophilia, and child/adult pornography, necromancy (sexual acts with corpses)[16], nudism, sexual abuse of animals, sex dolls; LGBTQ+ brain washing support or participation in any way with their groups, political actions, or voting for candidates that support this agenda. This is direct conflict with the admonition to "be separate and come out from among them". Don't forget drag queen activism, same sex prostitution, blackmail, and self-pleasuring habits.

- Adherence to ungodly worldviews. The '-isms' of organized human philosophies forced on other such as feminism as goddess worship, politically motivated constructs of socialism, Communism, Fascism, Marxism, Antinomianism, Racism, anti-Semitic hatred, Islamism, Humanism, Denominational and the like, restrict the mind into a no-other-options way of conducting life. Organizations like Black Lives Matter (a Marxist front) uses an erroneous construct for protest and fund raising because we know that all lives matter including the pre-born, disabled, and elderly. Antifa[17] is a funded New World Order hired mob using violence to loot, eradicate cultural symbols and history. There are many groupings we see daily in the news that are soul-enslaving systems that sets one's mind against God, His correct ways of doing human living, that distract from realizing one's destiny planned by His will.

- Weaponized 'health care' eliminates the liberties of choice and worship by volunteer then mandated posturing, distancing, and wearing of ineffective costumes. Related are the extreme environmentalism views, all theories and controlling systems that exclude Yahweh God. Believing in special rights while denying rights to others, the perceived entitlement rights to rights or funds that are earned by others, is an advancement into a poverty that results from no work effort. Actually, these signs indicate rejecting to fully trust in God who promises to give us purpose and meet all our needs in order to do so.[18]

- Prostitution of the Soul. This can be a snare to those in Christian ministry and happens when trading or giving part of one's soul away for unseemly gain by commercializing a once God-given ministry. The Christian intellect, music ministries, and abusing spiritual gifts, the most common being healing and coaching techniques given in pretended structures without gospel clarity. These are hirelings sold out to motivations for power, finances, popularity, fame, denominational standing, and self-empire-building.

Further areas of hidden fraud in the last times churches include white collar schemes, general criminal cyberspace action, tolerance for pagan social philosophies and corrupt politics, Christians promoting civil demonstration--say for 'women's reproductive choice'--masked as peaceful protests.

Some have established charitable foundations that may raise millions, but with very little allocated to the stated objectives of the kingdom principles set out by Christ in His commission. Aren't these ways how non-profit corporate tax structures are built, to gain profit no matter if religious or secular?

The heart of the Church is not watching leadership. These pseudo works and many more, bring chills to the purposes of Christ's kingdom principles. Carnal Christianity is the demonstration of human soulish ways for working the Babylonian system under the public pretense of Christian service. Wait until survival is based on taking Antichrist's mark.

Meanwhile, it is unmistakable that by diluting the punch of the gospel of Jesus Christ in order to become seeker-friendly and not Cross-centered, that denial of the power of the cross equally dilutes or eliminates the possibility of having Christ's supernatural lifestyle. Souls are lost here.

Where has the authentic Body of Christ gone that is to be the ambassador for the Kingdom of Jesus Christ?

Next, we explore the natural nature of fallen spirits wanting to express themselves around and sometimes within humans. All people are the targets of the demonic destiny and picked off to become conquests. We are aware of that, but it will become helpful to understand how demons work and understand their limitations, weaknesses, simple goals, and self-demonstrations. They are not almighty boogeymen. The human body soul, and spirit are their showgrounds.

[1] Look up John 20:19-22 and Acts 1:1-8, 2:1-4, 2:14-21, 8:14-17, 10:44-48, 19:1-7 for a deeper understanding.

[2] John 19:30

[3] Isaiah 53:5

[4] 1 Corinthians, chapters 12, 13, 14

[5] www.SpiritWarriors.us

[6] Matthew 12:43-45

[7] Daniel 10:10-13; Daniel 12:1-4;

[8] John 8:37-39

[9] *The Lie* is the first one and the most powerful one in Satan's arsenal today found in Genesis 3:4, *"You shall not surely die".* Oh yes, their spirits did die.

[10] Amos 2:4 – lies lead them astray; Matthew 18:10-14 shows the will of the Father in cases of one going astray from Him; Hebrews 3:7-10 and 1 Peter 2:25 within a passage of (verses 21-25) remaining faithful to their call.

[11] Mark 1:12-13

[12] Hebrews 2:10

[13] Daniel 11:32

[14] Ephesians 5:8-21 tells believers how to walk in the light within the world and within the fellowship of faith. Exposing evil is a major weapon we have that takes courage to speak against, rally the Ekklesia to action, and support those who are so doing in the law, medicine, arts, politics, and on the home front.

[15] Luke 13:11

[16] Deuteronomy 18:9-14 [Strong's #1875, 4191 for Hebrew definitions]. See the grouping of wicked customs that are hated by God.

[17] Antifa has been funded as a New World Order mob mastering in lawless violence to loot, terrorize, eradicate cultural symbols, and historic blessings. There are many groupings we see daily in the news that are soul-enslaving systems that sets one's mind against God, His correct ways of doing human living, that distract from realizing one's destiny planned by His will.

[18] Philippians 4:11; 1 Timothy 6:8; Hebrews 13:5

| 5 |

The Demonic Nature and Portals

"A loving person lives in a loving world.
A hostile person lives in a hostile world;
everyone you meet is your mirror."
~ Ken Keynes, Jr. 1921-1990

An Outside-the-Kingdom View

By this section in the book, you will have gotten an idea of the length and breadth of the spirit world as a closed in and broken one, wherein humans are captured by sheer gravity and body mass. Right now, I want to give you an outside-of-Christendom-analysis regarding one man's opinion of demonic functional identities.

His name is Francis Barrett[1], an Englishman by birth and an occultist by profession, penned *The Magus* that was published at the height of the Age of Reason in 1801. Once, it was considered the primary source to properly study ceremonial magic. Even today, the book is in use by those who seriously practice magic. In it, Barrett gives nine divisions he thought were diabolic positions to bring the question of how he formulated his list. Did it result from his direct interaction as an occultist?

Spirit Warriors, you too, will learn many characteristic strategies about the diabolic after directly confronting this dark spirit realm. For interest, let's compare our biblical knowledge of demonic characteristics with Barrett's categories as quoted.

1. *The False Gods*, who wish to be worshipped like a god;
2. *Spirits of Lies*, who use divination and predictions to trick and deceive;
3. *Vessels of Iniquity*, the inventors of all things evil such as cards and dice;
4. *Revengers of Evil*, who are ruled over by Aslmodeus,
5. *Deluders*, the demons under the command of Prince Satan who mimic and imitate miracles as well as work in conjunction with witches;
6. *Aerial Powers* who live in the air and cause lightning, thunder, and pestilence as it suits their prince Meririm;
7. *The FURIES*, who are led by Abaddon and cause discord, devastation, and war;
8. *The Accusers,* demonic spirits led by Prince Astaroth;
9. *The Tempters*, who reside in every man and are under the command of Prince Mammon.

Well, some of this looks like the Bible was used in his studies, but we cannot vouch for the whole truth of his list, dotted with speculation. It is interesting, though, that unnatural beings were recognized with the attempt to understand their power positions at the beginning of the 19th Century. Barrett was a professional occultist—he made money (Mammon) for his knowledge of the occult powers and it is certain that he channeled what they wanted him to know and tell.

Primary Purposes Assigned to Evil Spirits

When someone brings up this question to you in a session, *"Why did God cause this terrible thing to happen to me? He could have prevented it but didn't."* Jesus answered this question with the example of a tower that collapsed and killed many people as a common happenstance. Good and evil are indiscriminate, just as rain falls on everyone: as a blessing to quench a drought or as a tragic flood carrying away people and possessions.

Simply grasped, when negative things happen, understand that it is not in God's nature to do the wicked works of Satan. Nor does Satan do the good works of God. And, sometimes, life stuff just happens. All the possibilities of every situation have variables, so we do not automatically accuse our Father of bringing about evil for evil's sake.

Only humans and Satan operate that way. On the contrary, God is forever trustworthy and not capricious. Living and staying alive to fulfill His purposes in the spirit battle are very serious to Him. So, take Jesus' principle when you hear the question asked.

With that understanding, consider looking at the real sources. Who does cause evil as a lifework?[2] Is it natural consequences to the laws of the universe, or of a spirit nature? We learn to recognize the singularity of a demonic attack, its strategy, their preferred entries, who is targeted, the human interactions, and other factors according to what their story is, by recognizing that these tactics are not the ways in which the Holy One operates. So, when you see the opposing kingdom's infiltration, you know you are witnessing the behind-the-scenes network that really tilts the world.

What is Natural to a Demon?

How do evil spirits act or react when opportunities show up for them? Do they have specific liberties along with God-made boundaries? What are their assigned tasks from their master as revealed in their naming, and how does their obedience to their agenda impact Christians who are in the very world which lies in their sphere of activity?

Let's take a biblically look at their attributes and abilities in order to also understand their limitations.[3] Messenger-angels that chose to side with Lucifer eons ago became corrupted in that decision and left their heaven-assigned places. Looking at the following bible references, we see that demons have these true characteristics:

1. They have intelligence that produces knowledge. Matthew 8:28-32; Mark 1:24

2. A will and determination. Matthew 12:43-45; Luke 11:14-15

3. They express passion and emotions. James 2:18-19; Luke 9:38-43

4. The abilities to speak, cry, wail, convulse people violently, and shriek. Mark 1:26, 34

5. Recognize Jesus Christ as the Holy One of God and is God and obey Him. Mark 1:23, 32-34; Luke 13:32

6. Demons have self-awareness. Mark 1:24

7. The power to inhabit human-worshiped idols that masquerade as "gods". Deuteronomy 32:16-21

8. Authority to inhabit humankind. Luke 22:3-6

9. Drive people into physical and emotionally solitary places. Luke 11:24-26

10. Teach deceit through the soul-gates of hypocritical liars. 1 Timothy 4:1-5

11. Perform counterfeit wonders and signs. Revelation 16:13-14

12. Receive sacrifices as personal worship including the shed blood of innocent aborted humans. Deuteronomy 32:17; Psalm 106:34-39

13. Are subservient to Christ's Name. Luke 10:17

14. Communicate with humans who sense their voices "speak" or impress them to evil deeds. John 8:37-43

15. Satan can be a father authority to the unsaved. John 8:44-47

16. Demons believe that Jesus Christ is God. James 2:19

17. Have their own dwelling haunts. Rev. 18:2

18. Fellowship with Christians if allowed, creating negativity. 1 Corinthians 10:19-20

19. Have religious communion rites. 1 Cor. 10:21-22, 28

20. Receive rebukes and re-directions. Matt. 17:18
21. Will not obey unbelievers. Matthew 17:14-20
22. Cause mental and physical illness. Matt. 17:14-15
23. Able to possess unsaved humans and animals. Matthew 10:1
24. Rule by higher principalities and powers in the dark ignorance of this Age. Ephesians 6:12
25. Are not limited to bodies of flesh and blood. Ephesians 6:12
26. Are associated with sickness and disease. Matthew 10:1

As Spirit Warriors, you will want to make a more thorough study of the abilities and nature of demonic spirits as revealed throughout the whole bible in order to recognize their telltale identities. Demons, just like Satan, have the characteristics of active, viable personalities that exist to deceive and destroy.

Lucifer-Satan is the highest power level of the evil spirit world but all demons are *natural spirits* and do not have supernatural powers. They are restricted to their natural state of a spirit entity with some tremendous influential skills to deceive, delude, destroy, and lead into death. Be assured, they will receive their just punishment and be contained eternally in the Lake of Fire which Jesus Christ has prepared for them.

Only Jehovah, in all His dimensions, is supernatural; meaning, He creates all we call "the miraculous" in our world because He alone is divine. That is His nature. Satan and Jesus Christ are not equal in any sense of the meaning! In fact, by Christ's name, we have more power than Satan and all evil spirits.

Demons are not now, nor ever have been, human spirits. They are not ghosts, the walking dead, zombies, space aliens, vampires, greys, ghouls, poltergeists, witches, warlocks, apparitions, sub-heroes, mythological gods, or the many fabrications of imagination so popularized by writers of horror and science fiction productions.

Indeed, demons have no concept of, nor experience with, being souls eligible for salvation through Christ as we do. Jesus Christ did not die for angels, good or evil, for animals, the earth and vegetable kingdom, or for inanimate objects. He died for all human persons who alone have the opportunity for redemption by believing Him to be God, and confessing Him as the rightful Lord of their submissive will.[4]

What Do Demons Crave?

Demons do exist as fallen evil spirit beings (without tangible bodies but only capable of rebellion, evil attitudes, wickedness, causation of fear, torments, illness, and terrors. As well as with Satan, they do not have even one attribute of Jehovah. They openly reveal themselves as often as possible by acting through willing witch doctors, mediums, wizards, witches, warlocks, so-called zombies, pagan idols, in hallucinatory drugs and by religious traditionalism. They are creatures that will face a dreadful eternal judgment.

They do act out their personality abilities through inhabiting or tormenting open and willing humans. They promote godless theories and philosophies, practice an ever-increasing debauchery with an astounding array of sexual perversions, push death at all stages of human development from conception to old-age euthanasia, and are known to abuse animals if needful to them[5].

Demons seek human minds (souls) to act through to display their presence and limited controls. These spirits want to be recognized, called on, adored, and known. They crave what belongs to the holy that will never be theirs so it is to be marred, tormented, led into early destruction and final death.

NOTE. The authentic Holy Spirit wants to be recognized, called on, adored, and known. He trains and empowers His children to reflect His nature with the objective of building a family for Father God and making able warriors of the kingdom for the challenged of life right now. To do this, Jesus formed His kingdom within us by which the ekklesia works. Jesus in us is to rescue and redeem the ignorant and rebellious from the most remote primitive jungles to the cement, steel, and glass jungles of grand cities who are just as lost in their sin natures, intellects, greed, and carnal lusts.

We next explore the battlegrounds for mind control that leads the personality. Can you identify some of the gates demons constantly crash against to infest a human mind for their mild and wild exhibitions?

[1] Quoted from *The Encyclopedia of Demons in World Religions and Cultures* (2012), by Theresa Bane, Introduction, page 7.

[2] Foundations of George Soros, Bill Gates, Rockefeller, Margaret Sanger, World Economic Forum, et. al., are examples.

[3] Luke 9:1 the believer's authority over all demons.

[4] John 3:16-17

[5] Matthew 8:26-34

| 6 |

Battlegrounds for Mind Control

*"It is impossible to mentally or socially enslave a
Bible-reading people."* ~ Horace Greeley

Four Mind Positions of God's Order

Satan, as the false god of this world system Babylon), is organized
as he continually sets his will against God's will and against God's
children.[1] He is the archenemy of all that is godly and is against all that
God favors. He uses or attempts to use the human spirit, soul, and body
to exercise any or all control possible that will expand and enhance his
own kingdom of death.

> **The BATTLE is won or lost in your MIND and by your compliant WILL.**

Walking in righteousness does not vanish by a devil's tricks made in
his serpentine mind. All spiritual takeovers begin and continue in the
decision field of the human mind. He knocks, and you either answer or
ignore him. Sometimes, one must run from a powerful temptation that

will set you to following him. And, as Jesus told us, we cannot have two masters at one time, even in one area.

The human tripartite of body, soul, and spirit in which all battles rage, shows the effects of the struggle for control. In each of us, without exception, there is predominantly either a wealth of God's peace, love, joy, and healthy soul that is clearly discernible, or else cursed living revealed as depression, disease, failure, addiction, and recurring mishaps that haunt almost their every move.

The following list of God's order helps us to examine our own lives first in order to determine our position because we will need this ability to assess the Seeker's mindset. In assessing the spiritual position of one's self to enjoy a life of peace and joy, we should first recognize exactly where Satan is waging war against us. Is it from within or without? Are God-ward efforts resisted by his constant accusations to the Father against you?

Or, are the vile vexations of his demon horde consistently at your mind to tempt and throw you off God's plan for you? These are normal assaults but how we believers counter them by His Word, is the path to learning how to overcome the enemy's schemes.

It is only when we learn to recognize in our spirits what is of Jehovah God, what is of the human spirit, and what is of Satanic origin, that we can begin to agree with the Lord. Our hunger for being and remaining over-comers is a full-time job it seems. Encouragingly, you will begin to recognize what the battle is about, before an engagement in warfare is necessary, in order to bring into His light, the causes for conflict on behalf of yourself and others.

Once it is deeply internalized, we embrace the spiritual victory that has already been freely given to each Christian but at an exorbitantly high price to the person of Jesus Christ. In the end of all the other sacrifices, it cost Him His very lifeblood early on in His amazing supernatural ministry to those who were dead, diseased, possessed, hungry, and craving for freedom.

After His resurrection and promenade of victory in hell and paradise, the lost personal opportunity to ensure that His new Church could be freed and able to free others from enemy onslaught, was preplanned and pretrained into the hands of Pentecostal empowered disciples. Nothing was lost, not even His Presence. But it was a rough transition from a previously God-ordained prophetic era into the radically new Church era that is now after 2,000 years swiftly coming to its end.

Furthermore, to claim that deliverance requires us to get the reality of what the cross-victory encompassed, He had to release His body, His call, His mantle, His physical Presence, and all His human family and friendships, to personally implement the Ekklesia to safeguard His future family. This had to be completed by His Holy Spirit's Pentecost implementation in order to continue interacting in the lives of His family.

I really wonder just how long Jesus could have personally spread His ministry for the next so many years had not the hatred against Him consumed religious men to deliver Him to murderers? When you embrace this knowledge, it will produce the basis for becoming a victor over the Babylonian world culture, over your carnal compulsions, and certainly over Satan's efforts to destroy you.

These are the normal cutting edges of the spiritual battles of life. It is here where the deeply cut scars of successful soldiers of the cross are gloriously created, or where the losses of defeat are revealed. We begin the determination process next.

The Mind Must be Changed. The unregenerate, natural, unsaved mind which is the self-natural soul, is hostile toward God and utterly unable to subject itself to God's laws.[2] The natural mind rejects the true teaching of God because it perceives them as foolishness.[3] Unless this kind of mind is *changed*, a person cannot get his or her thoughts off the pleasures and problems of life and will remain occupied with the cares of the world and not with seeking God. The natural *Unchanged Mind* never comes to salvation.

What is REPENTANCE? It radically changes one's mind from self-destruction to God's direction. It is a gift or mercy from the Father and accomplished by one's act of faith in Him. It is the decision at God's prompting to stop the self-nature behavior, and turn to Christ Jesus with the whole mind and heart (soul). Repentance recognizes the human inability to help oneself in any way and leaves that mi position completely. It is the decision to not only *turn away* from sin, but to *turn to* the Lord and His purposes for you. After the step of repentance is made, the *Changed Mind* begins the spiritual relationship with Christ because the human spirit has been opened and birthed to communicate.

The Mind Must be Renewed. For born-again believers starting on their journey, the *Renewed Mind*[4] has the same attitude as God's will. We are commanded to PUT OFF our old self, which is corrupted by its own deceitful desires; and be made new in the attitude of our minds. But it is not possible to just put off a corrupted mind in our own strength: this mind must be replaced. The apostle Paul continues to add, "PUT ON the new self, created to be like God in true righteous-ness and holiness".[5] The Greek translator used the word *ananeoo* in this passage by which we see the intention to *"renovate, reform, and make new again"*.

The renewing process is an on-going endeavor of practical sancti-fication on the Christian's life journey. We never stop being renewed because it produces in us the look and behavior of "Christ-likeness" at ever more complete phases. We are growing into the image of Jesus Christ that is seen in the display of Holy Spirit generated fruit.[6]

The Mind Must be Controlled. First Peter 1:13 gives us three instruc-tions regarding controlling the thoughts of the mind: *"prepare your minds for action; be self-controlled, set your hope fully on the grace to be given you..."* Further, controlling our minds (by the soul's decision center) re-quires action to retain this position by, *"Casting down imaginations, and bringing into captivity every thought to the obedience of Christ"*[7] Herein is the battle for control or loss.

The *Self-controlled Mind* keeps us balanced and poised for godliness by reinforcing the *Renewed Mind*. Guarding your mind from the two extremes of either passivity (I don't care anyway) or fanaticism (I'll kill to get my way!), protects access to the spirit through the soul gate. An uncontrolled position can easily be conquered by destructive emotional imaginations into unclear and unstable thinking. *"What was I thinking?"*

The Mind Must be Occupied by Godly Thoughts. A blank, neutralized, and uninvolved mind produces a passive will that Satan takes rapid advantage of. This is a sure way to allow entrance of any idea or agenda another person or group wants to force and push on us and our children who are especially susceptible. We are not created to do the will of others, but only of the Lord. Philippians 4:8 tells us to, *"...think on what is pure"*. THINK in this verse is a command of active engagement. Again, we are told[8] to *"...SET YOUR MIND on things which are above, where Christ is seated at the right hand of God...not on earthly things"*. Earthly thoughts spell death and captivity.

This last, Christ-centered, and focused mind is an active, doing mind, able to defeat outside attempts by evil tormentors to continue to build and nourish *The Renewed Mind* by its athletic vigilance. A God Mind loves to discover and live by Scripture. It craves God's fellowship and hearing His voice that continually builds the soul-man in strength.

NOTE: Every thought suggested to the mind by evil spirits and accepted, is permission to steal from you. Blank and misused minds invite the attempted takeover by evil forces. In the case of many drugs, even some so-labeled vaccines (rDNA) that changes the chemistry of the brain, will create the mind-vacuum of an unused and misused mind that seeks to be filled with almost anything.

The preceding four controls of the mind will be stronger or weaker depending on what the Seeker chooses to be of most importance to them. Do they wish to remain unsaved? Then they choose to have an *Unchanged Mind*. Have they decided with God's grace to repent when confronted with their hopeless position without Christ? Then they choose to be saved and possess the *Renewed Mind*.

What about the believer who fills his or her mind with junk data, mindless electronic surfing, hours on social channels, taking selfies, subscribing to endless not-news feeds, frequent entertainment sites, and hours of gaming, exotic webcasting, occult mysteries, star gossip, with hours of mindless chatter spent on little known people to no purpose?

What are they looking for? These chosen activities to fill their minds have set them up to be undisciplined and uncontrolled in their thinking, absorbing what passes off as titillating truth. It just seems easier for carnal Christians to ride through life with a minimal relationship with Christ and foolishly think "to let life just happen since God is in control". Not so. He gave us the stewardship of our minds directed by His purposes.

Seven Mind Positions of Influence

Next, we turn our focus on the following seven mindset processes that are the battlegrounds of control Satan and his minions engage in. We will learn to recognize them. Remember, to the degree a person has yielded personal authority or has not come out of a negative mind posture, will determine the extent of domination he or she has given permission to the devil to maintain his own defeating agenda.

The Corrupted Mind. At this stage, unbelievers are at the complete mercy of Satan and generally anyone else stronger than they are. This mind is fleshly, unregenerate, and is naturally set to war against the Spirit of God in whatever forms that takes. It gives the enemy total access to run them.

The Corrupted Mind is a dead mind to the Spirit of God so it is cut off from wisdom and common sense meaning, it is cut off from God's input. *The Corrupted Mind* is the fool's mind and thoroughly saturated in the world cultural system naturally submitting to self-referential lusts that bend them toward final destruction. It cannot know God.

The Ignorant Mind. A person with an *Ignorant Mind* does not and cannot believe God's truth if they are totally unaware of what Truth is. They lack knowledge and recognition of Truth. Ignorance is a condition. All of us as newborn children are ignorant of almost everything except being hungry and uncomfortable. Survival instincts take over. However, for those growing out of childish years, it is fool hardy to retain an *Ignorant Mind.*

This mindset confounds truths with lies so that wrong things look just like right things. Examples include transgender mutilation, pedophilia, abortion, progressive political agendas, religious philosophies, and much more. These positions one is convinced of seem to be right (especially when legalized) as outside pressure or popularity mounts.

By not even exploring God's Word or asking for help, *The Ignorant Mind* chooses to go its own or others' ways. This can be the most dangerous mindset because it often wrongly (ignorantly) reacts to circumstances hammered at them by an assailing culture, instead of knowingly acting from knowledge, purpose, sanity, and self-control.

The Blinded Mind. We are instructed[9] that those of the world have been blinded by the god of this age like false light against the gospel of Jesus Christ. This compares to foolishly driving on a flooded roadway after a hurricane passes through as waters fill your stalled vehicle. The environment can be deceiving. It no longer matters your panic reasoning for being blinded to danger!

Satan is in his business to blind minds where all change occurs. *The Blinded Mind* is found in unbelievers who will sit under the preaching and sharing of the Gospel yet never "hear" or understand it. *The Blinded Mind* is a state that can be broken in the unsaved by a Spirit Warrior who will press through that mindset for them to gain understanding of what true salvation is.

In the believer, a *Blinded Mind*[10] is comprehended as a person's refusal to deal with specific sins of commission and omission that are painfully obvious to others in the ekklesia, or by rejecting what is truly the will of God for them. How many times do we see professing Christians openly living in relationships of heterosexuality or homosexuality and claiming that it is "alright with God who loves them"?

Or, you will find pressured believers to have had abortions along with the men or family members who 'help' young women to choose abortion over trusting God. Is it not our duty to stand against the clearly written hatreds of God into a clear mind to save lives?

Basically, the seeker-friendly and liberal churches of our era, is where everyone is spoon-fed on lopsided themes of "God is Love," or, pushed into entitlement attitudes so prevalent within bless-me notions. Why are blinded minds never impressed by God's hatred of the very things they are trapped by? God is a Judge, too.

The positive news is, that *The Blinded Mind* can be self-recognized, repented of, and verbally confessed in exchange for a *Sane Mind* that agrees with God's Word and forsakes the willful blindness. Here is another grand obligation for the ekklesia to show grace and train in righteousness.

The Untutored Mind. This mindset belongs to an immature or spiritually undeveloped Christian who has not, or has only partially yielded, his or her mind to the Holy Spirit to continue to renew.[11] It includes those believers who have no access to the bible in their own language with no fault of their own, but as they seek others to teach them, will become tutored or discipled in God's word.

Otherwise, persisting with an *Untutored Mind* locks the believer in the world's view where they came out of. It is this dangerous, fence-sitting ground that makes it difficult for the Spirit Warrior to determine if these people are either saved or unsaved.

An *Untutored Mind* is a truth-vacant area. It a demon's play-pen to plant many levels of erroneous misinformation and deceptive philosophies making them unable to distinguish truth from untruth. By intentionally not making time to read or deeply study God's truth, discipleship is delayed often resulting in the loss of that person's faith to believe God.

This may be a momentary period in one who accepts Christ and immediately passes into eternity by physical death like the example of the thief on the cross with his *Untutored Mind*. The point is, Seekers must be directed into discipleship opportunities to avoid ignorance, confusion, and double-mindedness.

The Depraved Mind. *The Depraved Mind is* fully classified by Paul in his letter to the Roman church.[12] The motivation of depravity is the result of, *"...since they did not THINK it worthwhile to retain the knowledge of God, He gave them over to a depraved (reprobate) mind..."*

Using Paul's list, Spirit Warriors can identify this Seeker as a person--to some degree--does what ought not to be done; they are full of envy, murder, strife, deceit, malice, and gossip; are slanderers, God-haters, insolent, prideful, arrogant, and boastful. They invent ways of doing evil (sociopath bent); disobedient to parents (or higher author-ity), and are senseless, faithless, heartless, and ruthless.

The Depraved Mind is marked by moral corruption, works evil (perhaps even against the Seeker who comes for help), and totally sets itself against God by thriving on willful rebellion. They are unsaved. Depraved Minded ones can join undiscerning believers that become church-wreckers or can escalate into criminal behavior.

The Suggestible Mind. Suggestions are not truths. The Internet and cyberspace are brimming with suggestions of truths, speculations, sur-mising, misinformation, and just wild guessing that many credit at face value. Some believe that what they read on the Internet replaces what the bible states and will argue their 'truth' with you! Suggestions are the hint, the intimation, the insinuation, the implication to something real, making it close to, but not God's pure Truth.

Professing believers who do not search out bible truth are, or increasingly can become, gullible by easily believing whatever they are told. This is especially true if it sounds "religious"; e.g., cults are religious and so are most broadly cast popular ideas. Knowing that Satan is the father of all lies, he speaks into a blank mind by filling it with false thoughts that naturally attract humans who are curious about their future and personal circumstances. This accounts for the enormous fortune-teller's market.

Fostering an openly *Suggestible Mind* will lead to deeply harmful trails of deception and becomes very difficult to learn how to conform to Jesus Christ's ways. The requisite need is the removal of all the falsehoods they have already stacked up.

A global example of *The Suggestible Mind* in action is witnessed in millions of people in the error of non-scientific Climate Change movements or political pressures to cause people to deny God's error-less control of His own creation (follow the money). Darwinism, Critical Race Theory, White Privilege, or extraordinary "rights" for special people groups. Many ecological green, mother earth honoring organizations began and maintain these lies. Repentance for allowing the *Suggestible Mindset* is the beginning point for these Seekers caught in these lies. They will require earnest discipleship follow-up to keep their deliverance as their minds are conformed to the mind of Jesus Christ.

NOTE: *The Suggestible Mind* is a normal state in youth who can be easily taught in the principles of Christ or flexed toward evil suggestions by others to use and abuse them. For example, they will be confused by adults who suggest they may choose their own gender status or male or female, if they "feel like". Childhood (under 12 years) is the best time to win them to Jesus, beginning with your own family and guarding their heart (soul).

The Passive Mind. Christians, use your minds! Our minds must be actively engaged. One indication that a mind is passive shows up when action is called for, but no decision to move on it is made. These become procrastinators who allow opportunities to pass them by, even

God's opportunities to obedience. An opposite sign is behavior that is rash or over-reactive in emotional ways after long periods of indecisive non-operation. Anger can build aggressively or passively.

In believers related to an ekklesia community, there can be many rationales given for lack of involvement or for Kingdom interest. It may be disobedience to God's voice or ignoring it when He requests their immediate action. You can recognize this attitude of being blinded ('whatever happens, happens'), and a lack of concentration, glazed eyes that will not focus on what others are saying, the use of poor or no judgment, with excuses of "having a bad memory", being chronically tardy or absent at set appointments and promised responsibilities.

The Passive Mind is easily out maneuvered and remains confused.[13] Areas that can be turned over through passivity are: the will, emotions, judgment, reasoning, feelings, passions, and decision-making abilities. Other areas of the mind affected by passivity are the conscience, spirit, body, whole personality, imagination, and refusal of creativity. *The Passive Mind* does not attain to full maturity because that person is unwilling to risk leadership by taking a position which would mean sacrifice to build character.

Evil spirits are well acquainted with *The Passive Mind*. They can both impart ideas and steal ideas away from them.[14] This mindset rarely lives in right-now reality, will not confront a bad situation head-on, and is oblivious, by design, of areas in life that others are acutely aware of and will address quickly to avoid disaster. This mindset can become habitual as a personality construct.

NOTE: The primary cause of DECEPTION taken by demonic influence happens when the soul is compliant and yielded to their operations. The number of liberties willingly yielded to evil will determine the extended endeavors demons are free to torment with. The bible says we have the position as "kings and priests to God". Do not yield.

One Mind That Cannot be Defeated

There is great news, though. True believers have *The Mind of Christ.*[15] This is the only mindset that cannot be defeated. It is an active mind, attuned to the Holy Spirit and ready to launch into obedience. The most straightforward and consequential law of the spirit realm is that nothing pertaining to a believer, either for or against them, can be accomplished without the consent of his or her will. We must give permission.

To recover lost territory previously relinquished to the enemy, will mean that an exercise of that person's will (triggered by repenting), is to be reinstated with a resolve to follow the lordship of Jesus Christ.

Request that confession them to vocalize that by declaring their consent of having *The Mind of Christ* during their first deliverance session. You will find a guide in *Appendix B* or encourage them to declare their position in Christ using their own words. By this means, the Lord Commander assumes His rule over the territory of the Seeker's soul by their discontinued tolerance of all demonic action formerly authorized to them.[16]

Most believers and all non-believers, will be conscious of the mammoth part their own soul-mind plays in keeping them sane, alert, directed, watchful, righteous, and aware of whom they are and where they are headed in God's plans or outside of them. Many come to the altar to seek, "God's plan for my life" or ask, "What is my destiny?" How will you answer them?

With use of the *Mind of Christ* within them, the ability to be aggressively willing and able to make definitive decisions to follow Christ becomes primary to knowing and obeying Him with intentionality and purpose. *The Mind of Christ* is pleasing to the Father for that is the God-position and announces that you are onboard with His will and ways; and indeed, are thirsting to know Him better and be closer.

There once was a popular (and profitable) trend to ask yourself when found in uncharted waters that needed a decision: *'What would Jesus do?'* This is a highly flawed and erroneous question because the answer you come up with is subjective to what your level of bible knowledge might or might not be.

The real question to ask is this one: *"What DID Jesus do?"* and that is clearly stated in the four gospels, Acts, and The Revelation of Jesus. *The Mind of Christ* is within us by the grace and guidance of the Holy Spirit Who can only agree with the inerrant word of God. Access Christ's mind for every situation.

At the end, we may be at odds with the Holy Spirit's faithful and continual maturation process working within us, until we yield our preconceived and wrongly learned doctrines. By choice, as unbelief is eliminated, He is free to let us recognize Him for the supernatural God He is.

Believers in Jesus Christ will at last, be residing in the peace of liberty to enjoy Him in all His glorious manifestations--working through us--to a needy world of people, most of whom expect a supernatural answer to their distressed and unlivable conditions.

We next investigate the possible sieges against the human spirit that works to prevent us from becoming who we are created to become.

[1] James 4:4-7; 1 John 2:15-17

[2] Romans 8:5-7

[3] 1 Corinthians 2:14

[4] Romans 12:2 *"...be ye transformed by the renewing of your mind..."*

[5] Ephesians 4:22-24

[6] Galatians 5:22-25; Titus 1:15; Titus 3:1

[7] 2 Corinthians 10:5; Hebrews 10:16; Hebrews 12:3 and 2 Cor. 1:10

[8] Colossians 3:1-2; 1 Timothy 1:7; 2 Peter 3:1; 1 Corinthians 2:16; 8:18-19 and 1 Corinthians 13:11

[9] Second Corinthians 3:14 and 4:4

[10] Romans 11:8

[11] Romans 12:1-2

[12] Romans 1:28-32

[13] Matthew 13:23; Isaiah 26:3

[14] Luke 8:12

[15] Philippians 2:5; 2 Peter 3:1; Revelation 2:23; 2 Timothy 1:7

[16] Romans 7:25 and 12:2

| 7 |

Assault Against the Human Spirit

"Now may the God of peace Himself sanctify you completely; and may your whole spirit, soul, and body be preserved blameless at the coming of our Lord Jesus Christ." ~ 1 Thessalonians 5:23

Created for His Intentional Purposes

God created we humans as three-part beings; meaning, our composition consists of three distinct capacities of spirit, soul, and body. These reflect His likeness that equally operates in the three capacities of Father, Son, and Holy Spirit. Theologians have called Yahweh as One God in three capacities, *The Trinity.*

Humans are not divine nor ever will be, however we are created to function in the image of God as one unit in three distinct elements. Let's explain this a bit.

The Spirit-heart is the unique gateway to a spirit-to- Spirit relationship with God, able to respond to His Spiritual side when birthed to life by the key of faith. This is the area that is described as the place the unsaved are always trying to fill up with all sorts of stuff that never works in a quest to become a whole. The faith of Jesus Christ births the spirit[1] into perfection, completion, and purpose.

When it happens, we are filled with a flood of God's peace as our dead human spirit opens into the new person we were meant to be. This is the portal to interconnecting with Father. It is the only way out of the closed human system of eternal sin and death. Our born-again spirit is empowered to discern the spiritual world as the Holy Spirit joins with those who seek Him.

The Soul is constituted of the mind, a will that chooses, an intellect, and emotional expression. The soul is our core personality. It is the command center for the body and acquires God-intel via our spirit as it is alive in Christ. The soul capacity responds to human and animal relatedness; is highly creative, imaginative, and sensitive. Each soul manifests one unique personality that can reason and deduce solutions, make decisions, and express love, passion, aspiration, fear, aptitude, and feelings.

The Body. Obviously, the external body is our contact with the physical world by using its senses of touch, taste, smell, hearing, sight, danger, pain, and pleasure. It is a marvelously God-created instrument with unique DNA and unique imprinting of the eyes, voice, hair and finger-, palm-, toe-, and heel prints).

Humans are dependent on survival with the needs of food, air, water, ambient temperatures, and shelter to keep alive. It is regulated to maintaining physical life to survive danger and disease in an earth-bound environment. One of God's most treasured gifts in fashioning us is the high privilege and physical ability to reproduce our succeeding generations.

As we begin to expand our knowledge of religious sects and how they hinder and stop the flow of the human spirit to live in obedience and harmony with Father, we will be better equipped to discern the confusions of Seekers who have believed that exact deception.

Distinguishing the Spirit from the Soul

It is at the point of division between living in the renewed spirit and battling against the self-lusting soul life as the point of either your victory is won or a defeat that must be challenged to rise to the next level of perfection. While by the sword of the Holy Spirit this distinction is made, each person must consent with his or her will (soul agreement) to the process, beginning with repentance for the trespasses.

Let us pose a question and answer it to help clarify the necessity for determining the division of spirit from soul in the Seeker. What is it about the expression of the soul that separates a person from walking in the Spirit? Chiefly, there are several things to consider.

First, it is in the soul area (mind, affections, emotions, will, intellect) that sin is wrestled with or outright practiced. When a Christian knows it is time to take up the cross of Christ—denying the pleasure of the soul to have its own way—a battle comes between the human spirit and the Holy Spirit who requires the Cross life.[2] For example, Christ says we are to leave our father and mother and follow Him. A choice must be made by the disciple. Do I choose the family inheritance or forsake worldly offers for Christ alone? These choices may be in many areas.

Now is when the soul puts up a mighty fight to keep the choice (e.g., family in our example). The sword of the Lord comes through to divide this soul-position from the God-position. But it can only happen with the person's understanding and consent. The beauty of this is in seeing the affections of the soul put under subjection to the Lordship of Christ: the lower life exchanged for the higher.

Second, the human tripartite has an order of organization and authority. Each of us are a dominant soul with a dead (not born-again) or a living spirit (born-again) which is designed to fellowship and happily comply with the Holy Spirit. Soul and spirit together makes us a Personality living within a material body able to communicate with the physical world.

When the soul in or outside its proper order, God will move to correctly direct us (for we are without a clue of life at birth). For Seekers who need that balance reinstated, it must be clear to no longer loves their wrong choices. The frail and volatile human love thread needs an exchange for the supernatural love of God.

Now, here the soul-life is summed up in the one word *himself*. It is the fleshly self-life that is contrary to not only God's will, but is against our own best interests. The sword of the Spirit must divide here, putting the spirit in command to desire to obey the Holy Spirit with its own soul the adversary. This establishes the Lordship of Christ.

Third, the soul-life clings to the innate possessions and people of earth. It loves material and people things: Houses, lands, motor vehicles, fashion, technology, professional sports, businesses, education, religion, safe retirement--whatever. This is the part within us that relates to self-interests, the natural instincts to self-preservation and the self-grasping of goods. This is the self-referential life (me, mine, me first, me only).

Immediately, when the Lordship principle is shared, the soul love of its idols is put to the sword. Lot's wife turned back to--familiar things and to a lifestyle, perhaps faithless family members--she didn't want to leave. Choices are made daily between renouncing this soul-tie to possessions and people or by giving them wholly to the Lord.

The undue absorption of the children of God with this carnal aspect of the soul denies his or her own spirit to submit to the Holy Spirit for its over-occupation with the affairs of this world. Soul ties must be cut by the knife of the Spirit to become a circumcised heart.[3]

Fourth, soulish self-love is another area[4] that spells eternal loss because it proceeds from the first Adam's corrupt nature. This grasping to "me" is manifested through the personality of the soul that had not been brought into submission to the Holy One. *"Is it a sin to keep it?"* they may ask. Yes, when the Light shines in and you see Truth.

This is the place where the will of the believer must be set to be on God's side, no matter what death occurs in its soulish idolatry. The very will (as choice maker) of the soul, bows before its own human spirit, abdicating the old Adam afresh so the new Adam might come forth.

When you minister to Seekers who have refused God's will and ways, part of that will be this breaking of the soul-ties to their idols by willingly allowing the Holy Spirit access to move in their renewed spirit. Warriors, as you minister the grace of God in His name, maintain this centering on His only Son, Jesus Christ as True Lord. He is the only Deliverer able to dispel the forces of sinning self-interests for the long-term.

The key is, that the whole person must lineup and team with the Lord Jesus Christ in His Lordship of them. Our spirit facilitates that aligning process with the Lord's intention for maturity. In the next chapter, we will focus on the important and correct position of the human soul and its potentialities amid assaults from within and without.

Religion is a False Model of Worship

Concerning the outbreaks most common against our spirit, further understanding is critical to define *religion,* the most perilous antagonist. Religion is the rationale and activities humans employ attempting to reach a god(s). In this quest, they do not know about the only possible connection to Yahweh, the One and only True, Most High God.

All that can be offered is every corrupted resource they possess or promise. From pagan nations to Christianized citadels, we witness their ignorant, fruitless, and often deadly efforts. That is why Kingdom servants are sent to preach, heal, disciple, raise the dead, cast out demons, and bring the light of the full Gospel to batter the gates of hell and release them.

AFFLUENZA.[5] A painful, contagious, socially transmitted mentality overload; habitual debt, anxiety, and waste resulting from the dogged pursuit of MORE. This could be religious.

RELIGION-1.[6] Any system of faith and worship. In this sense, religion is a concept that encompasses the beliefs and worship of pagans on an equal footing with Christianity; any religion consisting in the belief of a superior power or powers governing the world, and in the worship of such power or powers; we speak of false religion as well as of true (Christian) religion.

RELIGION-2.[7] Greek thrēskêia; a ceremonious observance: -- religion, worshiping. #2454 is Iŏudaismŏs, Judaism, the Jewish faith; #4576 sébŏmai: to revere, adore, be devout or religious. In short, religion is a false paradigm that simulates a possible God-connection; yet, it is impossible to deliver for it is humans reaching for God. Our Father is after relationship with the family He died to redeem from all our inadequate efforts. His only way is to reach for us with great love, grace, forgiveness, and mercy.

The Human Spirit Enthrones and Dethrones

In stark contrast to vain and false religion, is the born-again Christ-follower who begins with God reaching toward humankind through the finished, satisfactory work of His only begotten Son Jesus, the Christ.

God initiates this transaction, not we humans. It is a gift received by the utmost belief (faith) in Truth. It is an outright gift so no person at judgment will be able to accuse Father of demanding of us what no person can provide. All who have ever been conceived have had their sin redeemed. Thereafter, it is a question of availing oneself of that redemptive provision.

Salvation is free and freely given but it was not cheaply provided. Once it is received by faith, then believers give life-long effort to become conformed to the image of God's Son as a joyful and blessed consequence. The good works come after salvation, never before it as "earnings of good works or through insincere confessions to "get to heaven".

The one test that separates Christianity from all other religions, cults, sects, and philosophical ideologies, is the apostle's doctrine of God as the Father, God as the Son, God as the Holy Spirit while being

One whole God. Christianity stands with the Triple nature of God. That truth is uniquely foundational.

Assaults by evil spirits against the human spirit, if allowed, soon becomes a threshold of Satan constantly working to violently disfigure the very sanctuary of the Lord within us. Attacks against the spirit are particularly repugnant because they interfere with, and hinder, our closest relationship with our Spiritual Father and could delay or pervert the formation of the mind of Christ within.

Remember, born-again believers cannot be possessed (owned) by demons since we are possessed (owned with our permission) by God. Christ redeemed us from the hand of Satan and the penalty of death, replaced by His grace by the unique outlay of Christ's divine blood.

The Holy One dwells with us in our spirit man. We abide with Him there and are eternally safe though any part of our being can come under assault; however, our human spirit was *sealed as God's own*, at salvation.

The born-again human spirit sits enthroned with Jesus Christ in heavenly places[8] sending and receiving new intelligence and prophetic communications with the Holy One.

This is our position, *"for we are His workmanship, created in Christ Jesus for good works, which God prepared beforehand that we should walk in them"*. When the Word of God exhorts us to, *"Guard your hearts,"* the possibility of being pushed around is actual. By actively guarding our spirit, we have an ongoing barrier set against attempted take-overs to dethrone us from our places of influence and position.

Major Oppositions to the Human Spirit[9]

This level of opposition is demonic spirit against human spirit, so the methods of attack are on the spirit level. The most direct way this is approached, is through the deception of mystical intrigue and religious false doctrine. A little Truth mixed with a little False: the proportions of either one results from the amount of faith one puts in error or rejects error.

There are ways believers open themselves to the most subtle attacks imaginable. One of the most pernicious is prostitution of the inner man. This occurs by trading or giving part of one's self away for unseemly gain by commercializing on a God-given ministry, the intellect, or their spiritual gifts.

We've all seen or heard about those in kingdom leadership positions selling out the truth of the gospel for various rationales: sex, money, fame, liberal ideologies, fame, or whatever else. Two examples from the bible come to mind with Simon the sorcerer to use a demon-possessed girl for business and the servant of Elijah who lied to gain a gift of apparel in payment for Elijah's miracle, not his own.

There are many examples of destructive choices in life and in scripture besides what is on this short list of paths that cause temptation to bloom.

1. Persistent or recurrent evil or destructive emotions and attitudes that can dominate a person even contrary to his or her own will (compulsions); resentment, fears, hatred, envy, jealousy, pride, self-pity, tension, suicide, anger, impatience, rejection, meanness, a bullying attitude or actions, filth and abusiveness, rage, and a lack of conscience.

2. Various forms of religious error: bondage and submission to unscriptural doctrines and/or groups, cults, ideologies; included are all types of material and psychological idolatry, false worship, and attraction to error.

3. Consistent or violent opposition to the truth of Scripture, to the Name of Jesus Christ as the only wise God, against the Church (body of believers worldwide), or in advocating anti-Semitic that posits that the Church replaced Judaism.

4. Activism in culture, rights, and by political manipulation opposed to the Word of God and its teachings are often manifested as a raging rebellion against Godly spiritual, parental, and public

authorities. As was stated before, our world culture changed in 2020 by the attempted transition to a New World Order.

Technology was now in place to do so. We stepped into the future where conditions that could only happen at the end of the church age were now sliding us into the tribulation's edge of impending judgment.

There is no biblical doubt that we are in tremulous times. We will begin witnessing the rage of man and nations battling for control of food, water, health, banking, technology, information flow, liberties or not, and death on a global scale. People are anxious. Demons are stirred up.

Millions felt the radical shift against God that was long and quietly scheduled and engineered by a small cadre of the mega-wealthy thirsting for complete control of all world resources. They have plans to have less people access to 'their' world space. Look at the Georgia Guide Stones.

Disturbingly, we have observed some very prominent evangelical, Pentecostal, and liturgical church leaders being enlisted as community influencers to link their congregants with their new world agenda. Some openly marched with proven Marxist ideologues, LGBTQ+ causes, or paraded fabricated and false science often using misgender, environmentalism, or reverse racism as wedges for national conquest. "That don't play" as we say in the South.

More than a century has passed in their global control efforts for establishing a New World Order to replace the traditional Judaeo-Christian framework. Now they have moved to tighten the noose of control that only the advent of technology has been able to accomplish.

We are inside the satanic agenda for economic, religious, and secular cultural overthrow at this moment. Of course, the pressure is immense and the spirit world is gleefully active.

We are the targets.

[1] John 3:1-21.

[2] Matthew 10:38.

[3] Colossians 2:11-15; Romans 2:28-29; Philippians 3:2-11.

[4] John 12:25.

[5] Bob Mumford, *Dealing with That Other God*, Plumbline Vol. 40.3, page 21.

[6] Webster, Noah, American Dictionary of The English Language, 1828, Definition 4; Parenthesis are from the author.

[7] James Strong's Exhaustive Concordance of the Bible, Religion: #2356 (Acts 26:5, James 1:26-27); #2854 (Gal. 1:13); #2454 (Gal. 1:14). Religious: #4576 (Acts 13:43); #2357 (James 1:26).

[8] Ephesians 1:3 and 2:4-10.

[9] Lewis, Jessie Penn, *"War on the Saints"*. Lewis faced spiritual warfare during and after one of the most powerful revivals in history over 100 years ago: The Welsh Revival and what she said then applies today.

| 8 |

Assault Against the Soul
- Part 1

*"...Resist him, steadfast in the faith, knowing
that the same sufferings are experienced by
your brotherhood in the world."*
~1 Peter 5:9

Soul Language

When the human spirit is birthed and immediately sealed in the Lord of Glory, He initiates our spirit to grow in knowledge, wisdom, and spiritual power. That is the automatic shield, unable to come under the control of the spirits of evil. Therefore, being transformed into spiritual creatures, we are translated out of the closed kingdom of darkness into the open kingdom of God's Son. It is a spiritual operation.

In such the same way, the soul and body that had been totally exposed to the poison of Satan, learns how to shut down Satanic influences as the new spirit rises to rule under the Holy Spirit's direction. This is how in Christ Jesus, we become unified as a whole spirit, soul, and body established into the vital readiness and aptitude for God's higher purposes and indeed, fitted for spiritual warfare.

During the time a person is spiritually dead to Jehovah God before this rebirth milestone, the human soul is, nevertheless, able to communicate with demonic spirit forces, have non-God spiritual experiences, and be confronted and controlled by netherworld dynamisms sometimes manifested in signs, psychic abilities, and mind-soul control. Witches, warlocks, and pagan worshipers know of this power and are quite able to contract with this dark side.

Those who follow non-Christian religions, Hindu gurus, channelers, and the like, can move in overt Satanic societies. They do have real spirit contact, but not with our Lord Christ. They remain spiritually dead to God because they have not opened the door of faith. This is the corrupted mind that must come to repentance to claim Christ as lord. Jesus is the Door, the latch, the keyhole, the hinges, the bolts, the facing, and door frame—He is the only way into freedom!

This is the core purpose of intercessory prayer for deliverance: translating people from a spiraling state of darkness into the brilliant state of open spiritual freedom. I repeat, the Spirit Warrior team always begins a session by explaining and offering the opportunity of salvation to all who come for help. You will run into this admonition throughout reading this guide: begin at salvation!

When you begin there, what will shortly become clear, is the underlying reason of what got them into their situation: seeking wrong gods in wrong ways. Even if the Seeker is someone you know and had thought was saved, press in here by helping him or her find Jesus again, the only Source in more aspects than as Savior. Be satisfied with your outcome before continuing.

It is at this point that a division between living in the renewed spirit and dealing with the soul-life is made. While only by the sword of the Holy Spirit this distinction can be made, each person must consent with his or her will to the process. Let me pose a question and answer it to help clarify the necessity for determining the division of spirit from soul in Seekers.

What is it about the expression of the soul that separates a person from walking in the strength and ways of the Holy Spirit? Chiefly, there are several ideas to consider:

It is in the soul area (mind, affections, emotions, will, intellect) that sin is wrestled with or outright practiced. When a Christian knows it is time to take up the cross of Christ—denying the pleasure of the soul to have its own way—a battle comes between the human spirit and the Holy Spirit Who requires the Cross life.[1] For example, Christ says we are to leave our father and mother and follow Him. A choice must be made by the disciple. Will it be the family inheritance or forsaking worldly compromises to stand with Christ alone? You will hear a variety of choices in many areas.

Now is when the soul puts up a mighty fight to keep the former choice; e.g., their family allegiance in our example. The sword of the Lord comes through to divide this soul-position from the God-position. But it can only happen with the person's understanding and consent.

The beauty of this is in seeing the affections of the soul put under subjection to the Lordship of Christ: the lower life exchanged for the higher. Thus, the soul becomes dominated by the spirit which wishes to comply with the Holy Spirit. Now, with the soul in its proper order, God can move and bless so that the Seeker no longer worships his choice out of human, frail love, but has exchanged it for the love of God toward them.

> "Then Jesus said to His disciples,[2] 'If anyone desires to come after me, let him deny himself, and take up his cross and follow Me. For whoever desires to save his life (GK. psuche-soul) will lose it, but whoever loses his life (psuche-soul) for My sake will find it. For what profit is it to a man if he gains the whole world, and loses his own soul (psyche)? Or, what will a man give in exchange for his soul (psyche)?'"

Now, here the soul-life is summed up in the one word *himself.* It is the carnal and secular self-life that is contrary to not only God's will, but is against his or her own best interests. The sword of the Spirit must divide now, putting the spirit in command to desire to obey the Holy Spirit with its own soul as adversary. This decision to forsake all for Christ establishes the Lordship of Christ.

The soul-life clings to the innate passions, possessions, and custody of earthly domains. It loves material and people things: houses, lands, transportation modes, technology, fashion, the sport world, commerce, information, exotic religions, winning the lottery, fame, safe retirement —whatever the heart lusts for. The soul has a leadership position that attaches to self-interests, to the natural instincts of self-preservation, and the self-grasping of whatever is marketing for sale or conquest. The soul directs the self-referential life (me, mine, me first, me only).

Immediately as the Lordship principle is shared with a Seeker, their soul's love of its idols is put to the test. Which god/God will win? Lot's wife turned back to--familiar things, to a worldly lifestyle, perhaps to faithless family members who wouldn't go with them. She didn't want to leave.

Choices are made daily between renouncing this soul-tie to possessions and people or by giving them wholly to the Lord. The undue absorption of the children of God with this carnal aspect of the soul denies his or her own spirit to submit to the Holy Spirit for its over-occupation with the affairs of this world. Soul ties must be cut by the knife of the Spirit to become a circumcised heart.[3]

Last, we look at soulish self-love as a strong position[4] which creates eternal loss because it advances from the first Adam's corrupt nature. Holiness cannot come from corruption. This grasping 'for me' is clearly the personality that has not come by repentance into submission to the Holy One's wishes.

"*Is it a sin to insist on my way?*" they may ask.

Yes, when the Light of Christ shines in and Truth is evident. This is the place where the will of the believer must be set to God's side, no matter what death occurs to its soulish. The very Will (as choice maker) of the soul, must bow before its own human spirit, abdicating the old Adam afresh so the new Adam might come forth.

When you minister to Seekers who have refused God's will and ways, part of that will be this breaking of the soul-ties to their idols by their willingly allowing the Holy Spirit access and move in their renewed spirit. Warriors, as you minister the grace of God in His name, maintain this centering on His only Son, Jesus Christ as True Lord and as the only Deliverer able to dispel the forces of sinning self-interest for the long-term. The key is, the whole person must lineup and team with the Lord Jesus Christ in His Lordship preferences.

Let's next expand our knowledge of some of the strongest demon empires and how they hinder and the flow of the human soul to live in peace.

The Soul is Indestructible

God does not destroy the human personhood core at salvation or at any future time including death of the body. We are forever blessed with holy permission to choose to serve self through carnal pleasures (the will), or to serve God in love of His righteousness. Satan will dominate the area(s) of any life willed to him through fulfilling lusts of the flesh, the pride of life, the sensual love of money, or the unassailable attraction to the Babylonian world system's treasures he claims to control.

Believer-Servants must not entertain thoughts concerning what is contrary to the will of God, all revealed in His Word. Evil spirits will dominate those areas as time and authority is ceded for their development. Ignorance will not be an excuse that holds up with the Lord. Time must be set aside for the study of God's Word in order to build discernment.

Some entertain sin thoughts for so long, roots and inroads into the personality are molded. Deception can thus come that, that sin is, "just a part of me". So-called besetting sin mounts a defense like, "I'm always crabby (abusive) in the morning—that's just how I'm built". Or,

"Duncan is a fighter. He has the Irish temper, doesn't he?" There are no inherited sins: we choose at our will how we want to behave.

Another deception that is thought to be part and parcel of the personality is attractions to homosexuality. This sinful lifestyle can never be thought of "as natural"; not one person is born with it (or God be called a liar) and it is not just another area to culturally or theologically tolerate with an indifference pass given. Homosexuality is an evil root of sin that can be cast out of with sincere repentance and a vacate command!

Demons who do reside, reveal themselves through activity in the body. It happens through a series of events which begins in the mind (soul) by pondering temptations to commit wickedness. When giving in to these thought patterns, it a recurring temptation over time, as it is mentally caressed and toyed with before a decision to act is reached. Then, when once it is acted on by choice, it takes form as full-blown sin.

Persisting in sin invites demonic control because that is in their realm. You are now a sin slave. Demons will help you persist until it becomes the idol that replaces the living God. And that sell-created monster will disable you for God's service and kingdom living. Our grandparents called this 'living in sin'. Very popular to this day.

Idol worship is spirit-sin achieved by taking the soulish lead into avenues of apostasy. Idolatry turns FROM God's position of righteousness, His direction, His answers, and His provision of needs, TO relying on humans, governments, or spirit forces to satisfy those same needs. This exchange process guarantees fruit unto death.[5] For the reprobate believer, their salvation is never lost but the ungodly works will hit the burn pile.

Battered by the Tyrant of Fear

In the Hebrew language, *yare* and *yirah* define the good, and positive reverence of the fear of the Lord. At is contrasted to *morah* and *mora* meaning, "to have dread, be terror-filled, and a fearful deed or thing".

Emah is another Hebrew Old Testament word used to connote, "fright of an idol; as a bugbear like zombies, werewolves, space aliens, ghosts." The body expresses these fears when it has dread, horror, anxiety, quaking, trembling or to be exceedingly crushed, dismayed, broken, and fearful in spirit. Another body manifestation is to shutter violently.

While *guwr means* to turn aside, shrink from, and have fear to be in a strange place, it also meant to gather for hostility. People affected by fear will abide in, assemble in fearfulness and dwell or sojourn in fear itself.

New Testament writers used the Greek words *eulabeia* and *eulabeomai* meaning to fear reverentially and with caution; to be circumspect and religiously reverent (pious). This is the life-giving, positive side of fear/reverence. Other New Testament words in contrast to positive fear, are the negative side of "apprehension or dread to come".

The words *deilia* and *deilos* describe timidity, fearfulness, faithless, and strange. *Phobos* and its companion word *phebomai* are used elsewhere to mean "to be put in fear of and exceedingly alarmed". These connote seeing a frightening thing with terrific portent or to experience a fearful sight. Really, really, scary.

The fear of God (godly respect) is spoken of as a positive trait—high respect going toward God or as a negative destructive emotion—going toward the flesh, the world, and to Satan. Negative, crippling fears coming from human nature may not be demonic at all and disappear with the reading and affirmation of the Word of God, by prayer, and the self-discipline of putting fear on the run. This is ensured by exchanging a perceived fearful situation to becoming a person of faith that develops the *Renewed Mind*. Practically speaking, when we know what the real dangers are, we can deal with them rationally. That's how military troops are trained to handle the expected and unexpected outcomes of engagement.

Another positive type of fear is sensing danger and preserving your life and limb. We would not even survive all the pitfalls of childhood were it not for this God-given, natural fear of danger. *"Fear not"* was a constant admonition Jesus expressed to His disciples.

The spirit of fear is rampant. It was spoken by God to His people over 360 times in the Bible. It seems, then, that fear can be easily introduced into a life that is not fixed upon the Lord or when one is faced by great stress, threat of bodily harm to self or those he is protecting, or as a result of doing what is known to be a wrong choice with ominous consequences.

Fear is one of the first emotions evidenced after the choice to sin against the Father made in the Garden of Eden. Fear plagued different men and women of God like Moses (fear to speak), Saul (feared the people), Abram (fear of remaining childless), Jacob (feared his brother would kill him), Ruth (feared famine, rejection, and lack of provision), and the Apostle Paul at perilous times, feared shipwreck and loss of lives.

We can all harbor a damaging level of fear that hinders free trust and reliance on God to protect, care for, and deliver the necessities of the whole personality.[6] These outstanding men and women did overcome their fears through God's provision and remain as examples to our generation as over comers of their valid fears.

At those particularly crucial points in their lives, they were paralyzed with dread until they let go, and let God take the situation they could not control anyway.

Demonic spiritual fears invade to rob faith and faith-living. Its strength lies in hitting at our weakest moments with suggestions that seem bigger than life. Often the devilish suggestions prove more to reckon with than fear itself because suggestions are lies. Facts, however, prove Truth and never come from the pits of evil.

When Fear suggestions are embraced, believed, and allowed to take root, another principle of God comes into effect as follows:[7]

> *"...They have chosen their own ways, and their souls delight in their abominations; so, I also will choose harsh treatment for them and will bring upon them what they dread. For when I called, no one answered, when I spoke, no one listened. They did evil in my sight and chose what displeases me."*

Willful disobedience opens one up to fears and the very things feared *will come upon you.* It is a lightning rod fastened to the highest peak of your roof, inviting lightening to strike. And sure enough, it does! Negative fear has no place at all in the Christian's personality.

Fear is the device of demons. It gives a great license to gain entrance to the soul. Demons come right in to torment with the very request of fear. It can be either the strongman or a lesser demon who is invited by another strongmen-demon in search of unoccupied places. Jesus gave us much insight into the world of displaced spirits[8] and how they act in concert together to inhabit and tag team to create human misery.

Positional Fear is Negative Faith

Fears are expressed in various ways and evil spirits use these expressions as points of vexation. Take these examples of guilt, doubts, condemnation, passivity, social timidity, suspicion, indecision, bondage, restlessness, shame, superstition, insecurity, superiority, worry, haughtiness, aggressiveness; over-educated ("I need two more doctorates, just in case"; hoarding, selfish use of possessions, the fear of man (peer pressure), threats of suicide, loneliness, reticence to venture out, defiance to any authority figure, not exercising your own opinions, unreasonable denial, withholding sex from spouse.

Others include an unwillingness to participate in groups for prayer, fellowship, or to complete projects or tasks. There are many, many fears that can be listed but you know your own most crippling and tiniest fears where the battle takes up and combat must be launched. A chief place fear expresses itself is in social attachments.

There are Christians who will marry (or live together unmarried) not for love or from obedience to God, but out of fear of loneliness and insecurity. The culmination of that union of misplaced faith is one of substituting a reliance on God to supply ALL needs by placing trust in another human person who should not and cannot meet most needs. What an insult to God and how dishonest to yourself.

Young people who are afraid to grow into the role and responsibilities of adulthood never learn intimacy. They are most comfortable searching for a non-risk life. Fear causes Christians to bury their talents taking as truth a faulty consideration of other's opinions or expecting failure instead of success. They are unsure of what is right and wrong, cannot take criticism or punishment for misdeeds, are manipulative and often small-minded.

Fear annoys us with doubts. Fear is the motivating factor in overbearing, smothering parents who are afraid of losing their child' and his or her love. These parents are determined to create fear in the child to keep them home, keep them from rough sports, from dating, or from getting on with any of the risks (and rewards) of coming into adulthood. We have spoken with many people who suffered from a controlling spirit of fear that had reached across the years into the child's own marriage causing pain and soul ties to be broken so that both parent and child could go into maturity as separate beings and intimacy with the Lord where it belongs.[9]

The Bible is literally filled with faith verses that can be quoted, memorized, and used as battle weapons against all kinds of fears. Negative fear is unreasonable so do not try to reason it out and understand it. Reject its intrusion into your mind and act in faith in these situations. God never brings fear. Humans do not seek or naturally act in fear. Satan is the master of the strongman of fear as proven when he gripped the whole world with irrational fear of the global experience of 2020 with a microbe that has less than two percent (2%) death rate if contracted naturally. Children have even less of a chance of death.

Positional Fear is Negative Faith.
Positional Fear must be Replaced by Godly Faith.

As an example of someone speaking their fears onto you when you happen to sneeze and a cat is nearby, they say, "Oh, you're allergic to cats." No, everyone is not allergic to cats. Don't accept that suggestion. We take precautions around anything to be harmful to a great many people, but we do not assume a fear of allergies, disease, pandemic misfortunes, or family curse syndrome. That is a capture attempted on you. This will be good news for Seekers with fear issues.

When we grasp the principles laid out for us in 1 Peter 5:8-10, it becomes sound weaponry for Seekers who have unanswered questions and expect you to address them. Begin with verse 8: *"Be sober, be vigilant; because your adversary the devil walks about like a roaring lion, seeking whom he may devour..."*

Right off, we are warned to maintain a soberness (seriousness) of mind and spirit; to be vigilant, observing what is around us. Then we are permitted into the devil's operational schemata for believers. He walks about slowly. He roars like a hungry lion; meaning, all noise and trash talking (fear-garnering, using deception) to scare its prey out of hiding to take advantage of a created vulnerability. Does that ring true in culture today?

What does the devil strive after? He wants to devour and waste anything in his path that hinders his overall program of world-conquer. Is that really the best he has?

Really?

But in the natural, we know that the lion will get its prey or starve. In the spiritual, those hiding under the wings of the Almighty Jehovah[10] as a refuge from all harm, are not vulnerable unless they move away from that abiding place.

There's always that decision amidst the roaring that Spirit Warriors face in Seekers and in themselves. But Christians have the Good News that we never need to face the assaults alone or without supernatural power to resist and conquer.

ADVERSARY.[11] In Scripture, Satan is called *The Adversary;* by way of eminence; an opponent or antagonist, as in a suit at law, or in single combat; an opposing litigant; contrariness, opposition; the enemy position.

ADVOCATE.[12] To plead in favor of; to defend by argument, before a tribunal; to support or vindicate; defend or maintain.

When the devil is coming after you as your adversary, remember that you have an Advocate Jesus Christ who is maintaining your cause and your authority in that situation, by His own blood. The tribunal is in the supreme courts of heaven, and standing against that prosecutor is your Defender Jesus Christ. Don't move from His bench in the roar of accusations. This is our position in Christ.

As believers move from under the substantive lordship of Christ, bad things can happen and often do. This is when the spirit is attacked to disable and interfere with the communication system to the Holy One. Should the accusations be true, repent and stay closer than before. Continuing with 1 Peter 5:9-10, we get the direct commands needed to overcome the assaults of the spirit of fear in all circumstances:

> *"...Resist him, steadfast in the faith, knowing that the same sufferings are experienced by your brotherhood in the world. But the God of all grace, who called us to His eternal glory by Christ Jesus, after you have suffered a while, perfect, establish, strengthen, and settle you."*[13]

Whether you are in a deliverance session confronting the spirit of fear or hearing its whispering of accusations or directions for you to leave your place of righteousness under His wings, the answer is the same: RESIST! Peter should know and his counsel is spot on.

Our active faith in Christ must hold steadfastly loyal to Him because, *"the God of all grace...called us to His eternal glory by Christ Jesus".* What this implies is that one day, this type of suffering at Satan's will, so common to all believers, will be vindicated by our Advocate and settled eternally. So, hold on. Resist it with this understanding of our hope ahead of us.

Alternatives that are satanically offered believers out of his arsenal of great fears, very likely will be positioned against your survival, against the possibility of losing someone or something of much value to you, or will confront your mental stability or physical life. Don't believe *The Lie* but rather hold on to our Good God fiercely. These are the concerns of Seekers needing consolation and enlightenment on the devil's tactics.

Peter's reassurance is that, *"the same sufferings* (coming from a spirit of fear) *are experienced by your brotherhood in the world."* And, *"after you have suffered a while,"* these very types of challenges will, in fact, result in underpinning us to higher levels of warfare and victory. Recognizing and foiling demonic attacks against the inner spirit will, *"perfect, establish, strengthen, and settle you"* in your true faith. To master the fears of life, we undergo testing to develop strength.

A report was given to the granting agency by scientists whose project was to grow sustainable plants within a biosphere with man controlled perfect conditions. Every plant in the biosphere that separated it from the external (real) environment were watered consistently, provided with plenty of organic fertilizer, proper temperatures, and turn-on sunshine were in hand. The plants from the smallest moss to the tallest tree grew outstandingly well. After time though, the scientists noticed that the young trees were falling over at a certain height of growth. This puzzled them greatly when all the elements for success were provided. What was happening?

Finally, after exhaustive investigation, the obvious turned up. The scientists determined that the trees had never experienced a prevailing wind—or wind resistance of any kind. The perfection of the biosphere prevented negatives. Trees began toppling under their own weight with nothing more than untested shallow roots for support. We need the balance of testing, effort, and success and repeat until success.

This is a good example for not enabling sinful behaviors in self and others or for denying the secular insistence that bad is good and good is bad as we are warned would happen. That time is now here. Embrace your ability to resist the devil's bad outcomes in life so you can walk in the liberty of God's good.

The Luciferian Spirit of Narcissism

No amount or quality of exposure or involvement in Christian living, teaching, counseling, ministry, spiritual service, and good works is effective in the one who resists a complete surrender of his or her will to God for His use. Jesus Christ is Lord (owner, chief, boss, controller) of your life or--you are continuing in your own pride and self-centered habits.

A narcissist is centered on life befitting him or her and is only self-intentional (honors self-first, last, and always). Generally, the more easily offended and hurt a person becomes, the more pride-filled they are and thought to be above it. People who are dead to their first Adam life cannot be hurt: they are dead. It is a historical fact in nations that pride can be so strong over losing face in a situation that suicide is contemplated and often accomplished (especially oriental, and Indian societies).

Pride is a tenacious and destructive root that can sprout in many directions and specialties. When one feels empty, threatened, insecure or dejected, pride raises its head in false comfort. It will attempt to justify the inadequate feelings by putting these thoughts into the mind of the hurt one.

It will reason: "I wasn't 100% wrong!" and, "I'm tough enough to handle this alone." Or, "Look at them—what right do THEY have to criticize ME?" Pride comforts the soul by attempting to bring down the offenders to a level of pseudo-guilt brought on by the pride-filled person. When that does not work, the blame is shifted to the victim of the accusations.

Christ's way is humility. Humility is the extreme opposite of pride. A humble spirit quickly submits to Father, does not assert itself in self-referential preferences, and thus reflects the very nature of the Lord's relationship to His Father. Humility is a fruit developed in the Holy Spirit and goes hand-in-glove with wholeness, harmony, contentment, and order. It seeks nothing for itself and is not easily offended.

Look at pride in the form of self-centeredness. This attitude upsets unity from the sandbox to the corporate boardroom to the marriage bed. Pride in one's self and abilities, neutralizes the release of God's authority with power to right a situation. It undermines faith and begets the sin of unbelief. Pride is fashioned on exalted misconceptions and shadowy pretexts. Satanic truth says that a person can become a god and pride buys into that error. Snap! the trap shuts.

As pride strengthens itself from situation to situation, soul-dominance develops to continually assert itself to lead and not submit to the spirit. Pride is a huge door for Satan to enter and is often the strongman in many people's lives. After all, pride caused Lucifer's great fall[14] and is the antipathy to Jesus Christ's humility.

The lust for materialism is often expressed in high-risk gambling or through hoarding. We have all heard of the millionaire who deprives themself of decent housing, clothing, and nutritious food—the basics—all the while with a bank account bulging with provision. This level of lust is a selfishness that replaces the life God can bless and provides for when faith is forthcoming.

Pride is enhanced by a familiar spirit that feeds the fear behind a lust for money. It becomes reinforced and can build or be lost immediately. You will detect its presence when a Seeker is bound by either gambling that risks its loss, or hoarding that holds materials too dear. First look at these two: pride and lust for money, as strongholds (addicting) that deplete the godly life of simply trusting the Lord to provide work and funds for one's self and family.[15]

Again, either Jesus Christ is Lord of the life or an idol like money and what it brings will displace Him. Another facet of pride is covetousness wherein the love of wealth and materialism leads to greed. When one loves these things and points their whole life toward their attainment, the demonic force behind the object is worshipped.

[1] Matthew 10:38.

[2] Matthew 16:24-26.

[3] Colossians 2:11-15; Romans 2:28-29; Philippians 3:2-11.

[4] John 12:25.

[5] Romans 5.12-14.

[6] Proverbs 29:25.

[7] Isaiah 66:3-4.

[8] Matthew 12:43-45.

[9] Ezekiel 11:8; Jeremiah 42:13-16; Job 3:25; Proverbs 1:7; 8:13; 9:10; Psalms 46:1-2; Deuteronomy 31:8; Psalm 34:4; I John 4:18.

[10] Psalm 36:7; Psalm 17:8-9; Psalm 57:1; 91:4, 147:3, and Malachi 4:2 (healing in His wings means restoration to health, remedy, cure, medicine; tranquility, deliverance and refreshing comes from the verb *raphe* salvation is God's cure for the entire person.

[11] Webster, Noah, American Dictionary of the English Language 1828.

[12] Ibid.

[13] 1 Peter 5:9.

[14] Isaiah 14:12-17.

[15] Philippians 4:11; 1 Timothy 6:8; Hebrews 13:5.

| 9 |

Assault Against the Soul
- Part 2

*"But I (Jesus) tell you that men will have to give account
on the day of judgment for EVERY CARELESS WORD they
have spoken. For by your words, you will be acquitted,
and by your words you will be condemned."*
~ Matthew 12: 36-37

Gossip, Slander, Foul Talk, and Lying

The assault against one's core being, your soul, is the most serious threat possible. Sometimes this assault comes from outside forces. Or, we can consent to either beneficial or damaging mindsets that morph into patterns of behavior. These personality traits can be godly, character building or self-opposing choices when the soul is trained to cooperate with defeating the process of sanctification that the Holy Spirit is working on so hard for life's entire journey.

A few of these negative characteristics in this chapter are common and will be discovered in the Seeker as they come to you for help. Self-opposing traits are not demonic but carnal in nature. It is up to the team and the Seeker to determine how to pray in these situations.

Self-imposed harm to the soul means a trespass has occurred of property that was purchased by Jesus Christ. Repentance is needed and personal responsibility taken for participation.

When the soul is stormed from exterior forces, recognition of the assailant with resistance is in order. For instance, some in the church membership seek you out continually to bring gossip or slander about another person. The permission for them to continually find you as a willing ear to the negativity is our responsibility to warn them, resist their messages, and reject their input.

Many scriptures are given for counter-attack of these soul killers. No one needs to entertain the depressive results of not guarding your soul. Open doors from passivity to act will expose a willingness to believe the enemy's lies and accusations. Sometimes it is good to just understanding how these forces work.

Gossip. Both the telling and listening to hearsay or rumor against another's reputation and character is abusive. The attack on God's other children is a serious way of keeping believers from pure fellowship with God. Gossip usually comes from people whose hearts are bitter or fearful, having a lowered esteem for the one spoken against. This lack of the fear of God (respect) to use untruth, mild or wild exaggeration in order to elevate themselves into a better light with whom they are gossiping.

Interestingly, the Greek word for devil is *diabolos* meaning *slanderer*. To slander means, 'to make false charges or misrepresentations; to defame and damage a reputation'. Slander and gossip do not wait for facts, truth, or proof. Satan is known as the False Accuser and father of all liars who stands before God night and day accusing the brethren.[1] Do not join his quest to divide and conquer.

Slander is willful. It is usually premeditated, and does spiteful harm for another's downfall. Slander is so commonplace that there are public laws protecting individuals and corporations against it. Slander—as verbal abuse—is a stronger, more aggressive sin used for attacking to wound or kill. It can be lethal against family members or when used in dependent relationships against spouses, employees, Christian leadership, and children where little protection is possible. Satan has used slander induced by the false media and social networks on a corporate and national level to subvert truth through propaganda and deceit. Whole nations have staggered from the effects of public slander right into the end time plans of Satan.

Foul Talk (verbal abuse) is a very caustic form of hatred that is a carrier of curses. This sin can be so subtle in the Christian's mouth, that much injurious declarations are demonically energized. Verbal abuse will defeat friendships, marriages, careers, families, and nations. It does so by the disintegration of the souls to whom it is leveled against and is most grievous to children, spouses, spiritual confidants, and soul shepherds because these relationships are basic to unity and happiness.

Intentional Lying[2] has the grimmest spiritual consequences because it falsely validates gossip, slander, and is what the bible calls foul talk.[3] All are species of The Lie Lucifer told to capture us all in Eden. Speaking lies is the devil's native language. Lying is never cute, white, or told "for one's best interests". A lying habit must be broken in children and not tolerated in adults. Liars are Satan's coworkers who extend his dark captivity and keep ourselves and others in bondage to not finding God's truth.

Keep awake on this!

The more believers open themselves to participating actively (talking) or passively (listening) in gossip, slander and lying, the greater territory Satan conquers within them until they cannot recognize what bitter waters are springing from their hearts and mouths. This is one practice believers shoot one other down and keep the wounded sick. Warriors: these sins are to be confessed and repented of to turn away from impurity.

In deliverance of these poisonous traits, understand that using Lucifer's "*The Lie*" is a root demon principality. Reconciliation should be encouraged between those involved in the telling and/or listening to gossip. In the case of verbal abuse, much rebuilding of trust will be in order in family situations by apologies and true repentance to the Lord Who does not allow the use and abuse of the tongue.

> *"Then there came out a spirit, and stood before the Lord, and said I will go out, and BE A LYING SPIRIT in the mouth of all his prophets. And the Lord said, thou shalt entice him, and thou shalt also prevail: Go out, and do even so... the Lord hath put a lying spirit in the mouth of these thy prophets, and the Lord hath spoken evil against thee."*[4]

As we mature in the Lord's ways and will, self-control demanded by the soul over one's body (lust which is sexual impulse), the eye gates, and mouth, the easier it becomes to live in sanctification.

Who's in Control: Anger, Rage, or Wrath?

We have all experienced the soul emotion of anger. Being most commonly negative in its natural outcome or corrective (righteous anger that Jesus used), anger is expressed when a person's perceived rights or their soul's will is questioned, countered, or imposed upon. Therefore, anger may be used as a protection for self-dominated territory; it is often aggressive behavior used to govern others and retain the lusts of the flesh.

With another motive in mind, we've also witnessed aggressive anger glorified, funded, and forced by activists' violence to change the culture or mob to their worldview. This happens in medicine, business, politics, religion, or banking, and leads to a warring spirit.

To the ambitiously unsaved population, it is an acceptable contrivance to win the prize of what they want at all costs, even to murder or mass murder as in the cases of experimental pesticides, drugs, human-into-animal research, and human fetal tissue exploitation. These are certainly ways we see the devil's hand in the world today.

ANGER in OT Hebrew is: *qatsaph* and *chema;* meaning, "To crack off, burst out in rage, fret self, provoke to wrath, vex, be furious;

splintered off by rage or strife; foam, indignation, sore, tempest, vain whirlwind, windy; heat, poison from its fever, hot displeasure."

ANGER in NT Greek is: *orgizo* and *cholao;* meaning, "To become exasperated, provoked, be contrary to a friend; be rebellious, irritable, enraged, and choleric."

Anger can be passively directed at others in pretense of friendship or family love, but be assured, it is never born out of genuine love. Anger hides behind the attacking, dominating, fear-provoking behavior that is a fleshly response for keeping one's self, possessions (even spouse and children), and their concepts aggressively used in order to control the situation for one's own insecurities or paid response.

Anger may result from have your will crossed. When this challenge comes up, becoming angry handles the stress wrongly,[5] it appears in distinct characteristics of the carnal nature. Some examples are malice (ill will), bitterness, resentment, bullying, consistently argumentative, intolerant, rebellious, and clamoring for attention. Through verbal or threatening body movements, they will be loud or shouting to cause fear that is especially destructive in small children and animals.

Other expressions of anger emerge as physical and verbal cruelty, by envy, gossip, revenge, or emotional violence. The person who walks in anger as their personality trait comes across as judgmental by expressing harsh and directed criticism to control a situation to their comfort. They think their solution in negative, hurtful ways are constructive but the corrected person will be devastated and diminished.

As you listen to these observations made by wounded Seekers, you will learn that the aggressively angry person's temper is quelled almost immediately by their release of abuse while the recipient can be deeply wounded for days into years and grow to hate them. Most evident is the abusive spouse who is "immediately sorry" after an outburst and asks forgiveness with promises it will never happen again. Oh yes, it will happen again because it is a spirit and certainly out of the management of the abuser.

In childhood or youth, temper tantrums have not been broken. Cruelty to pets and animals has not been addressed and forbidden on threat or execution of punishment. Animal violence is not acceptable. As the highest expression of creation, we were assigned by our Creator to respect, tend, and compassionately care for domestic and wildlife as valuable to His reasoning to exist and fill their roles in sustaining life. When anger in these people is justified and excused, they will never learn to conquer this negative soul force until harm to self or all else results. Prisons are filled with violent and angry people.

When the Seeker talks about unforgiveness, contempt, impatience, displeasure, contrariness, irritability, sexual frustration, jealousy, stubbornness, blocked mind to the truth, murder, war, rape, swearing, cursing and foul body language, look at anger. In the area of challenging authority, you will hear exaggeration, confession to aggressive-illegal driving habits, meanness that is often seen in business and sports, and befalling to fractious and frivolous lawsuits.

An angry soul cannot be pleased no matter what is done or said to appease them. They are unruly, quarrelsome in public to embarrass someone close to them, and grossly socially immature. Young children and teens will display screaming fits, or may take on destructive substances that can often escalate into self-harming acts to 'punish others'.

Angry adults shout others down or talk over them. Angry children stamp their feet, run away, and won't speak to you for hours and days. Anger can be passive, like depression that is anger turned toward oneself.

Other signs can be gross obesity, pouting, refusal to communicate, cold hard stares to intimidate, or those who will undermine business deals calculated to cripple or topple empires, small or international. Passive anger generates addictions and self-destructive diseases such as excessive sleeping, exercising, or in eating disorders.

The demonic strongman of anger can hold other and lesser evil entities with it. Demons like to have their influence over humans to be seen. Anger outbursts coddle and accommodate demons if allowed to take on forms of behavior which are thought to be "my natural personality trait". Often fear rides on the back of anger because that abuser is fearful of losing his or her control over the victim, so speak against both spirits as coupled in strength

How different it is for Christ's followers! Believers surrender to God at salvation, have given over all their rights and control of self by acknowledging the Lordship of Jesus Christ in all life's future decisions. When we Christians begin to realize that we do not own one thing of this world—that all things (and persons) are temporarily allowed to us and ultimately taken from us, we will stop struggling to possess and cease becoming angry when threatened.

Any calamity can come and remove all possessions from us and most rapidly. ALL OF EVERYTHING belongs to the Lord. In His love and by design, we are allowed responsibility to use things and love people, for a season. After all, we are the servants, stewards, and managers He placed here to multiply the fruit. We were never told we may keep the fruit of our obedience. It disappears beautifully into the kingdom.

Those who have learned to be willing to give up whatever know they temporarily have this possession know that God has promised back many-fold everything freely given to others in the pursuit of His Kingdom. Certainly, a reaction of anger against someone who is trying to take what is "ours" leads to fights, murders, stealing, lies, lawsuits or whatever seems necessary to hold on to the possession.

Here is a final word to those of you who live with or around angry people and become the victim. You must seek God for relief from this environment because it will eventually kill love in a relationship and must be tackled. Tolerating destructive anger in a. life partner, child, or in any relationship is being part and party in the anger. We are not to support weaknesses in others but seek to help them out of the bondage they are in and get out of it ourselves.

The Heritage of Virtue

God advises us to let go and allow Him the pleasure of meeting your best needs. Second Corinthians 4:18 expresses the truth that whatever we can see with our eyes will pass away. And what we cannot see, passes into eternity. It is obvious that the importance of living rests with the eternal valuables: the invincible values of the Spirit. Because of this, we can give up anger.

Happily, God can be trusted with your life and their life! Participating in this anger-bond must be confessed as a lack of trust in the Lord. Repent of it. Soundly reject anger out loud and cut the soul-tie to this person.

Spirit Warriors: after praying for deliverance from spirits of anger, the Seeker should be advised that at their first opportunity (since anger is so often used against others), is to ask forgiveness for this behavior from those offended. That may be hard to do but it is the only way to allow true, loving relationships be established.

Pride will be broken in asking for forgiveness and a Renewed Mind will change the behavior to that which is acceptable to God bringing peace and harmony in that life instead of constant upheaval and destruction.

Anger is contrary to the gentle, Holy Spirit of God and has no place whatever in the believer's life. Repentance and forgiveness are the antidotes for that very insecure person's soul health. As important, there are multiple scriptural antidotes[6] to the victims of anger. Forgiveness, not to be confused with reconciliation, releases the power of God to act on our behalf to correct the abusers while bringing comfort to the victims to live free of them.

When thinking about the roots of sin the Bible speaks about, the Lord compares them with the roots of plants. Some strong plants and trees have a taproot that reaches further than any of the other roots, going for life in the forms of water and needed nutrients. We are to put a taproot into the Holy Spirit. Still other plants have more complex and scattered root systems.

For example, an oak tree does not have a taproot like other trees but it will have a network of large to smaller roots the same length and pattern underground as the branches, limbs, and leaves have above ground. This is for balance and efficiency. Likewise, root sins in a life may go deep into the spirit, soul, and body or branch out touching many auxiliary areas that are only externally seen.

The next chapter will establish the principle concerning the attack against the body and how deeply or broadly the roots of sin are taken advantage of, by evil forces.

[1] Revelation 12:10.

[2] James 3:5-12.

[3] Colossians 3:8.

[4] 2 Chronicles 18:20-22; Exodus 20:16; Matthew 12:36-37; Revelation 12:10; Colossians 3:8; 2 Chronicles 18:20-22; Exodus 20:16; Exodus 23:1; John 8:44; Matthew 12:36-37; Matthew 5:39; Psalm 34:18.

[5] Matthew 5:39.

[6] James 1:19-20; 1 Timothy 2:8; 1 Corinthians 6:1-8; Hebrews 12:14-15; Proverbs 10:6; Galatians 5:22.

| 10 |

Assault Against the Soul - Part 3

"...they mouth empty, boastful words, and by appealing to the lustful desires of sinful human nature, they entice people who are just escaping from those who live in error..."
Jude 16-19

Rebellion *is* Witchcraft

The importance of understanding the role of rebellion in deliverance is seen in: "They rebelled against the Lord, scorning Him who is the God above all gods. That is why He broke them with hard labor; they fell and none would help them rise again.[1]

> Rebellion cannot be healed. Rebellion must be broken.

To be rebellious is to take a position in opposition to the Lord's will by either not listening to Him or listening but not obeying what He has shown you to be righteous behavior. A toddler who challenges and rebels at her parents' desires for her good, indicates the attitude, if unbroken, she will carry into adulthood toward the heavenly Father. Rebellion compounds its strength if it is not broken and dealt with in its earliest stages.

Let's face it. Everyone knows when they are being contrary. They know when they are forcing their own ways and opinions, desires, or to control on others. It goes on in Christian fellowships, marriages and often is acted out against our heavenly Father. An intensity of rebellion against the Word of God causes suffering and demonic vexation within and without the personality.

Rebellion in the soul-life says, "I will have my own way no matter what the cost to myself or to you!" In your mind's eye, can you not see the "bratty child" within that adult standing there and insisting on their wishes, trying desperately to overcome all objections? But they will not be moved off their position of rebellion.

But praise God that as a loving Father He will not allow His headstrong, willful child rush over cliffs to self-destruction without attempting to redirect him or her to the peaceful path He has planned for that life. Conversely, Satan will jump on every opportunity left open by that strain of rebellion to keep him or her headed for the, cliffs of destruction.

Rebellion against God has root causes in pride (I am sufficient to meet the needs and demands of life), in self-centeredness (I will do it myself, my way), in carnality (I will walk, dress, talk, sin in the world's way), and in immovability through a wounded spirit (I will put up walls that no one—

not even God—can surmount). God's desire for His children is a broken heart (soul) and a contrite spirit[2] that will quickly hear and obey Him without hesitation. This obedience to quickly respond comes with maturity and from a profoundly deep love of the Lord God for Himself.

There is much Bible teaching on the linkage between rebellion and witchcraft contrasted with hearing God and obeying Him. Take for example this strong warning that carries consequences: *"Now, if you will fear and worship the Lord and LISTEN to his commandments and NOT*

REBEL, against the Lord, and if...you follow the Lord your God, then all will be well. But if you rebel against the Lord's commandments and refuse to listen to him, then His hand will be heavy upon you as it was upon your ancestors."[3]

The Co-dependent Spirits of Ahab and Jezebel

God is Order and has clearly set boundaries for His earth in the animal and plant kingdoms, and for humankind in its domain. He has unmistakable benchmarks regarding authority and submission, what is higher and lower, the holy, and the unclean. A perversion of God's order is chronicled in 1 Kings 16-21 in the history of King Ahab and his wife Jezebel, who both confused their roles of God's order. This is the first clue we can utilize to identify the Jezebel spirit in action, whether spotted in males or females for spirits have no gender.

New Testament epistles uphold male spiritual leadership with its attached authority in local ekklesia structure. Both men and women may have leadership positions, be called as apostles, prophets, missionaries, and teachers but they are positioned there by others in higher authority. Godly order demands a submission to those who have the rule (spiritual elders) over the flock and will not seek to steal that authority for themselves by their own will and scheme.

The Jezebel spirit gains control in two ways. First, using the 1 Kings story as the example, Ahab willingly relinquished his ruling responsibility and God-given authority to be king of Israel, by allowing his Philistine wife Jezebel to usurp[4] it. Secondly, Jezebel seized it for her own purposes but without the benefits of the call, so she had to rely on other means (and she choose the demons spirits of Baal), to keep that leadership position going.

What do we see? Ahab, from his lack of faith in God, gave up his kingship with its authority, its access to prophetic wisdom, protection, and the provisions of that call, all relinquished to a weaker thief. This was a major trespass and put him in danger on the battlefield, his chief role. The call of God with its benefits to complete it, can only belong to the person of God's choice. It is not transferable. The Jezebel spirit attempts to, and sometimes succeeds at, stealing the ministry of another person's calling with their willing or passive consent if possible: an Ahab must have a Jezebel.

Jezebel manipulated a weak, vacillating Ahab to subvert her husband's ordained, kingly authority to uphold Yahweh. Instead, she turned him to use his ordination by God as king into a force to destroy Elijah the Prophet who was the voice of God to Ahab. But she immediately ran into trouble thinking a position was equal to a calling.

As a Baal-worshiping pagan, she would not tolerate God's message to preserve Israel, the enemy of her own people. She wanted to remain in her rebellion so maliciously and with evil intent, pursued the bringing down of God's authority and voice to His people in Elijah. This is how the Jezebel spirit tries to destroy servants of God (those in the ministry operating in the gifts and calling of God).

The Philistine Jezebel was the high priestess of Baal and intent on subverting the Hebrew ways of Ahab into Satanic rites. She used cunning, sweet words, probably sex, and the most subtle manners to outright deceive, hatred, rebellion, murder, fear, and governing authority. She mobilized hundreds of false prophets to bring down Elijah.

It was a frantic situation for the Prophet of God who was so overcome with *fear* that he errantly ran from God (though it looked to Elijah like he was running from Jezebel), set aside his holy prophet's calling, and became spiritually impotent in the face of the Jezebel spirit operating within Jezebel, the usurper. This same spirit is mentioned in the New Testament:

> "...nevertheless, I have this against you: You tolerate that woman Jezebel who calls herself a prophetess. By her teaching she misleads my servants into sexual immorality and the eating of food sacrificed to idols...and I will make those who commit adultery with her suffer intensely, unless they repent of her ways. I will strike her children dead."[5]

While the Jezebel spirit goes after the prophets (the mouth of God) first, they will then seek out the Godliest intercessors to try to deceive and if not dealt with there, will next go after the elders and pastors as the overseers of the flock. Often you may find these people in bible study groups, on worship teams, and ministries; or in beginning leadership positions that are always close to those who are in authority appearing as credible volunteer servants. Their objective, either known or unknown to them, is to undermine the authority of God by twisting influence to promote Satan's kingdom from within, and to spiritually weaken or disable the fellowship.

These spirits will eventually bring confusion, uneasiness, false tales, argument for scriptural positions distorted to fit their opinions, or offer pseudo-prophecies using political maneuvering to cause discord and splits within the body. Jezebel is the spiritual spawn of all who pursue libertine doctrines and practices to usurp the authority of God in the church by justifying it with the doctrines of demons.[6]

Males and females can be driven by a Jezebel spirit. Spirit Warriors will encounter them and must remember that these are people caught in the sticky web of Satan needing to be floodlit of their precarious positions of error and given opportunity for repentance and deliverance.

Another closely aligned spirit to influence leadership is called the Judas spirit. These people put themselves in positions close to leadership like Judas did with Jesus for several reasons. The danger here is when they are not satisfied with "how things are being done" they often turn on that leader in betrayal...just like Judas.

Thankfully, the body of Christ is biblically empowered to overthrow the spirits of Jezebel (the aggressor) and Ahab (the compliant) in its gatherings by recognizing and disciplining them through the elders' vigilance and engagement.[7] Should these disrupting people remain unwilling to confront and repent of their sin of harboring spirits which cause the fellowship so many conflicts, a confrontation by the elders is necessary. If they refuse the help that is offered, biblical dismissal[8] may be decided.[9]

Paul, as an apostle, reminds and freshly challenges his protégé Timothy, as senior leader of one of the local churches with these words:[10]

> *"I charge you therefore before God and the Lord Jesus Christ, who will judge the living and the dead at His appearing and His kingdom: Preach the word! Be ready in season and out of season. Convince, rebuke, exhort with all long suffering and teaching, for the time will come when they will not endure sound doctrine, but according to their own desires, because they have itching ears, they will heap up for themselves teachers; and they will turn their ears away from the truth, and be turned aside to fables. But you be watchful in all things, endure afflictions, do the work of an evangelist, fulfill your ministry."*

This was Paul's description of Timothy's calling and how to lead those under the wings of his ministry. Only he could complete his role here in this location to these under his care. Overseer Timothy and church elders will be accountable, *"at His appearing..."* for how seriously he overcame the challenges, the usurping spirits, the degradation of his work in those whom he thought he taught well when they go off the rails to deviant doctrines that just sound better to them.

The office of pastor is not an occupational role: it is a calling of God with attendant authority and spiritual and material resources to accomplish the assaults and blessings ahead. A husband and wife are not automatically "co-pastors" as has become so popular. No, this brings confusion to the congregation and especially to the wives we have counseled who are burdened with a title and expectations unrelated to their personal gifts and kingdom purposes.

The offices[11] that the Lord Jesus as king of His kingdom gave are: apostle, evangelist, prophet, pastor, and teacher. These are not ecclesiastic career positions one goes to seminary to learn how to function in, according to some professors' denominational opinions and textbooks. This paradigm will end in the traditional one-man/woman church governing as lone head that ignores and suppresses the functioning of all the gifts and callings within a true Ekklesia.

The Python Spirit

This is an ancient spirit type that got its specialized powers from the pagan worship practices of foretelling, mental and thought control, seen as a strangulating method often experienced in traditional religious rites. In the natural, python non-venomous snakes (also boa constrictors) wrap their strong musculature around the prey, squeezing the air out of it for the kill (by suffocating), and keeping them from doing things they should be doing. After complete control and with no danger of escape, pythons will then consume the corpse at their leisure.

Pythia[12]~ The priestess of the mythical Apollo who was able to deliver the oracles (precepts, demonic prophecy of the future) of Delphi; a sort of witch or pythoness; ventriloquist, soothsayer; geomancer; druid; astrology. In Greek (#5172/75), it is known as *pytho*, a dragon or serpent; a hissing snake; i.e., whisper a magic spell; pretending to foretell, forewarn, or predict what evil spirits tell them as a psychic, of future or past events (pythonic); a conjurer. The root of this demon spirit is pride/control and is common to preachers both political and religious.

When people feel gagged and suffocated by life with no perceived options out of their unwelcome situations, we suspect a python spirit. This takes tracing back to their wrong choices of how and when this spirit obtained the authority to have a grip on them. This can sometimes manifest as intense mental control, fueled by pride. Severe headaches can occur or be especially aggravated when the person is determined to know God more closely or just before or during serving Him.

We have personal testimony of one preacher traveling out of state to speak and teach and every time he crossed the property line toward the guest church door to minister, instant piercing headaches would overcome him until he had to lay down for twenty minutes before platform delivery.

He testified that this activity only happened at this one church and never anywhere else he visited to preach. Later, upon sharing this with the elders there, he learned that the local Wicca coven had walked the property line raining down curses on the people and property. A python spirit was identified by intercessors and the property was cleansed by the congregation in a prayer walk and verbal exorcism.

We handled another situation when a young woman came for prayer for a complaint of movement in the front of her skull. We three asked permission to feel it and it was truly amazing to feel a large marble-sized mass cross under the skin, and see it travel back and forth across her forehead. She experienced headaches, brain fog, and lack of concentration for bible study.

This manifested just when she had committed to becoming the youth director in her small church. The python spirit was bound as we laid hands on her forehead and cast it out. There was a lot of shrieking and whipping of the head (be mindful to support the head when this happens) as we prayed for deliverance and got it, but more counseling time would be needed in follow up appointments with a prayer team.

Any time you learn of witches' involvement, try the spirit of python which is there to curse and kill a ministry, squeeze the breath right out of your ideas and creativity for God, and destroy by intimidation, interference, and fear of failure as a snake would when you come upon it suddenly.

Master Demon Strong Holders

Master demons are sometimes known as "the strongman" that holds onto its demon team. No amount or quality of exposure or involvement in Christian living, teaching, counseling, ministry, spiritual service, and good works is effective in the one who resists a complete surrender of his or her will to God for His use because of pride.

Let this be true: Jesus Christ is Lord and He alone is the owner, commander-in-chief, shepherd, and authorized controller of our living and planned destiny. The alternative to His lordship is the use of our free will to continue to self-lead by our own pride and self-centered habits, blindly carrying us to multiple attempts "to get it right".

For example, a pride-filled person is centered on life benefiting him or her and is very self-intentional; e.g., thinks of himself first, last, and always. Generally, the more easily offended and hurt a person is, the more prideful they can be. People who are dead to their first Adam life are not hurt: they are dead. It is a cultural reality in several nations that pride can be so strong not to 'lose face' that their failure in a situation will leave suicide as the misguided solution. When there is a history of suicide as a pattern (especially seen in Asian culture or homosexual rejection), be aware that if they are talking about it, it is contemplated and often accomplished.

Pride is a tenacious and destructive root and pairs itself with control. When one feels empty, threatened, insecure or dejected, pride raises its head in false comfort. It will attempt to justify the inadequate feelings by putting these thoughts into the mind of the hurt one. It will often reason, "I wasn't 100% wrong!" or, "I'm tough enough to handle this alone;" or perhaps, "Look at them—what right do THEY have to criticize ME?" Pride comforts the soul by attempting to diminish the reputation of the "offenders" and pass blame to a manageable level for them.

Christ's way to victory over our temporary fails, is humility.[13] Humility is in active opposition to pride. A humble attitude quickly gives way rather than assert rights, does not override others' views, and evaluates challenges by reflecting the very nature of the Lord. Humility is a rich and hard-won fruit of the Spirit, going hand-in-glove with sanity, harmony, contentment, God's peace, and order. A humble heart seeks nothing for itself and purposefully not easily offended. When these virtues are absent, look for pride.

Assess egoism as a formulation of self-focus. This attitude upstages unity from the sandbox to the corporate boardroom, from the platform to the marriage bed. Pride neutralizes the release of God's power to correct a situation. It undermines faith and begets the sin of unbelief.

Pride is crafted on exalted misconceptions and shadowy pretexts unlike any other soul expression. Satanic myth claims that special people can become a god. Pride buys into that error. Snap! the trap shuts and just like that, you just crossed the threshold into neopaganism.

As pride strengthens itself from situation to deeper situation, soul-dominance develops that will continually assert itself to lead and not submit. Eventually, it will not bow to God Himself. Pride is a huge portal that demon's access and is often the pivot man in many people's lives. After all, pride caused Lucifer's great fall[14] and is the antipathy to Jesus Christ's humility.

The soul is a huge attack area because it is the core of our personality. It is "who we really are". The next chapter will come at this from different angles. Why are humans so prone to the lustful, love of money? It seems to be predominating in many societies and a necessity for food and shelter.

Does the Lord have an answer for us and for the Seekers you will be meeting?

[1] Psalm 107:11-12.

[2] Psalm 34:18.

[3] 1 Sam 12:14; Proverbs 17:11; Numbers 22:32; Ephesians 2:1-2.

[4] Usurp: to confiscate; to steal away by force or by consent without having the legal rights. Ahab prostituted his commission from God. The benefits of that were taken from Ahab but were not transferred to the usurper who now became his enemy and God's enemy.

[5] Rev. 2:18-23.

[6] 1 Timothy 4:1-5; 2 Timothy 3.

[7] 1 Timothy 1:1-11.

[8] 1 Timothy 1:18-20.

[9] 1 Timothy 4:1-7; Matthew 18:15-19.

[10] 2 Timothy 4:1-5.

[11] Ephesians 4:11 and 1 Corinthians 12:28. See our website for audio teachings on these church appointed offices: www.SpiritWarriors.us.

[12] www.demonbuster.com.

[13] James 4:6; Luke 1:51-52.

[14] Isaiah 14:12-17; 1 Timothy 3:1-7, Titus 1:5-7, 1 Peter 5:1-4.

| 11 |

Assault Against the Soul - Part 4

*"Love the Lord your God with all your heart and with
all your soul and with all your strength."*
Deuteronomy 6:5

The Love Affair with Money

Pride is enhanced by a lust for money to build it. This is often expressed by gambling that risks its loss, or hoarding that holds it too dear. and is a stronghold (addicting) that robs the blessed life of providing for one's self and family. Again, either Jesus Christ is Lord of the life or an idol like money will be.

Pride and what it represents will displace Jesus Christ. Another facet of pride is covetousness wherein the love of wealth and materialism leads to greed. When one loves these things and points their whole life toward money attainment (no matter what it takes), the demonic forces behind the objects are essentially what is craved.

The love of money in its use and misuse has caused great hardship and hardening to God's Spirit. There has been more violent division, war, moral decline, jealousy, murder, soulish depravity, slavery, and diabolical violence manifested through the love and conquest of money than from any other vice I am aware of. Jesus said that *the love* of money is a root of ALL evil. True, there are other roots, but this one is pervasive, idolatrous, and certainly can prove to be the strongman.

Money itself is not evil. On the contrary, using money as a tool is useful in broadening the Kingdom's exposure. But wealth cannot be enshrined as controller and goal-setter or it will cause too much vexation from driving spirits who will literally wear a person out physically with a shortened lifespan, ruined family relationships, and mental distress. It will deaden their spirits to the freedom of Kingdom living and make true, honest relationships impossible as it supplants human love with object lust.

Should God entrust you with wealth, it is a secondary blessing to your spiritual storehouse in heaven and is to be respected and kept in circulation of the kingdom economy. Be generous. Share this disappearing resource into God's kingdom where it puts a credit balance on your obedience account for eternity. Give only as the Lord directs specifically for the Shepherd said, *"For you have the poor with you always, but Me you do not have always".*[1] Make the most of your relationship with Christ.

A Seeker who expresses trouble with handling money, its misuse through compulsive credit spending or exorbitant and flashy prideful attainment or possession of it, will ensnare them to live on a spiritual poverty level. Seeing the problem and hearing God's call for repentance and deliverance from it must be followed up with a radical change in the lifestyle to block further entrapment.[2]

Advise Seekers not to throw their money into causes with a motivation of receiving a greater gain of benefit. We call that gambling. Or, to follow the false prosperity-gospel of carnal teachings that have materially enriched illegitimate ministries as they religiously steal from God's sheep. Recognize them as wolves claiming to represent the Lord's interests. Hear Him for yourself! God's blessings are eternal and mostly come later at reward time. Expect His blessings of genuine love coming into and out of you in the economy of His kingdom flow.

As a suggestion for walking in freedom from bondage to the love of money, it may be helpful to make up a family budget that is reasonable to provide needs and repay all outstanding debts until you are free of debt. This alone breaks dependence on money as a substitute for God. Then, as God leads, save a prudent amount for emergencies and family goals but be open to sharing the overabundance within His body. At first, giving even a small portion of the funds God is trusting you with, may seem an impossible undertaking. But the higher law of love will reach beyond this as you listen and have more faith in Him.

As you walk (and then run) in this truth, it will become difficult to keep up with God in His blessing on your life. But don't expect money for money. Expect His blessings of true love and provision coming into and out of you by a generous and humble hand.[3] We know everything seen will burn up on earth and what is unseen is eternal. We are only here a very wisp of time, so nothing is that dear. Stewardship, not ownership, is more realistic.[4]

Mind Gatekeepers: The False Ones

Spiritual ignorance sets up the immature for planting doubt of God and is a primary and essential condition for deception by evil spirits. Why? Because false teachers and even pastors can get away with planting deviance from God's Word, even small ones.[5]

Unbelief is the thief of victories that could have been won through believing prayer. Unbelief blinds us to the true causes of life's troubles by hindering a clear vision of who Jesus Christ is as the consistent and faithful Healer, Deliverer, Provider, Strong Helper, Savior, and Advocate. That is who He is on behalf of His children but if you don't believe those divine positions, you won't receive those dimensions critical for ministry.

In short, those who are deceived and willfully remain so abide in a state of unbelief and are prone to false teachings that reinforce deception in God's revealed Persona. In this state, they cannot enter the miraculous, peaceful, and guilt-free life God intends for us until the light of the Lord breaks through this sin against the human spirit. Often, they do not even know how to recognize what false teaching is and how to reject it before it has a foothold in the soul.

The main characteristic of those peddling false doctrine can be identified as falling short of qualifying as righteous teachers. According to God's will, righteous teachers are born anew in their spirits to the communication to the Holy Spirit is open, they hear the voice of the Holy Spirit, and are equipped and supplied for ministry, then appointed to the teaching ministry—best by the recognition of a local body of believers as in early ekklesia times. If this is not happening, you are dealing with a false spirit.

False teachers may have great followings, chat groups, and electronic friends, but that does not qualify them that Christ's kingdom influence is growing. This is a matter of quality, not seeker-friendly crowds, millions in offerings, or star recognition. They cannot, in fact, worship the Eternal God or be anointed of the Lord no matter how much their PR declares it.

Be aware of the broad way with the flashy road signs of false doctrine that never lines up with God's word. One of the most obvious examples is how the LGBTQ$^+$ adherents will bend the bible to defend their sin position. False teachers will mishandle the bible to fit their opinions and religious goals.

Sometimes, new bible translations with man's commentary will produce the many fractures of religious sects and whole new denominations. Bible translations not linked to the original transcripts are mass produced yearly. There is money to be made, fame to be had, a career to foster, and prove a fool is a fool.

Second Peter 2:1-21 describes false teachers in detail. Only part of that passage is quoted, so read the whole scripture for yourself.

"...there will be **false teachers** among you. They will secretly introduce destructive heresies, even denying the sovereign Lord who bought them...Many will follow their shameful ways and will bring the way of truth into disrepute. In their greed, these teachers will exploit you with stories they have made up.

Their condemnation has long been hanging over them, and their destruction has not been sleeping...they are ungodly...despise authority, bold and arrogant, slander celestial beings; blaspheme in matters they do not understand; they will be paid back harm for the harm they have done; they seduce the unstable, are experts in greed; have left the straightway and wandered off to follow the way of Balaam; ...are springs without water and mists driven by a storm;

...they mouth empty, boastful words, and by appealing to the lustful desires of sinful human nature, they entice people who are just escaping from those who live in error...they promise them freedom, while they themselves are slaves of depravity—for a man is a slave to whatever has mastered him."

Then Peter gives a chilling reality: "...they are worse off at the end than they were at the beginning and ...it would have been better for them not to have known the way of righteousness, than to have known it and then to turn their backs on the sacred command that was passed on to them."

We are told that these false teachers once knew the truth and believed themselves to be Christians with a message from God (you need to ascertain which god?); however, they are now deceived and espousing the doctrines of demons whose chief job is to deceive and move in for the kill. Their teaching brings death. It does matter which bible version you consume and with whom you fellowship.

False teachers bear poisonous fruit, Jesus taught,[6] *"Watch out for false prophets. They come to you in sheep's clothing, but inwardly they are ferocious wolves...A good tree cannot bear bad fruit, and a bad tree cannot bear good fruit."*[7]

False teachers cause their followers to worship at the feet of the idolatrous shrines they build in their minds and many times, they themselves become the idols. We see the world doing this with fear, political nonsense, lies, hypocrisy, underhanded manipulation of the media for mass national and international manipulation and truth blackouts.[8]

We are open to deception only to the extent we insist on living our own way and harboring unconfessed sin. False teachers must be exposed as agents of Satan. *"Come ye out from among them and be clean of them,"* shows false teachers are imbued with the ideas, teachings, and satanic creeds he wants proclaimed. In other words, professing Satan's agenda to the world. These teachers—in these last prophetic days— will seduce poorly grounded and undisciplined believers away from the truth of Scripture to fall into their incorrect interpretations. Follow the money. Fake prophets are included here.

Mind Gatekeepers: The Right Ones

Righteous teachers, in contrast to false ones, are identified by their unequivocal persistence to present the straight and extremely narrow way to the Father: *"Ye must be born again in Christ Jesus alone".* They possess a personal maturity in the Lord and recognize the many snares of the world. They have learned by putting the whole bible together as a unity, bringing them into total, unqualified doctrinal agreement with God's Word.

Righteous teachers maintain an attitude to spiritually guard and protect those for whom they are called by teaching Truth and not a lie.[9] They have no other motive than to honor God even when they do not fully understand all they study and will change their own concepts to match God's Word.

True, godly teachers unveil Christ to their hearers and cause the Ekklesia to grow, bear godly fruit, and flourish in righteousness[10] even under persecution. Righteous prophets are included here.

Ten Faith-Killer Doctrines of Demons

Listen to what the bible says: *"Now the Spirit speaketh expressly that in the latter times some shall depart from the faith, giving heed to seducing spirits and doctrines of devils."*[11]Deceptions in today's churches are doctrinal untruths taught by false teachers basically derived from evil spirits through whom Satanic doctrines are presented. That is when discernment and bible knowledge should cast them aside.

False doctrines always come with the purpose this verse identifies as the purpose of causing believers to *"depart from the faith"*. False teaching has purpose and it is seductive, drawing away from God's strict Word by curiosity or just what we want to hear. For instance, a practicing homosexual will read into the bible doctrine quite differently than what Spirit-filled believers find. If their interpretation was the same, they would repent and turn from practicing this obviously God-hated sin.

Demons play with the human open souls to bring a brain murkiness that sounds so good, so correct to them. When their error is listened to or studied, a willingness to embrace error adheres to the target's soul area. The false teacher's motivations are not to be factually accurate or else deception could not take place.

Rather, motivations may be for personal greed, the thrill of creating a power trip, controlling others, or other impure self-gratifications. We must question what results evil teachers want to achieve (purpose, again) that operates because of their proffered demonic doctrines. And much broader than that, what is the conjunction with the world system they are perpetrating by using a local church social network? These are the snares Seekers find themselves in.

Following, are short summaries of the most common counterfeit doctrines being circulated in religious circles. Some are ancient going back to the First Century, but all were formulated and perpetrated by human and often demonic influences designed for control and profit.[12] Most certainly, many more demonic doctrines will arise as these ending Church Age times are concluded as the world gets compacted by hand-held electronics, medical experimentation, global financial leaps, and lawlessness replicating the violent days of Noah.

What makes doctrinal lies so insidious? Is it their psychological intrusions against the soul to supplant faith, implant error, and neutralize the Holy Spirit's influence by preventing or interrupting godly communication.[13] Let's evaluate this concept further:

■ **Trials and Tribulations Doctrine (Stoicism).** This deception proclaims that all bad or negative life experiences (sickness, rejection, trials, financial loss, cross-sexual attractions and perversions, global disasters, family deaths, imprisonment, and you-name-it), comes from God who is sovereign and "could have prevented them". It sounds plausible at first glance, but removes the believer from the reality of free-will liberty. We are not created to be puppets on strings of God-control. No, life happens and consequences develop. This deception refutes what God declares in Job 2:3-10: "*Shall we accept* (only) *good at the hand of God and shall we not accept* (also) *misfortune and what is of a bad nature?*"

In the testing and challenges of life (better understood as spiritual growth periods), we begin to recognize what our Father is dealing with us to course-correct us onto higher success. Blaming negative happenings on God or Satan causes us to miss what the Lord really has in mind for His big picture. The bible advises us to, "*...count it all joy when trials and temptations befall you,*" because as we learn to listen to God amid living it out, we mature in faith and become the spiritual warriors He requires.[14]

Obviously, the devil isn't interested in our growth but in our destruction. His powers are very limited by the authority we now possess and use through the name of Jesus Christ. Most obviously, demons who hang around us use the negatives coming from whatever direction the source that is upon us to twist us out of miracle ground for God.

Rather than believe circumstances and demons, negative friends, or false hopes, let's believe in His good character and perfecting love for us.

Yes, God's children are rewarded for their suffering caused by stepping up in outward actions that can only be taken by raw faith. We are to expect these natural, negative attack responses hurled at us from living in a wicked and bent-to-evil world. Suffering persecution is consequential to deliberate faith choices on our part.[15]

Even Jesus Himself warned us[16] that at times Christians can expect to be hungry, thirsty, strangers, needing clothing and shelter, ill in body, and perhaps imprisoned and even beheaded for our beliefs. This certainly means we are on track. This is the Cross-way, the path outlined for over comers to receive eternal reward.

- **Secular Humanism**. Let me quote this partial definition of secular humanism as, "...regarding, the particular belief that humanity is capable of morality and self-fulfillment without belief in God".[17] Of course the 'morality' is subjectively made up by them.

This secular, atheistic worldview is the attempt to dethrone the Supreme God of the universes by enthroning human wisdom and morality as an adequate substitution as a new god. They postulate that all people are born good but somehow can go wrong in life by denying the inborn DNA of a sin nature.

In effect, Humanism is an explanation for becoming God in one's own world with the notion of producing what they consider the highest good for society. This intellectual soulish doctrine slips into churches and is rampant in education as a "professional and ethical" way to properly socialize our culture. Its purpose starts with a basis of believing the lie that people are naturally born with the capacity to be good.

In local fellowships, Secular Humanism has gained credibility by placing less emphasis on God's Word that would dispute their humanistic beliefs with emphasis on social diversification as humanly goodness.

Affected churches experience little, if any, real worship of the Lord but have, "*a form of godliness,* (yet) *deny the power of God*". The supernatural aspects of true worship and practicality of the cross live of Christ are distinctly denied while Biblical concepts such as blood sacrifice, sanctification, repentance, the sin nature from conception, and eternal judgment are grossly missing or more comfortably redefined.

Secular Humanism explains social works apart from those Kingdom-assigned, godly works, as counterfeits to the commission of Christ. Some may bring temporary changes to people's physical needs but cannot facilitate eternal change. *Secular* itself means not-God. Add humanism to that as the combined theory and we witness many works-oriented cults, government programs, religious sects, and independent ministries coupled with self-serving and unbounded humanistic goals like providing free or forced genetic modification injections under the guise of false, curative "vaccines".

Secular humanists produce charities and foundations demonstrating great social, athletic, medical, and entertainment complexes instead of houses of prayer and powerhouses for reaching the lost. Their impossibility to satisfy God is simply humanistic do-goodie that will burn up in judgment. Remain apart!

For Christians, proper response to human, physical need arises from an apologetic foundation by giving help to needy fellow believers as the Scripture admonishes. Needs can be met (food, water, shelter) in the context of Gospel witness. On the other hand, Secular Humanism is a vain and worldly gesture that comfortably slips people into a Godless eternity.

- **Positive Confession and Demand Healing.** There is a demand belief in health and wealth doctrines that smack of witchcraft. It is presumptuous and testing God. In these services, the audience is instructed to say some of the following in the name of positive confession: "I WILL receive my millions. It is my right as a child of God!" Or, "I speak the word of faith to claim that I am a king's kid and deserving of _____". They might even threaten God with, "If You don't answer my positive confession and heal me (or, provide money, get me a job, bring me a spouse, or whatever the demand), "I'll fast until I die." Unexpectedly, people have died waiting on their falsely declared claims to work for them.[18]

■ **Civil & Social Justice Gospel.** This is currently very popular-- that justice is a human right no matter what the newest 'right' is invented. These new social rights make allowances for sin choices that are or were once, illegal in society. Equality is now defined as not being equal or of the same value, but repositioned through the lens of the LGBTQ movement that decidedly suppresses Constitutional rights which all Americans enjoy. Deep within its hidden motivation is the removal of the full gospel that can expose and eliminate the false.

> *The Equality Act (2021) would amend existing civil rights law—including the Civil Rights Act of 1964, the Fair Housing Act, the Equal Credit Opportunity Act, the Jury Selection and Services Act, and several laws regarding employment with the federal government—to explicitly include sexual orientation and gender identity as protected characteristics. The legislation also amends the Civil Rights Act of 1964 to prohibit discrimination in public spaces and services and federally funded programs on the basis of sex. Additionally, the Equality Act would update the public spaces and services covered in current law to include retail stores, services such as banks and legal services, and transportation services. These important updates would strengthen existing protections for everyone.[19]*

The United States Civil Rights Act of 1964 was inclusive of and protected everyone and, if passed *H. R. 1* (2021) defeat those freedoms in favor of the sin they want to federally protect. If passed, this *Act* would eliminate preaching and teaching of the full and open truth of the Bible. It comes with penalties for ignoring its authority—up to imprisonment—for those willing to preach against perversion, anyway. It is a politically-obtained federal protection for one of the oldest fertility religions.

So far depending on the fluctuating leadership of the United States per fair elections, America is considered the leader of the world for making an appeal for justice when other nations won't provide it.[20] Justice rises and falls by the will of ambitious, power-controlled greed or by godly patriots on the side of our God-inspired Constitution. The critical need for Christ-dominated world rulers is to bring leadership from biblical standards as the unique way to uphold God's justice for all. This is a Kingdom stewardship responsibility and worthy of a lifetime effort.

The Civil Justice Gospel is false: it has no validity for it purposefully prevents the involvement of Jesus Christ as the One who uses His ways to bring justice to law, trade, the high seas, world peace by making a lack of war by the suppression of terrorism and tyranny. Peace comes when there is a stop of genocidal aggression through military, medical, and other channels.

In contrast, the Church's job is to bring God's justice to bear on the affairs of the secular fields of education, media, medicine, government, science, law, social behavior, religion, and in all aspects of human interface.[21] After all, we live in the world but are not of this world. Let God off the hook because He provided salvation for the whole unsaved world, and gives the additional bonus of eternal life to those who believe Him.

It is an incentive for the body of Christ to guard its position zealously and be alert to step forward at any cost, to preserve the fabric of liberties under constant demonic and human incursion. Spirit Warriors will encounter many who have endured indoctrination to contend for false systems.

- **Replacement Theology.** This theory is also known as Supersecessionism that is a false doctrine asserting that the New Covenant church of Jesus Christ supersedes (overtakes, succeeds, replaces) the Old Mosaic Covenant made exclusively with the Hebrew people. They assert that only the Church is now the definitive people of God. This view directly contrasts with dual-covenant theology which holds that the Mosaic covenant remains valid for Jews and the Church is open to all who believe and worship Jesus Christ that does not replace any people or religious group as exclusive.

For instance, Islamic tradition views Islam as the final and authentic expression of Abrahamic prophetic monotheism; of course, Allah is a fallen principality and not even close to the One True Jehovah God.[22] It and all religions fabricated by humans can ever replace Hm.

- **Secular Psychology.** Psychology is a pseudoscience that can be highly rational. By mixing secular psychological theories with biblical mysticism, the mixture impersonates biblical wisdom with attempts to cram the world's corrupted views into a new mindset framework. As a deception, Christian Psychology makes some sense and easily appeals to utilizing faith explanations for resolving problems but it avoids the fact that Jesus Christ is the only solution, not their theories. Psychology is not only fundamentally warped by humanism and speculation, but produces a double minded substitute when it uses theological language.

Just what is secular psychology, anyway? Briefly, it is the study of why people are the way they are and how they can change or adapt their behavior in any of some 10,000 psychological methods and categories on record. The secular world, however, does not recognize the One God we know, but calls their gods 'the universal mind', 'Mother Nature,' 'The Force,' 'We are a Village', 'the collective unconscious,' and 'individuation'. These and others too numerous to list, are not just other names for God but substitutes for God.

What followed along the paths of ancient spiritualism in the early 19th Century onward, was the creation of psychoanalysis by Sigmund Freud, Eric Fromm, Carl Jung, and multiple others. Each laid a questionable intellectual base for their introduction and integration of "science" with the powers of occult spiritualism. It became more developed in the next century by a growing number of new theories adding to this body of knowledge, exacerbated by cultural changes, and turned into a professional career path with educational studies and certified licenses.

■ 'Christian' Psychology is a contradiction in terms. It is a mixture of secular pseudoscience enveloped in Christianized terminology. Since the psyche is the soul, we either operate out of the soul-life (flesh) or from the renewed human spirit that is in direct contact with the Holy Spirit and directed by the Lord. A pure vessel cannot operate from both.[23]

This is not to be confused with sound biblical counseling meaning, the sole word of God is applied to the challenges and sin-choices people entangled themselves in.[24] Sometimes, redemption is what is needed that allows the emergence of a new creation in Jesus Christ, with the mind of Christ applied. Besides salvation, releasing the influence of the hindering spirits by repentance and exorcism may be the real answer.

Take the popular 'Christian' philosophy of Possibility Thinking. It is one such false coaching that uses meditation as a launching pad (PTM for making the human attitude by meditation responsible to change the person into something better. This brand of psychology errantly appears as self-improvement as "the realization of full human potential". How much strengthening of the soulish life is needed to walk as a Christian? You are right, none. The cross-life is what is demanded to assist the human spirit to follow God's way by the grace and mercy of our Father.

■ The Social Gospel. This is the doctrine that all people are God's children with no need for salvation since there is no punishment or hell. Both nonbelievers and some very immature Christians adhere to a social gospel. Its good works are efforts to provide bodily needs such as free food days, donated clothing, help with job location, legal support to facilitate abortion or chemical abortifacients medical care, and temporary shelter. But just as quickly as it meets temporary bodily needs, it eliminates the true Gospel of Jesus Christ, who is the only Source for permanent provision. These are liberal and intentional human works. But as Dr. Adrian Rogers once quipped on secular works: "Soup and soap gets a sinner clean into hell."

■ **Sexual Perversions are Normal.** Finding few or no answers to relieve confused mental dysphoria regarding sexuality, activists joined with secular psychology to redefine once labeled mental illnesses, as "preferred lifestyles". Maybe the answer is sex re-assignment surgery? Or, forced legislation for extra rights? Or, constant media blitzes, pornography, and open gay parades to re-shape Judaeo-Christian culture into tolerated acceptance? These, and other militant approaches, flared across the world. What was once understood as sin was now postured as socially normal behavior all the way down to pedophilia.

Within the past five years, thousands who had once openly con-fessed to believing The Lie went back to their natural DNA-driven bio-logical sex identification. They tasted and spat out the bitter misguided lies from Big Gay of same-sex attraction theories running its full course all the way to body mutilation and a lifelong chemical dependency to maintain the charade of being the opposite gender.

Time for reconsideration and the horrors of living that lie, took a sane turn for some. Many found Jesus Christ as believers reached out in love and not condemnation. Within two decades, a good number of surgically and chemically mutilated transgenders were coming out of the indoctrination of Big Gay's recruitment tactics and propagandized programming. These were willing to confront reality openly and re-verse their decision of false-gendering.

Re-gendering was courageous, difficult, and emotionally painful as hormone treatments were eliminated. But in some cases, although it was physically impossible to correct the surgical mutilation, they recovered their minds and could fulfill what God had planned for them. Deliverance can help.

One newly born-again woman, a former lesbian with a re-gendered group demonstrating in Washington, DC (Spring 2021), said it took five years for the male hormones to wear off and when they did, she was undoubtedly now attracted to males in a healthy way. On top of the ongoing personal vigilance and political strife to keep up the expensive pretenses and medical manipulations, is the constant natural pressure of fighting one's own gender DNA stamped in every cell of the body. On top of that, the movement's constant attempt to force society--who readily sees *The Lie*--to validate a false sex-gender unreality with pronoun corrections, with pretend marriages that have higher divorce rates, and the pain of birth family alienation.

It's impossible to fight what God has implanted in the soul and natural body. Our gender is God's undisputed will for our lives. Embrace and celebrate it! We will only function in a gender role until our translation to eternity and get our new bodies fit for the next assignments.

You may meet Seekers with many questions of gender dysplasia. It is just another selection by the sin nature. By pointing them back to the obvious biological will of God in their natural bodies, the first relevant step for them is repentance and choosing salvation. Then it is possible to address the conflict controlling their perceived identity that left a trail of social and mental crises, depression, suicidal attempts, and soul fractures. This can be healed.

Find out if they were either alienated by family or affirmed by family in *The Lie*. This linkage keeps them bound to the demonic controls. The saddest part of choosing that sin path is supporting propagandizing innocent, pre-pubescent children to *The Lie* that replaced the truth of their bio-gender, and convincing children they are a mistake or that God made a mistake. Demons are experts at this. This is qualified child abuse.

God has a predetermined plan for each life and will never make mistakes on gender but parents, non-experts, and psychoanalysts do. We must call this deception out as trespass abuse. The adult and young Seekers who are severely wounded and disillusioned will show up at your door broken and needing love and acceptance for a new way back. Demons must be exposed and expelled with the Seeker's cooperation.

Secular psychology may identify the tormenting demons and give them scientifically fancy names but they can only try to train people how to best live with these demons or recommend secular rehab and false step programs. Their psychologically considered routes will demand time with great personal and monetary cost. But the world's knowledge can never provide freedom as Christ does by putting them together again, body, soul, and spirit.

- **GAIA Mother Earth Worship.** Mother Earth worship is nothing new and continually repeats its pagan entrance each generation with new, updated crises on the critical need to, 'save the planet'. Lately, scare is planned as a global taxation system to fund the illegitimate United Nations consortium to remain in power over the peoples of the world. Personifying the physical world that God created as *mother* earth, is alone heretical. The worship of created beings, even inanimate ones made from stones, wood, or metal images, is ludicrous; it is enmity in God's view.[25]

Female goddess worship became more center stage when the global Feminist Movement was dressed in modern guise advancing in the 18th century onward. Witchcraft was no longer persecuted with stake burning and disfigurement. It has fringe popularity and is a perfectly legal religion across the world. GAIA thrives on dominating males (the toxic male), uses child torture and infant sacrifice, has elaborate satanic worship rituals, and much more you can research.

Biblical Counseling in contrast, is how we reveal God's wise solutions gathered solely from within the holy scriptures. When this divine source of wisdom was usurped from pastors, priests, and the brothers and sisters in the faith by worldly, professional psychologists (with their State-approved licenses to earn thereby), the Church lost a great deal of its testimony and authority.

Sadly, some Christian parents are fearful to guide, discipline, and instruct their own children preferring or pressured into the indoctrination of leaving these responsibilities (and blessings) of parenting to "specialists" in child warping many times mandated by godless educational institutions that we Christians have not guarded against but placed onto school boards through naivete or disengagement.

Reflection Time. Spirit Warriors, slow down as you soak in this section of the manual to allow God to bring into your own minds those for whom you may have caused to have suffered a wounded soul, negative feelings, unresolved anger, or unforgiveness by reviewing things that have happened to you or because of your wrong decisions. As you review Appendix A, you will be able to take yourself and the Seeker step-by-step through the forgiveness process as outlined there.

Again, stop to listen as He tells you against whom you may have bitterness, hatred, hurt feelings, grudges, or an ungodly attachment. Bitterness is the mature offspring of decayed hurts in your soul that are kept alive by constant remembrance either by thinking silently on them or speaking them aloud. God does not bring failures to the mind as all sins have been forgiven and forgotten by Him, but Satan will accuse if you allow it.

Bitterness results in an unwillingness to release yourself from its torment or rebellion against God whom, you feel, doesn't understand how hurt you were or, "who allowed it to happen to you". Unforgiveness can also stem from the evil desire to continue to somehow think you are able to punish the offender in this self-destructive habit. This is true for Seekers, too. Get free from any animosity that can defile the spirit to the point of influencing the soul to maintain weak and unhealthy feelings. When biblical counsel is not sought, the body will be exposed to disease from fostering soul bitterness.[26]

Finally, Jesus told us to, "watch and pray". We have to watch deceptions and outright delusions the world is very aggressively pushing on others to support those delusions. At the end, the internationally stated agenda of globalists is to corrupt the human DNA that God imprinted in every cell of our bodies. We belong to Him. We are allowed to choose if we will belong to Him but until that CHOICE is made, the human creation belongs to the Father.

This is a tremendous battle. The Beast's mark will probably distort and corrupt the very genome of the identification of being human. Satan want's his imprint and when it is obtained, that person can never be saved and brought into Christ's family.[27] God's doctrines matter. They are life and death.

In the next two chapters, we are introduced to the specific assaults against the human body and how these demonic offensives (signs) can show up in the physical body.

[1] Matthew 26:11.

[2] 1 Timothy 6:6-10.

[3] James 4:6; Luke 1:51-52; 1 Timothy 6:6-10; Matthew 25:1.

[4] Luke 16:10-11.

[5] Revelation 22:18-19.

[6] Matthew 7:15-20.

[7] False fruit rises from the soul's character. See Galatians 5:22-25 to compare with the Fruit of the Holy Spirit.

[8] Deuteronomy 11:16, 27.

[9] First Timothy 4:1.

[10] Ephesians 4:12-13.

[11] Other Scriptures on False Teachers: 2 Corinthians 4:4 and 6:17; 1 John 2:9-11; Hosea 4:12; Deuteronomy 11:27; 2 John 7; Revelation 12:9, 20:8-10; 1 Timothy 4:1; 1 Corinthians 3:14, 18.

[12] Isaiah 5:20.

[13] An excellent booklet by John Ankerberg and John Weldon, The Facts on False Teaching in the Church is recommended reading on these cults but there are many others.

[14] James 2.

[15] Hebrews 12:4-12.

[16] Matthew 25:37-46.

[17] Secular humanism is a philosophy or life stance that embraces human reason, secular ethics, and philosophical naturalism while specifically rejecting religious dogma, super- naturalism, with superstition as the basis of morality and decision making.

[18] James 1:5-6; 4:2' Matthew 7:7-12 explains what prayers are answered. Asking for a stone will not get bread from God. This explains why selfish and harmful requests go unanswered.

[19] https://www.hrc.org/resources/the-equality-act.

[20] U.S. Senator Bob McEwen's speech heard on Dr. James Dobson's *Family Talk* radio program, October 8, 2020.

[21] 1 John 1:9; Acts 3:14; Romans 1:17; Romans 3:26; Hebrews 12:23.

[22] Wikipedia on Super-secessionism; a theology that argues Christians have replaced Jews as the people of God, and often refers to the quotation of Jeremiah 31:31-32.

[23] James 3:13-18.

[24] Word done by June Hunt is totally based on scripture and a rich resource for bible counselors because it is divided out in 50 topics in her first handbook. www.JuneHunt.org.

[25] Deuteronomy 4:28; 28:36, 64; 2 Kings 19:18; Isaiah 37:19; Isaiah 45:20.

[26] 1 Corinthians 11:27-33, 48; Mark 11:25-26.

[27] Revelation 13:11-18. This happens during the Seventh Trumpet judgment just before born-again believers are rescued from earth to join Christ in the clouds.

| 12 |

Assault Against the Body
- Part 1

"We have all eternity to celebrate our victories, but only one short hour before sunset in which to win them."
~ Robert Moffat, 1795-1883

Stewardship of the Body

It is exciting to consider the magnificent physical home for the spirit and soul God gave all humans at creation. The complexity and diversity of this marvelous wonder is still not totally understood by science yet we may enjoy our bodies with all its natural defenses, capacity for pleasure, and ability to take us where we wish to go.

What we do understand is that the body is to be used for His will and glory. It is the outward vehicle by which we relate to the physical world. For the Christian, the body is a sacred temple of the living God and must be treated with care, respect, and holiness.[1]

In the natural order of life cycles and reproduction, God ordained married sexual intercourse (interaction) for practical and recreational purposes. That is clearly seen in the book of Song of Solomon. God carefully planned and lovingly biologically and psychologically engineered the sexual privileges to be set aside for adult men and women within the context of the Sacrament of Holy Marriage.

Sex is not a past time for children as our culture dictates, but a serious, lifelong commitment made to God by married adults. Respecting sexual relations as God intended gives protection from disease and freedom from guilt. It brings the blessing of the Lord for life, health, and spiritual prosperity. When respect for the body is misused or abused, a person leaves his or her God-chosen place and is open to Satan's advantage.

He or she may find out too late that the devouring lion has been set free to destroy them from within their body. We must have a healthy love (not adoration) for our bodies to live long on the earth as free from pain, disease, early death, and suffering as possible: this is blessing.

Mentally healthy people accept the body God gave them as perfect for them. Contrary to this truth is the untruth spewed by pop culture, self-enriching marketing pressures to be dissatisfied. Body hatred is a real problem we'll discuss later.

A special concern to Christian parents in a highly permissive electronic environment should be to make available from the church or godly home, Christ-centered sex education. It is an absolute necessity to equip our children with scripture to escape the snare and pressures of illicit sex. Virginity for both sons and daughters is the only Biblical position. Any alteration of this direction can only damage their tender spirits and enslave the sacredness of their bodies.

Regarding Christian unmarried adults: a total lack of honor and respect for God's revealed will in your bodies will lead you to either a promiscuous sexual lifestyle or multiple monogamous relationships outside His will that lead nowhere close to His will for your life. Both positions are self-abusing and defile God's temple.

Instead, seek the Lord for the supernatural fruit of self-control to grow in your character so your testimony remains clean and pure from the guilt and torment of evil. We need to be unspotted by the world and in a clean relationship with God to gain meaning from the short time we live here.

Body Fixation

Something very popular in the world right now is an over concern for the body and body-fixation. Both are sin and idolatry. This behavior is manifested in pampering the body into unhealthy, over-developing it by extreme muscle use, tattooing or surgically changing it for vanity's sake. Has God demanded that we look young all our lives?

Then why believe the devil by chasing the elusiveness of youth?

Some believers are superficially engaged in constant discussion about illnesses, allergies, diets, and exotic diseases. They are robbers who steal time away from others who wish to speak on the things of the Lord. The Bible says to avoid them.[2]

Then there is the other group who are convinced that hating their bodies as evil, denying it nutrition, cleanliness, medical attention, proper rest, and exercise is "spiritually prudent". This old tactic of the devil to focus all a believer's attention on the physical was most successful during the Middle Ages but proved fruitless and ungodly, gendering false doctrines that have plagued the Church for centuries. How subtle and diversionary Satan can be!

But when the body is used naturally as a servant and gift from God in balanced perspective, all your much needed time and attention can be devoted to being used as a channel for the Holy Spirit without the encumbrance of centering on the physical plane. There is a time for fasting. There is also a time for feasting. Those led by the Spirit of God know when to do both.

Listed next are some areas of attack against the body which have been given particular attention here, but there can be many more. Remember, the mind is the battleground: it is in the mind that choices are made to sin or not to sin, to walk with the Lord, or to walk after the fleshly appetites. But the body carries out the will of the mind.

Self-ordered Murder

Especially in this area, Spirit Warriors must recognize and disclose to the Seeker that team members are not qualified as medical, mental health, psychological, or psychiatric Spirit Warriors. Mention this disclaimer at the beginning of all sessions and explain it in writing, with the signed acknowledgement of Seekers. For those who give handout material, write it out clearly and explain that the team is voluntary and not paid for ministering. Participation for exorcism is by the voluntary consent of Seekers.

According to Christian wisdom Spirit Warrior June Hunt,[3] these areas may be critical and possibly life-threatening. With that in mind, the range of self-ordered murder methods covered here includes anorexia nervosa, anorexia athletica, bulimia,[4] gluttony, tobacco use, vaping, addictive drugs, and self-abusing substances, including alcoholic beverages.

These categories are ways humans have allowed their carnal soul to be in charge of sin preferences that end in destroying their bodies. Seekers will explain that these choices were made for numerous reasons, delusions, fears, unbearable pain, made through ungodly, faulty wisdom, or peppered with excuses, rushing all the way to self-terminating suicide. Spirit Warriors will hear and/or see these conditions in Seekers who are finally reaching for help from the Lord and from you.

Eating and drug disorders are symptoms of the torment surfacing in their lives because of believing lies from the world ("Your size is totally wrong"), from yourself ("I can't be happy until I'm thin/athletic/young-looking enough"), and from the devil ("You will not surely die"). Those with eating disorders[5] experience some or all of the following:

- Confusion over values;
- Deception (pretense) of self and by others;
- Depression over feeling "fat" or "inadequate";
- Compulsion for some feeling of control;
- Loneliness because of the desire to avoid discovery;
- Isolation because of shame for being obese from gluttony;
- Lowered self-value because personal value is based on appearance;
- Perfectionism – everything must be just right; and

■ People pleasing with an excessive desire for approval.

What are situational causes? Here is June Hunt's list:

■ Feeling worthless from abuse in the home;
■ Feeling inadequate because of unrealistic expectations of others;
■ Feeling driven in a high-performance atmosphere;
■ Feeling hopeless resulting from depression of past behaviors;
■ Feeling powerless because of obesity or other disorder in family;
■ Feeling angry for past mistreatment; and
■ Feeling anxious due to stressful uncontrollable life changes.

Notice the word *feelings* in these situational causes. Feelings emanate from the soul-mind area. But we know that feelings are not facts or necessarily the truth. God has created us with three major inner needs: love, significance, and security. He is the ultimate Repairer so we would come to know and love Him.

As Spirit Warriors, seek the Holy Spirit's specific target need of the Seeker. Ask some gentle questions and get discernment on the tormentors that want to carry this one to death sooner than God's will. In the case of professing thoughts or attempts at suicide, get immediate, professional help for them. Have a list of practicing professionals to give for ongoing care.

Rainbow of Sexual Orientations

In the natural order of life cycles and reproduction, God ordained sexual intercourse for practical and recreational purposes. That is clearly seen in the Song of Solomon. He lovingly set these sexual privileges aside for adult men and women to be enjoyed within the context of the Sacrament of Holy Marriage. Sex is not a past time for children as our culture dictates, but a commitment made to God by married adults.

Respecting sexual relations as God intended gives protection from disease and freedom from guilt and brings the blessing of the Lord for prosperity. When the concept of the body is misused or abused, a person is out of his or her chosen place and has been opened to Satan's advantage. He or she may find out too late that the Lion has been set free to kill and destroy from within the body.

We must have a healthy love (not adoration) for our bodies to live long on the earth as free from pain, disease, early death, and suffering as possible: this is blessing. King David gave himself as a servant especially suited to meet God's purposes to his own generation. He continued to struggle with Jehovah until his relationship between spirit, soul, and body was put in proper balance. Because of this kind of discipline in David's early life, God's testimony sustained the Jewish nation at so critical a time. David blessed later generations through his blood line as a heritage to Jesus Christ.[6]

A special concern to Christian parents in a highly permissive society should be to make available from the church or godly home, Christ-centered sex education. It is an absolute necessity to equip our children with scripture to escape the snare and pressures of illicit sex. Virginity before marriage for both sons and daughters is the only Biblical position. Any alteration of this direction can only damage their tender spirits and enslave the sacredness of their bodies.

And to single Christian adults: a total lack of honor and respect for God's revealed will in your bodies will lead you to either a promiscuous sexual lifestyle or multiple monogamous relationships. Both are sexual self-abuse and defile God's temple. Instead, ask the Lord for the supernatural fruit of self-control to grow in your character so your testimony remains clean and pure from the guilt and torment of evil spirits. You need to be unspotted by the world and in right relationship with God to gain meaning from life.

Two questions you might want to answer are these: "Is sex outside the covenant of marriage important enough to kill for it (as in abortion should a pregnancy occur)?" And, "Is sex outside of marriage important enough to die for it (as in contracting AIDS or other sexually transmitted disease)?" These are questions your Seekers need answers for.

Sexual Immorality, Perversion, and Bestiality

ADULTERY is marriage covenant breaking sexual sin when at least one of the partners is married. It is in violation of the marriage vows and corrupts or makes poorer by mixing with an inferior strength. Sexual union is spiritual union and reserved for marriage only.[7] The marriage covenant is a three-way promise between God with the groom, God with the bride, and the groom and bride with each other. Adultery breaks this sacred triple covenant by introducing a fourth alien affection that is not part of it.

God's way is to keep the marriage covenant pure. As an example, the Church is a type of the spotless Bride presented to God's Son in spiritual marriage. Thus, a Godly marriage produces the fruit of love, children, pleasure and fun, mental and emotional stability, longer life, a partnership to stand against the powers of the world and Satan, companionship, and mutual reward of shared ministry in old age.

Love in a marriage is an attitude of the mind, not a weak sentimental emotion that is easily diverted by someone new. Lust is demonic and there is no love in it. Love is Godly.[8] The Lord continually declares that He hates adultery; in fact, He divorced His wife Israel for the spiritual whoredoms she committed with the world and His archenemy, Satan, by her idolatrous living.

This might be a burning question that Seekers come to you for counsel. First Corinthians 6:15-20 deals with a person (male or female) who is not in God's order. The physical body is spoken of as members (part) of Christ Himself. Even today, almost two thousand years later after this was written, Paul asks the pointed question to someone contemplating adultery like this one:

> *"Shall I then take the members of Christ and unite them with a prostitute? Never! Do you not know that he who unites himself with a prostitute is one*

> with her in body? For it is said, the two will become one flesh: But he who unites himself with God is one with him in spirit."

What possible level of hatred is needed to submit Christ—who goes everywhere within you—to illicit and filthy sexual experiences? He must turn away in deeply felt grief to see the damages to the human spirit which He has worked so hard to sanctify.

The marriage has now entered a lie and betrayal. Temptation to commit adultery must be rejected outright. If you are in a situation or work place where you are constantly tempted to sin, the believer MUST make direct assault against the demon and make his or her position known to the tempter.

Regard it as a direct and evil assault against your marital commitment and desire for godliness. Don't allow Satan to flatter your vanity by flirting with sexual temptation. You will lose. Do not even give the appearance of evil by placing yourself in situations with people that can be construed as wrong. Take responsibility for your marriage vows and for keeping the door shut in Satan's face.

Some tormenting demons that can come in with adultery are rebellion, lust, liar, covenant breaker, perversion, pride, unfaithfulness, anger, prostitution, Jezebel or Ahab spirit, selfishness, idolater, crime, regret, guilt, self-hate, spouse-hate, rejection, and jealousy.

> The solution is quick: "FLEE (don't walk but run!) from SEXUAL IMMORAL-ITY." ALL other sins a man commits are outside his body, but he who sins sexually really sins against his own body. Do you not know that YOUR BODY is the TEMPLE of the Holy Spirit who is in you, whom you have received from God? You are not your own; you were bought at a price. Therefore, honor God with your body."[9]

FORNICATION is all sexual impurity between two (or more) unmarried persons. The Hebrew words for fornication are *taznuth* and *zanah* meaning, "harlotry, idolatry, fornication; cause to be, to play, to fall to whoredom, to go a-whoring continually." The New Testament Greek word is *porneuo* (think pornography) as: "to act the harlot, indulge in unlawful lust (with either or both sexes); to practice idolatry and commit fornication."

I can find no place in Scripture where a pure, holy sexual relationship does or can exist between people who are not joined in marriage. It is explicitly given for Christians NOT to engage in premarital sex of any kind. That includes physical contact, petting, caressing, verbal, visual, and Internet sex.[10]

The Lord is concerned not only with our personally indulging this sin, but also places a high standard against forming and maintaining friendships with those who practice fornication. All who are controlled by the sinful nature (idolatry) cannot please God.

INCEST is to have willful sexual relations with a close relative by blood or within a close lawful kinship.[11] The Greek word is *porneia* and falls broadly into this perversion for God's normal lifestyle of order.

BESTIALITY is humans performing sexually with animals. It is an atrocity and dangerous portal for attack. Besides sinning against your own body, it debases the honor and position God has given the human being as it degrades the position of animals in His kingdom. Bestiality includes the scientific mixing of the species between human and animal in experimental vaccines, drugs, and commercial investigation.

The HIV virus and some venereal diseases are said to have passed into the human system as a result of participating in sex with animals or by vaccines with animal tissue. It is increasingly difficult to find remedies for sexually transmitted diseases (STD) when different strains are mixed from multiple partners. This deviant use of sex is forbidden for our own human good. Our body systems and immunologic strength are not designed for this.[12]

LESBIAN, GAY, BISEXUAL, TRANSGENDER and QUEER. The Old Testament Hebrew for this class of sin is *qadesh* as describe as, "a (male) devotee (by prostitution) to licentious idolatry; a sodomite, unclean." From the Greek word *pornos*, we get this definition: "A prostitute and debauchee (libertine); fornicator, whore-monger." Prostitutes are both male and female.

Consensual sex between the same gender, including within a licensed "gay marriage or partnership." Christian leaders do not perform marriage ceremonies since the marriage contract is three-way: God, man, and woman.

All homosexual and explicit sexual thoughts and/or activities must be confessed as sin by the Seeker. It is against God's rule. Continuing in denial or unrepentance is rebellion in this sense. Perversion becomes idolatry when the personal sacrifice of one's body and soul to another, is made. This lust is a personal choice, effectively displacing Jehovah's unique position as, *"The only one, true God"*. Until the Spirit Warrior can explain the "why" of perversion from the biblical standpoint, repentance might be impossible so that deliverance is halted.

In other words, holding on to any preferred sin, no matter what form it takes, blocks the expulsion of the demons who rule that sin choice so they will still maintain permission to harass, tempt into deeper darkness, and control. It is possible for someone to have these tormenting demons though never having physically practiced it. This is important.

It is often one of the prime causes that destroys normal male-female ways of relating because the question is always front and center: "Am I gay or not?" These unclean spirits arise through a person's confusion about body and soul connections sometimes brought through militant propaganda and assault on childhood ignorance. These demons are familiar (family) spirits that like to be the main attraction of attention and win new victims.

Many demons can be introduced into the person of a rebellious and practicing gays. The Bible refers to those who practice sexual intimacy with members of their same sex as sodomites. Genesis 19 reveals the awesome and complete destruction God visited on the gay-populated cities of Sodom, Gomorrah and another five towns close by, because of the prevailing area wide practice of open, rampant, uncontrolled homosexuality. It was a spreading cancer. Today, these sites remain uninhabited and covered with hell's Sulfur.

The Bible calls the self-abuse of unwarranted sexual expression to be an abomination. That's a strong term for, *"extreme hatred and detestation; hence, defilement, pollution in a physical sense; evil doctrines and practices which are moral defilement, idols, and idolatry."*[13] The repugnance to God for perverting sexual activity has been ignored and softened by using terms such as gays, lesbians, queers, transgenders, pedophiles, and other demeaning labels that serve to keep hidden the serious error of this sin choice.

Clergy who are in bondage to this area of sin and often very understanding as religious authorities which continues to affirm parishioners in captivity to their flesh. Attending these churches puts them in special danger that fortifies demonic bondage.

First, they have been betrayed by leaders who should know the Word of God more perfectly, and secondly, they are encouraged to continue (and sometimes defiantly so) to lead others under their care into a life choice that distances them from God by their tacit confirmation of sin.[14] Full repentance by turning away and breaking all ties to this lifestyle, is the solution to beginning deliverance.

The Spirit Warrior must be aware of auxiliary spirits that may support perversion in order to address them by naming them as the Holy Spirit gives the Word of Knowledge. Here are some of these clinging spirits that we have identified (the demons told us their names) and confronted in deliverance over the years:

Hatred, lust, fear of sex, lack of identity, shame, mental and physical perversion, pornography, sadism, unclean spirits of anal and orifice sex, child molestation, rape, vulgarity, voyeurism (peeping tom), indecency, torture, confusion, cowardice, fetish sin, a spirit of darkness, spiritual blindness, strip-tease, dirty dancing, attention-getting spirit, tattoo-scarification, defiance, promiscuity, an idol of physical pleasures, flashing and mooning (desire to expose genitals), transvestite, sensuality; alluring and enticing spirits, militancy, and anger. You can see that this is a large portal of torment.[15]

A huge area of concern across the world is the criminal area of adult and child sex trafficking which we cannot address fully here. But be aware that millions of children have been unwillingly forced into this abuse and misuse, even in circles and organizations self-identifying as "Christian".

Amazingly, a new class of compassionate warfare ministry is devoted and called to cross borders, locate and rescue the ravished victims from literal cages and venereal diseases and damages where paid services of the grossest perversions had been caused. Men who commit these sins, whether sellers or buyers, must be prosecuted to stop the torture and deaths to feed lustful demons possessing them.

Some children are so physically traumatized, their immature bodies cannot stand up to the abuse and they die long before puberty. Please study this area on your own and use extreme love and acceptance when a Seeker comes with their story. Believe them. Love them. Provide fellowship, discipleship to advice for overcoming their emotional soul traumas. Counseling will be needed.

As the sin-prone human nature that easily turns to these sexual choices is unwrapped, it is easier to avoid and not make it ingrained as a lifestyle or identity. The constant barrage of marketing for sexual encounters, confusing the innocence of childhood, pressing the god-less ideas and practices on conquests, and reinforcement from deviant religious entities, causes much emotional and physical pain. For some, it is an early death that they never escape.

No one is completely without the temptations and easy shortcuts to avoid facing difficult situations we have not encountered before. That's exactly how life in a broken world runs. But when we realize that we will begin as a novice over and over in each new area, we seek the Lord's help until they are conquered. This is normal.

Certainly, not all problems are demonic. Far from it. Learning to work life out with the possibility of the flesh nature gives plenty of times the process of sanctification is lived out. Controlling the body is where the godly paths are chosen and become normal as the image of Jesus Christ.

[1] Romans 12:1-2.

[2] Titus 3:9-11.

[3] www.Junehunt.org, Hope for the Heart radio ministry. *"There are no hopeless situations-only people who have grown hopeless. There really are biblical solutions for all of life's struggles!"*

[4] June Hunt, *Anorexia & Bulimia – Control that is Out of Control,* (2014). Hope for the Heart.

[5] Ibid. Pages 52-56. Psalm 116:3; Psalm 25:5.

[6] Acts 13:36.

[7] 1 Corinthians 7.

[8] 1 Peter 3:1-7.

[9] 1 Corinthians 6:18-20; Exodus 20:14; Matthew 5:27-29; Proverbs 6:32-35.

[10] 1 Corinthians 5:9-11; 1 Thessalonians 4:3; Romans 6:12-13; Romans 8:8; Col. 3:5; Lev. 18:6.

[11] Leviticus 18:6; Leviticus 20:11-21; Genesis 19:36; Deut. 23:2-3; 1 Cor. 5:5

[12] Deuteronomy 27:21; Leviticus 18:23; 20:15-16.

[13] Webster, Noah, American Dictionary of the English Language.

[14] 2 Timothy 4:3; James 3:1.

[15] Lev. 18:22; Deut. 22:5; 23:17; Romans 1:24-32; Jude verses 7, 9.

| 13 |

Assault Against the Body
- Part 2

*"Love one another with mutual affection;
outdo one another in showing honor."* ~ Romans 12:10

Addictions and the Double Mind

A big revelation is the use of the Greek word *pharmakía* in the New Testament with the definition of 'sorcery'. Drugs are poisons when given in certain quantities and were recommended and traded by witchcraft shamans (sorcerers) in very ancient times to today. They are dressed up now. Our good bible teacher and friend Bob Mumford[1] teaches us in his work on, *The Eternal Value System*, the following facts that are certainly expanded now:

> "The absolute avoidance of pain and the continual experience of pleasure is the soil in which addictions and obsessive life styles take root, grow, and bear the fruit of death...currently, this (opioids) crisis produces over 70,000 deaths a year from overdoses; destroys families and communities; and has an annual cost of over $500 billion in medical expenses, criminal justice costs, and lost job productivity." ~ *Market Watch*, August 16, 2014

Rejection: Bob Mumford's Black Hole Theory

People who suffer from the effects of rejection can have some or many of these twenty characteristics. The result is being off-balance in personal relationships and ignoring the correction of the Holy Spirit in believers. Many patterns of defeat stem from negative pride.

1. Is emotionally immature from short-stopping relationship development; there are patterns of divorce, constant move, career changes, and upheaval.
2. Displays a self-centeredness expressed by constant requests of: "pray for me, help me, love me, see me, teach me, listen to me, feed me, me, me...".[2]
3. Has an unstable back-and-forth Christian walk.
4. Shows a lack of commitment to the Christian walk, to the family, to a hobby, to someone special like a spouse, family, friends, to their Bible group, earning a living, or just present when needed.
5. Obvious negative self-identity with feelings of inferiority and an overwhelming need to question God's love and care for them.
6. Suffers from loneliness (even at a gathering) and continually builds walls through their language, actions, or body language to keep people distant.
7. May have grown up under perfectionism having to earn approval by their actions, grades, athletic skills, or outward appearance.
8. Is a people-pleaser without strong feelings that would counter someone important in life (this is passive side).
9. Feels betrayed easily and is offended at even casual snubs.
10. Worries, has doubts and fears of failure, shows anxiety and unbelief for success, and may bring actual financial insecurity on oneself to reinforce the rejection cycle.
11. Has allowed a physical handicap to dominate all of life.
12. May have been over-protected (smothered) as a child or as a change of life baby, as adopted; by being a child of the "wrong sex" according to a parent, or distorted by a broken home situation; guilt from having the mother die at their birth, or being

of mixed race. It is endless and easy to seek people or places to blame or justify feelings of rejection.

13. Feels, or is, unloved and unaccepted for just being me.
14. Is often suspicious of life and may feel persecuted.
15. Acts impatiently and is intolerant of slow movers, slow thinkers, inept drivers, the infirm, or anyone else who does not share their world view.
16. May develop stress diseases or take it out on the physical body by finding comfort in over-eating, under-eating, excessive alcohol use, smoking, drugs, or porn.
17. Is quick tempered, argumentative, angry, always right, and clashes easily with people; the passive types withdraw at the first sign of conflict and uses silence as a punishment for those who cross them.
18. Must constantly receive credit, adoration, stroking, the glory, and personal validation.
19. Has trouble submitting—will quit first—rather than work with others; drives to lead or withdraws totally if their perceived or real leadership is frustrated.
20. Is critical and a moralist; knows how to fix everything and put it back into order by their standards.

The Six Postures of Rejection

The following soul-positions that rejected people take, help them deal in their own strength with the stresses of life. This is not an exhaustive study, but serves to help uncover the camouflage that rejection puts into a personality to keep one from open and transparent living. Working from a posture whose core is soulish deters the human spirit from rightful headship and lacks that constant checking in with the Holy Spirit to correct personality alignment and development.

THE BRAGGART. Exaggerates even small accomplishments (golf scores, fish lengths, sales, amount of money in pocket, child's feats). Stories are told to get recognition, to become "bigger than life", to get self-worth. It is upheld by lying spirits, unfaithfulness, fear, and intimidation.

THE CRITIC. Easily adapts to his or her own situation because it is narrowly defined by their own concept of right and wrong; they are quick to point out other's faults, especially in areas they feel accomplished. A critical spirit is proud; e.g., "I'm not where you are, poor sod". This attitude promotes and sustains spiritual blindness, their lack of love, and intolerance.

THE LONER. Has a wounded spirit from real or imagined hurts and forms walls of protection all around? This manifests in a lack of faith in God to BE and DO ALL that she or he feels are needs. It fortifies unbelief, pain, loneliness, emotional atrophy, and creates a "little child spirit" which will hinder maturing. The little child spirit will speak back to the exorcist in a small, pitiful voice begging to be allowed to remain. Sometimes there are tears

THE DEFIANT and REBELLIOUS. Bucks the system; may become very aggressive or bullying to prove one's self worthy to authorities or in his or her own household. It often shows itself as a workaholic and overachiever to gain materialistically or goes all out for fame and public recognition which is believed to be a strong extension of themselves. Collaborating spirits are a deceptive spirit, and rebellion along with mean and abusive spirits, murder, pride, an overly competitive spirit with negativity.

THE SHY and RETIRING. This posture is very insidious and manipulative. Shyness is a controlling attitude masked in timidity, bashfulness, and wariness. This is normal in children until they gain confidence in their decision. But as adults, it is used in hopes of changing the behavior of others around them to do things to his or her own advantage. It manifests itself in a lack of courage to make decisions openly and reflects inward anger. Sickness, self-pity, and controller spirits are sometimes allowed to cohabit by this spirit of rejection.

Acting shy is an excuse and ploy to avoid becoming mature in demanding situations. Shyness should be prayed and trained out of children by allowing them to achieve. It is interesting to realize that Jesus was meek but never shy. Meekness is humility which is a strength of character.

THE SWITCH-HITTER. This is the hypocritical mask of rejection where, even though he or she is highly critical of others, cannot stand criticism directed toward themselves and are above being questioned. Or, if one behavior is expected of them, they will change to please even though they previously stood against it.

Taking a switch-hitting posture comes out of a lack of strong identity in Christ and the responsibility to take the good with the bad when motives, actions, opinions, or personal beliefs are questioned. Mature people will either stand by their decisions as correct or apologize for error when proven wrong but will not deny the action taken. Allied spirits are liar, double-minded, indecisive, smokescreen and hypocrite.

* * *

Our Father God desires us to have very strong beliefs and ideas of who we are. We get these healthy postures from simply evaluating ourselves and where we are regarding our character then looking intently at the Word of God to see our spiritual and (many times) physical and soul positions in Christ. The Holy Spirit makes this possible through the gentle prodding of our conscience that points out sin or a wrong path taken.

Godly character is formed when the Holy Spirit is obeyed and we consistently turn in God's direction. A person who knows they have heard from and have been obedient to the Lord will not allow the feelings of rejection to enter because of the misguided opinions all around. Security comes in knowing who you are in God's will and enveloped in His love. That is when you know your righteous standing. Expect to be different (godly) and at peace with that.

Depression: Why is the Seeker There?

Depression is what many call The Black Hole. It is an emotional prison that controls the body to react. The ancient way depression is described uses two Hebrew words: '*Ebal* describes a mourning, lamenting, moaning; to bewail, chant and wail. This is the acute stage of mourning coming after a severe calamity and is a natural and healthy expression of great loss.

Balah, however, brings with it the results of carrying mourning too far or falling into a depression. It means, "*to fail, decay, consume, spend, waste away; to make dusty and black as sackcloth, sordid garments.*"

The Hebrew[3] word *aven,* referred to the person who came to offer his sacred portion as a tenth of the first fruits for the priests, widows, and orphans, but did not do so when he was in a period of mourning. That type of mourning of the spirit (depression) was not a blessed attitude with which to offer to the Lord his sacred portion. God truly means He loves a cheerful giver with healthy motivations behind the gift.

Aven brings the meaning of, "to pant (hence exert oneself in vain; to come to naught); strictly nothingness; trouble, vanity, wickedness, an idolatry. Further, if brings affliction, evil, false idols, iniquity, mischief, brings mourners and mourning. It is a negative sorrow that is unjust, unrighteous, vain, and becomes wicked". Again, God was very careful that His peoples' attitudes were right as they gave themselves to spiritual service.

From Job 3:8, mourning is translated in Hebrew as *livyathan,* or, "a wreathed animal, a serpent; the constellation of the dragon; a symbol of Babylonia; leviathan, deep mourning." Dragons are symbols for Satan and for Babylon, representing the world's system in opposition to God's kingdom throughout the ages.

Look how closely depression (Leviathan) is intertwined with these two sources. In practice, Leviathan may have had more than one head. Ask the Holy Spirit to reveal how many heads (strongmen) are on the Leviathan lead spirit tormenting the Seeker and then ask their names. Cut these exposed heads off by the Holy Spirit then cast out the beast and all his heads together.

When researching *livyathan,* I found the subsidiary word *lavah* having to do with "borrowing, to unite with; to borrow as a form of obligation or to lend. It means to abide with the borrower, to cleave and join oneself with a lender". This financial relationship creates an unholy soul-tie to human providers.

This may help explain how destructive and depressive situation that credit borrowing has created for many Christians who must find enough money to pay debts or provide food, proper shelter. It may be from wanting tempting luxury items with funds for the Lord take a subservient place. This is real bondage.

Let's look at Ezekiel 2:10 where depression is spoken of as *hegeh,* "a muttering, sighing, thought, sound of thunder; murmuring (in pleasure or anger), sore imaginations." This subtle form of depression attacks the soul in the intellect and emotions with consequences manifested outwardly.

As we go into the New Testament Greek, *Duo* enlarges our understanding to include, "to sink, go down, and be set", while *oduremos* brings out the aspect of "mourning, to lament, sorrow and torment".[4] Next we find *patho* and *enthos,*[5] "to grieve, mourn and sorrow; to experience a sensation or impression (usually painful); to feel, have passion, suffer, and be vexed".

Depression is a very serious emotional condition that defeating and seemingly hopeless circumstances instigate. It may be caused by a chemical imbalance or body system disturbance that can be treated medically. Seekers should be made aware of other causes to depression than spiritual in nature. We are not doctors or therapists! All causes must be explored. One serious error we have all seen is the overzealous prayer team that suggests the discontinuance of medication "since God has healed you". Don't do that.

On the spiritual side, we often witness an outside interference by Satan. But he cannot do so without the Christian's consent. It is allowed to station itself within by embracing an unbelief in God to move on your behalf in some trying situation that is "depressing".

Unfortunately, we can become our own worst enemies by using fleshly interior motives to bring it upon ourselves. That is the embracing aspect of depression. The good news is that by God's loving grace, we can also be rid of it in the name of Jesus Christ by resisting it through the renewing of our mind. It takes work.

Depression, outside of medical causes, is anger turned inward. It is an internal temper tantrum that is damaging to the whole person. Medical science has found specific chemical responses in the brains of depressed persons unlike chemicals of the non-depressed.

This leaves us with the question: is depression caused by brain-manufactured chemicals or are brain-manufactured chemicals caused by the negative human response to the upsetting or unpleasant occurrences in life? What responses do we make in our spirits that can produce physical change?

Depressive spirits are usually strongly linked with the lead demon (most powerful demon or head of the demon gang). For example, Hatred can be a strongman which gains entry through the act of child abuse bringing about unresolved guilt and finally, depression spirits with it.

When Depression itself is the strongman, it will make room for, say, a suicide spirit because these feed on each other. Families of demons link themselves together for reinforcement and mutual feeding.

Fighting against what God brings into your life out of fear or rebellion at a possible negative result, is a secondary type of depression. It comes from feeling inadequate for what one views as a hardship instead of bringing the positive faith-attitude of experiencing a wonderful (if not, difficult), opportunity to know God more fully.

We are told in James 1:2-4 to *"...consider it PURE JOY* (not pure depression!) *my brothers, whenever you face trials of many kinds, because you know that the testing of your faith develops perseverance. Perseverance* (sticking to something tough until you get through) *must finish its work so that you may be mature and complete, not lacking anything."*

Here we see that the heart-attitude is to be one of cheerful abandon when trials come, not to get down under the circumstances and grovel there. It is imperative that the spirit of depression not find a home in a Christian. It is possible to be delivered of spirits of depression or never to contract them when a constant guard is mounted against entry or re-entry.

The nature of this demon gains strength when the same rebellious, lack of faith reaction to circumstances becomes a behavior pattern. Then it is much more difficult to break. It is preferable, although sometimes most trying, to push beyond depression into maturity. These are the phases of every believer's spiritual growth.

I believe the Lord wants all His children to go into maturity and He will make a way for them to do that: again, TRUST HIM. When a great change for you comes along like divorce, death in the family, the loss of job or business, a new baby in the house, or anything potentially depressing, you can begin right there to praise God for another step to being conformed to the mind of Christ. The victory is in your attitude and the battle is fought in the spirit.

NOTE: Never give in to a spirit of fear or the hopeless spirit of depression. Praise Father and believe Him for His best for you. Stay in the word of God and close to loving, believing friends for prayer and other support through these challenging times. Verbally, out loud, refuse, reject, and fight off depression spirits!

Keep busy with living! Discipline yourself to do the little hateful jobs you've been putting off. You will find that working through difficult times with praise in your heart is an act of faith. Get in the Word of God. Life can only be lived from one moment to the next, not years in advance. Depression cannot occupy where faith resides—there is not enough room!

The Triple State of Depression

Before the state of depression, comes repression, a mental pressing down. Repression warfare seems to be the initial sneaky method demons use to introduce themselves to humans when, perhaps their last human host dies and they are wandering, looking for new real estate. For the born-again-in-spirit believer, it is the most dangerous outer area for expulsion.

More likely, the soul as the decision center, is the more common temptation opportunity for them. There is so much more working for them in the soul to attach to. Finally, we see them antagonize the body with fear reactions.

This demonic entry offensive is limited and can only happen by the sole consent of the human. Here are telltale symptoms of the repression tactic and why they happen, before it becomes full blown depression.

The Human Spirit

This is the part within us that communicates in the spiritual realms. It is the core that cries out to worship God when everything else is not enough to satisfy the God-longing each human is created with. The spirit is filled with the Holy Spirit at salvation to quench the worship function.

In the not-born-again state, demons communicate with humans (spirit-to-spirit) with counterfeit worship to Satan with the tools of pagan idols, occultic activity, unrighteous religious sects, and more. These false gods are shut off by God when Jesus Christ is acknowledged as Savior from the power of sin and lived out with Christ as their Lord.[6] Being saved displaces demonic access or residence.

In believers, prolonged repression ripens into depression as a result of willful sin choices apart from God. What new idol was allowed to compete with the Holy One? The consequences of sin (guilt, curse, disaster, vexation) brings on a mourning in the spirit[7] that is healthy when we permit it to lead to repentance and reconciliation with Christ's place as Lord. However, if repentance is not attained, a person will mourn to the point of groveling in the guilt, curse, disaster, and vexation until depression is brought on.

Depression allowed to come to full bloom may attract demonic suggestions toward destruction, to the final point of suicide. If acted on as truth, this demonic manipulation could result in body death. What a road downhill! Instead of taking that path, doesn't it make spiritual sense to humble one's self, ask God's forgiveness, turn from the alluring sin, and reject depression?

We learn from these experiences how to overcome depression for one of any of the attempted captures of the spirit. Next, command Depression to leave you, forgive yourself, and then purposefully forget it as God forgets it. It will take time to walk through that process but health is assured.

Realize that humans do fail some of the many challenges and tests of life because we are created to be ever learning and trusting Him instead of the dark side. This is helpful to women who chose abortion at one time and the men (or others) who paid for or encouraged abortion of their child. It is a constant decision to regain their ground.

God made provision for our lapses, both present and future, as learning snags or as victories. Otherwise, we would never need Christ Jesus except for a salvation ticket to glory which He is not. Heaven is just a default. No! Rather He is after relationship and His blood provided us with continual cleansing of future cycles of growth that build on what we have learned through mistakes, miscalculations, and the correct choices.[8]

Think of your childhood. How many times did you fall down trying to learn how to walk upright for the first time? Were these fatal mistakes to get depressed over or just a series of learning steps to get the victory over? The same method repeats in all new growth opportunities in living as a faulty human to begin with.

It does great harm in the spirit to be angry and rebellious until you are out of fellowship with The Guide, made sick, or perhaps causing your ministry to be laid on the neutral shelf of inactivity. Satan loves that sort of conquest where believers cannot be as powerfully directed for God as they are equipped to be.

Demons linger in such human confusion and not kept on the run.

The Human Soul

Let me pose a question that may clarify the necessity for division of spirit from soul in the Seeker. What is it about the expression of the soul that separates a person from walking in the Holy Spirit? Chiefly, there are these things:

Soul Dominance. It is in the soul area (affections, emotions, will, intellect) that sin is wrestled with and conquered or not. When a Believer realizes that he or she must take up the cross of Christ—denying the pleasure of the soul to have its own way—a clash comes between the human spirit and the Holy Spirit who requires the Cross life to the soul.[9] For instance, Christ says we are to leave our father and mother and follow Him.

A choice must be made to become a disciple. Is it the old way of family that leads me or it now Jesus Christ who leads me? It could be any number of decisions but this is when the soul puts up a mighty fight to keep to the family in this example. The sword of the Word comes through to divide this soul-position from the God-position. But it can only happen with the person's consent.

The beauty of this is in seeing the affections of the soul put under subjection to the Lordship of Christ: the lower life exchanged for the higher. Thus, the soul is dominated by the spirit which wishes to comply with the Holy Spirit. And with the soul in its proper order, God can move and bless so that he no longer loves his family with human, frail love, but has exchanged it for the love of God toward them.

Soul-denial. Matthew 16:24-26 reveals that, *"if any would come after me, let him deny himself...For whosoever would save his life (psuche-soul) shall lose it: and whosoever would lose his life (psuche-soul) shall find it."* Now, here is the soul-life summed up in the one word: *himself or herself.* It is the fleshly self-life that is contrary to not only God's will, but is against its own best interests. The sword of the Spirit must divide here putting the spirit in charge to obey the Holy Spirit and bring freedom by separation of old ways, old thinking, old acting.

Soul-Materialism. The soul-life clings to the innate possessions of earth. It loves material and physical things like property, motor vehicles, social media, fame, fashion, careers, businesses, furnishings—whatever you desire most. This is the part within us that relates to self-interests, the instinct natural to self-preservation, and the grasping of goods.

Immediately as Light is shared, the soul love of possessions is put to the sword. Lot's wife turned back to "things or people" she didn't want to leave. Choices are made daily between renouncing this soul-tie to possessions or giving them over to the Lord. The undue absorption of the children of God with this aspect of the soul that denies its spirit to obey the Holy Spirit by an over-occupation with the affairs of this world, needs the knife of the Spirit.

Soul-love. This area means eternal loss of reward because it proceeds from the first Adam.[10] This grasping to "me" is manifested through the personality of the soul not brought into submission to the Holy One. Is it a sin to keep it? you might wonder. Yes, when the Light of truth shines in and you see Truth. This is the place where the will of the believer must be set to be on God's side no matter what death occurs in its soul. The very will (choice maker) of the soul bows before its human spirit, abdicating the old Adam afresh so the new Adam might come forth.

Spirit Warriors: when you can minister deliverance to believers who have left God's will and ways, part of that will be this breaking of the soul-ties that frees the Holy Spirit access to move in the renewed spirit and heal. As you minister the grace of God in His name, maintain this centering in His only Son, Jesus Christ as True Lord and the only force able to dispel the darkness for the Seeker's long-term freedom.

The Human Body

The physical body is the "outer man" and was created to be a source of delight, utility, and practicality for the housing of our inner soul and spirit. It contains the senses of sight, smell, touch, taste, and hearing. It relates us to the physical world of wind, water, fire, vegetable, animal, and human life.

Its place is one of submission to the spirit. This physical area reveals the spiritual attack of depression by manifesting itself in the body. It may be seen as obesity, bulimia, addictive disorders, drug-related sicknesses, uncontrolled mourning, and hysterics.

It shows up as a lack of interest in life affecting work habits and disrupts marriages and relationships with Father. Depression can be induced and will be encouraged by the person who abuses the body through overwork, under-work and improper or multiple fad diets, lack of rest, severe confinement of space or lack of privacy, giving in to peer pressure that goes against better judgment, and the like. You know what you allow to depress you and so does the Seeker.

Medication will not stop this behavioral response to difficulties but serves to mask them, making one far too weak to fight and resist in the spirit. Consequently, yet another host of masking demons will be allowed in from relying on chemical and psychological means. It only serves to strengthen the depression cycle. The folly here is the refusal to rely on God in trial.

Take care.

Depression must be recognized first and disowned as rebellion, enchantment, idolatry, and unmasked as unbelief that you have the answer in Christ. Do not allow it to damage your physical body!

Why? Because, our inner being (spirit and soul) is supremely important to God, remember, physical disabilities and what humans call, body imperfections, are invisible to Him.[11] God cannot reject His own creation no matter how damaged from Adam's rejection and your common accidents from just living in a broken world. He desires to take each of us just as we are--basic material—for His new molding. Even extreme beauty or handsomeness as the world defines it, can disable many from seeking a closeness with God through fabricated pride.

Know yourself and assure the Seeker that she or he is physically acceptable! Thank Him for your body and praise Him that He has allowed you to live and serve Him in the most unique ways that that exact body has fitted you to accomplish.

This is self-respect.

This is God-respect.

[1] Mumford, Bob, Engaging the World: *The Eternal Value System* (2019), Plumb Line Vol. 41.1, page 22.

[2] Bob Mumford's Black Hole theory. www.LifeChangers.org.

[3] Deuteronomy 26:14

[4] Matthew 2:18

[5] James 4:9 and Revelation 18:8

[6] Matthew 11:27; John 8:42-47

[7] Ezekiel 7:14-27

[8] 2 Corinthians 10:17-18; 2 Corinthians 3:17-18

[9] Matthew 10:38

[10] John 12:25

[11] 1 Samuel 16:7

| 14 |

The Call of a Spirit Warrior

"...that our God would count you worthy of this calling,
and fulfill all the good pleasure of His goodness and
the work of faith with power that the name of
our Lord Jesus Christ may be glorified in you..."
2 Thessalonians 1:11-12

Qualifications for the Deliverance Chaplaincy

The ministry and calling of an intercessory prayer Spirit Warrior for deliverance is worthy. Yet it is no more or less special than other specific callings of God. It is a call to death in the servant so that a response to life can be found by those who are helped. Its weapons are glorious yet sharp, unwieldy, and hidden.

It is a ministry that is frequently misunderstood even while the cry goes up for renewal in these latter days against the onslaught of the enemy. It demands a person to be worthy of this call.

The Greek word used for 'worthy' as found in the following Bible verses is, AXIOS meaning, *"Deserving, comparable, appropriately: as becometh, after a godly sort, worthily; to desire, think good and count meet; to draw praise and due reward."* God places a high value on this calling and none dare enter it lightly from self-serving motives. The arena is just too dangerous for that.[1]

Not all believers are called to a full deliverance ministry although every believer is authorized to cast out evil spirits. We cannot know all the qualifications and graces God bestows and grows in his servants for this type of ministry. While an admittedly incomplete list is included here, the basic considerations from our experience are presented. In all cases, the prayer Spirit Warrior should be under the direct authority of a pastor or priest and in constant contact with him regarding what the Lord is doing and how He is leading.

Having a spiritual director will provide the balance needed in the ministry and prevent a great deal of wasted effort and treading on dangerous ground. Intercessory prayer for deliverance is not an independent, maverick ministry that is done over afternoon crumpets and tea. It is a serious calling with an anointing, carried out under the authority of the spiritual headship of Jesus Christ.

Spirit Warriors who are moving in the walk of faith with spiritual gifts manifested should fall into this list or be working on weak areas, knowing that no one has achieved maturity in Christ. This is a only guideline:

1. You have personally experienced salvation.
2. You have followed the Lord in water baptism.
3. You have received the Baptism of the Holy Spirit and are already functioning in your gifts of the Spirit.
4. You have established a relationship with God and hear His guidance, obey it, and are an example to others.
5. You are walking with the Lord in no known or unconfessed sin and open to the ministry of others regarding sin in your own life.
6. You have a submissive, servant spirit, and the anointing of God for this ministry.

7. You are in the Word and prayer in a disciplined way.

8. You are willing to submit yourself for deliverance before beginning this ministry and at any time necessary in order to remain a clean vessel.

9. You are recognized by your pastor/priest and your fellow-ship as a servant worthy of this calling.

10. You have come under training and are prepared for the ministry of deliverance.

Ministering Deliverance in Love

Ideally, this ministry comes out of a church body set up for deliverance that can process the requests as they arise. There is an orderly way of handling counseling opportunities so that prayer ministers are not rushed (usually by the Seeker) or too hasty to minister before all is in place. Be assured that nothing will happen to the Seeker while those in charge are finding the will of God for the appropriate Spirit Warrior team, the place to minister, or for any spiritual preparations needed before and during ministry.

Satan and the flesh compel and propel. The Holy Spirit in contrast is gentle and timely, never pushy. In helping to form teams, for the ministry there are some basic common-sense considerations. For instance, intercessory prayer counselors (like all Christians) are to avoid all appearances of evil. For this reason and for self-protection that Satan has no place to trip you, counselors should be paired in groups of two or at the most three.

As a rule of thumb, it is advisable to use any combination of males and females on a team of three. Two women as a unit or two men together on a dual team is fine. A husband-and-wife team can prove very strong in this ministry and is especially beneficial in post-deliverance counseling for families.

Usually, a special room is set aside at the church where deliverance can take place in a controlled area that can be spiritually sealed. These rooms can be equipped with proper chairs, privacy (no telephones or video cameras), a rest room facility, if possible, tissues for tears, etc.

It is a neutral room that may be scheduled for specific prayer use and will not contain familiar objects or distractions. Having it in the church brings the blessing of the pastor and congregation by making it a body ministry.

Or, deliverance may be accomplished in a home setting that can provide the same privacy I have assisted in room deliverance (about 20 people) where people came forward one by one to sit in a chair directly in front of the prayer Spirit Warrior for personal ministry. It is highly effective after intense teaching has taken place. This does not prove to be the best place for deep ministry and must be done in a trusting communal atmosphere.

Before beginning any session, it is good to explain that at times the prayer Spirit Warriors may sound angry, commanding, demanding or intense. Remember that the Seeker is a PERSON with feelings, needs, perceptions, a capacity for communication, and is quite vulnerable at this point of need. YOU are the one who is mature, has understanding, and is walking with the Lord in holiness. It is up to you to present the Lord Jesus Christ and not your own personality or personal traits during these sessions.

While it is true that prayer Spirit Warriors are directly communicating in the spiritual, the Seeker is listening to every word and should be cautioned that team members are not speaking with them but against the forces of darkness in them. Communicate this clearly so they understand that warfare is a personal attack against Satan and not against them. The Holy Spirit in you is fighting the demonic while they listen in.

Be cautioned not to be side tracked by the revelation of some sin by thinking or speaking out an immediate answer to solve the problem. This is not called for. Actual deliverance is not the place to reform or train Seekers with problems. Rather remain concentrated on the war against Satan on their behalf. It is like a competitive game of chess: you can play around on the board, or you can steadily move in to capture the king piece and win.

Intercessory prayer for deliverance is a totally confidential ministry. There is no need or scriptural basis for a Spirit Warrior to share anything with anyone of what was seen or heard during the time of ministry. If curious people ask for particulars, firmly admonish them not to ask.

A simple, "I'm sorry, but that's between them and the Lord" should do it. You value the Seeker and would not purposely handicap him or her in their efforts to leave the past behind them. Be very strict about this. Once deliverance is a part of the fellowship and you remain hidden in the ministry, these situations will not arise.

Spiritual warfare can be highly exhilarating at times as victory after victory is won. Spirit Warriors must be careful to realize that whatever great breakthroughs happen belong to the Seeker's testimony—not to yours. Personal testimony comes from wanting to share what God is doing with and in them.

They may choose to never share. Respect their privacy and realize that the prayer Spirit Warrior is but a hidden and confidence-keeping servant of God, His vessel that the water of the Word passes through on its way to healing. It is amazing to realize that you will not remember much of what happens anyway. Leave it to the Lord.

Experience and maturity in the use of this ministry will serve to precaution those called to never seek "demons under every bush". They are not there. God will give you ministry through your elders who are in an authoritarian position to see what the Lord is doing in the whole church, and in agreement with other team members.

But people who seek demonic encounters without being in order thus protected, will find themselves open to deception and ministering out of season. This type of self-serving behavior will only bring discouragement and take the power of God away. Rather, wait on the Lord to see what He wants. You will be used as He sees fit in the right place with the right timing. Become a humble and submissive servant, one sensitive to God's direction and plans.

Orderly Policies for Private Deliverance

As a rule of thumb, it is advisable to use any combination of males and females on a team of three or four. Two women as a unit or two men together on a dual team is fine. Husband-and-wife team members can prove very strong in this ministry and is especially beneficial in post-deliverance meetings with families.

Usually, a special room is set aside at the church where deliverance can take place in a controlled area that can be spiritually sealed. These rooms can be equipped with proper chairs, privacy (no telephone), a small rest room facility, if possible, tissues for tears, etc. It is a neutral room that may be scheduled for specific prayer use and will not contain familiar objects or distractions. Having it in the church brings the blessing of the pastor and congregation by making it a body ministry.

Or, deliverance sessions may be accomplished in a home setting that will provide the same privacy. I have assisted in group deliverance (about 20 or more) where people came forward one by one to sit in a chair directly in front of the lead Spirit Warrior for personal ministry.

This public method can be highly effective after intense teaching has taken place to a congregational setting. Caution is needed to be aware that this does not prove to be the best place for deep, personal ministry. If the situation is not a trusting communal atmosphere, do not attempt it.

Before beginning any session, it is good to explain that at times, Spirit Warriors may come across with an angry voice, be commanding, demanding, or directly intense. Remember that the Seeker is a person with feelings, needs, perceptions, the capacity for communication, and is quite vulnerable at their point of need. YOU are the one who is mature, has understanding, and is walking with the Lord in holiness. It is up to you to present the Lord Jesus Christ and not your own personality or personal traits during these appointments.

While it is true that Spirit Warriors are directly communicating in the spiritual realms, the Seeker is hearing every word and should be cautioned that team members are not speaking with them but against the forces of darkness in or around them. Communicate this clearly so they understand that warfare is a personal attack against Satan and not against them.

The Holy Spirit in you is fighting the demonic in them while they "listen in". Be careful not to be side tracked by the revelation of some sin by thinking or speaking out an immediate answer to solve the problem. This is not called for.

Actual deliverance is not the place to reform or train Seekers with complex problems. Remain concentrated on the war against Satan on their behalf. It is like a competitive game of a board game: you can play around on the board, or you can steadily move in to capture the last piece and win.

NOTE. Importantly, as Spirit Warriors, we recognize and must disclose that the team is not qualified as medical, mental health, psychological, or counseling experts. Make this disclaimer at the beginning of all sessions and explain it in writing, with signed acknowledgement of Seekers if needed. For those who have handout literature, write this in it clearly. The team is a Christian voluntary unit and not paid for ministering. Participation for exorcism is by voluntary consent of Seekers and ministers.

Orderly Policies for Public Deliverance

This section is a practical application for church services that give altar time ministry for Seekers (members and visitors) whom you may or may not know. Written from our personal experience as a husband-and-wife team (Kurt and Laurel Massey), please fit it to your own situation. Your team in an ekklesia fellowship may develop a policy manual to train new Spirit Warriors using the guidelines fitted to your group.

You will find, as with many altar encounters, the first approach is to establish the point of personal salvation (or not) in the Seeker. Are you born again? What do you mean by that? Please tell us your salvation experience. By establishing this first, Spirit Warriors may discern the level of approach. If the problem is very serious, determine whether a third team member is needed and a separate room. Here are a few basic principles we follow.

1. Thank them for coming to the altar and introduce yourselves by your first name only. Ask for their first name only and be warm, helpful, and welcoming.

2. One minister should take the lead by opening the session with a very short, three sentence prayer. Then, slowly go through the simple plan of salvation explaining clearly--even over protests that they are already a Christian—the steps of salvation. We don't know what they really mean by "being saved" that until it is pinned down. Quoting *Romans 10:9-10* is all that is needed. This is not a seminary session! That scripture can be printed on a small card kept at the altar and given to the Seeker to keep.

3. Dig a little deeper. Has their life changed since salvation? If they do not know, go back to the gospel to make sure they understand and have done this the biblical way. Note: Delivering an unsaved sinner will only bring on more trouble for them later. The greatest deliverance of all is being born-again.

4. Right up front, explain that a major reason why deliverance sometimes cannot be accomplished is because of a Seeker's position of unforgiveness. Ask if there is anyone who comes to their mind who has offended or trespassed against them needing forgiveness. Explain that forgiving people (and forgiving God for some) is a decision of their will. Ask them to repent for a hard heart and then confess that person out loud before continuing. This establishes their clear position before the Lord and notifies demons of that position.

5. At the church altar, my husband Kurt and I minister together. Otherwise in a more private setting, we like a team of three or four with intercessors close by. Generally, women should minster to women and men with men along with a third team person of the opposite gender. This is mainly practical in the case of a

female Seeker. The male should stay in the background unless he gets specific discernment to try the spirits.

6. A three-male team for a male Seeker is preferred. However, it might be needful for a female team to have a male as the third person, since demons can act out physically, slide on the floor, or become threatening and over powering. Women may need protection, even the Seeker herself and he can help here.

7. Husband-and-wife teams work well together. In our case, Laurel takes a back position to the Seeker (out of his sight) when ministering to males, leaving Kurt to face him. We reverse these positions when it is a female Seeker.

8. Ask what they are most struggling with. Why did you come to the altar? You will find that especially women will bring a list of concerns but don't you allow that. Listen patiently, ignore the list, and refocus him or her on the one thing they most want the Lord to do for them *right now*. We do not deal with prayer requests for their children, friends, spouse, world peace, or for others. Short altar ministry is for the one who comes forward.

9. Get specific. Deal with one area at a time beginning with the most pressing need by identifying and naming the spirit involved. If you have a target sheet that Seekers can access online or a paper handout, this is the time to review it with the Seeker and begin with the most troubling one.

10. In private sessions when appointments have been made and you must begin without a pre-filled in sheet, one team member records the names of the discerned spirits so none will escape exposure and expelling. Bring them up one at a time for discernment and exorcism.

11. Every so often, take time for short breaks (2 minutes or so) with the Seeker. When appropriate, the lead should be handed off to another team member. Those present but not directly involved, should be praying, and discerning what the Spirit is revealing, with one recording the demons who are revealed.

12. Team members talking together and interrupting are not helpful but brings confusion. Loud praying in tongues, shouting out names, and constant movement hinders and distracts. Allow the Seeker the floor to discuss their concerns and reactions.

13. When we minister together, my husband Kurt is especially good at calming people and focusing them on Jesus as Savior even when the room is blaring with music, people walking around, lining up for prayer. He takes the lead first on. His calling as an evangelist is especially valuable as part of the team. Because of his background, he relates well to those who have military and law enforcement backgrounds (males and females), so look for areas in team members with a commonality to the Seeker.

14. It is demeaning and unnecessary to allow a Seeker to grovel on the floor, bent over looking at the floor most of the time, or passively disengaged from their own deliverance by shutting their eyes. They need to be alert and know what is proceeding. Gently ask them to sit up, breathe, and become cognizant of what is going on inside of them, and respond when addressed to help in their own deliverance.

15. Ask them to focus their eyes on the lead minister who explains that he or she is not talking to them, but to the spirit(s) hindering them. If they get an idea or name coming into their mind, they must speak it out. For example, "Jack, I want you to look into my eyes as I begin engaging the demon. I am not talking to you, but to any spirit that is around you. You mentioned you have a problem with _____. So, let's start with that demon and see where it leads." Then, take a position in front of them, looking in their eyes, and address the demon to confirm its name and job assignment. [2]

16. Always ask them to verbally, out loud, reject the spirit (whichever one you are working on), and cast it away from themselves. They must withdraw their invitation that had been made by the sin choice that opened the way of harassment to begin with. For example, "Demon of envy, I command you to come out and leave

me by the Name and Blood of Jesus Christ." Step in and continue with this line until the team seems relief.

17. Require the gang of demons that are attached to each other to leave as a unit, Strongman demon first.

18. The gift of discernment from the Holy Spirit is critical since this is a work of His. He knows the person and what they need to be freed from. Walking in the authority of God is all important and should not be limited to one person as sole lead. It is a team effort for many reasons.

19. Team members do not have designation badges. With man's authority structures, titles such as pastor, prophet, intercessor, evangelist, bishop, and so on, are designated. But we have experienced it to be a big hindrance when someone less experienced assumes the lead because they have a title on a badge for some seemingly higher position than other team members. Spirit Warriors do not need, nor should expect recognition but work as an equally chosen unit.

20. In heavy deliverance sessions, there should be a continual questioning of the Seeker to gain permission to continue with deliverance. Some elderly people need a breath and less excitement! Especially when several people are shouting to them or giving orders to do this and that which we do not subscribe to at all. But, for safety, we cannot detain or refrain a person against his or her will, so to speak. Parent(s) should be present and consenting.

21. Every thirty minutes or so, the team stops to again ask the Seeker to relax, breathe deeply and ask them how they feel. Do they need a bathroom break? Water? Do they rather wish to continue this later or continue at all? Do they have questions? Always supply tissues and encouragement on these breaks. Walk away for a while.

22. We do not subscribe to holding trash receptacles close to the face or body and directing them to vomit, hiccup, cough, weep, or display emotional (soul) or physical responses. When they look like they are spontaneously going to do that, it is alright to give

them leave and reassurance that these reactions are normal with some people. If a person is gagging, keep the trash can be close by, then remove it.

23. We do not subscribe to continuously touching Seekers with hands or bibles, or anything else. The best approach is not to touch them at all. Sometimes I will lightly take a wrist two seconds to get their undivided attention and ask them to look back into my eyes, but we do not maintain bodily contact.

24. Do not rub a bible on a person's torso, especially children. Use the powerful name of Jesus Christ. This is especially pertinent for those who have been physically abused, are in homosexuality, prostitution, have experienced incest, or faced any of the wrongful touching sins. For one thing, it stimulates the demons to act out instead of getting out.

25. When a demon is expelled, trust God that it happened and do not revisit it moments later, bringing it up again and again. Someone on the team is not paying attention! Wait until the end of the session when you can re-try the spirits to determine if they departed when they don't respond to questioning.

26. Again, deal with one demon at a time by name and work on expelling that one before going on to another. Repeating what has already been cast out seems to be common when too many people are in the room are learning and just guessing and blurting out. This is where the scribe comes in who records each demon name and checks them off.

27. There is no spirit to cast out when the Holy Spirit does not give you discernment, so guessing and yelling into the air is counterproductive. This shows a lack of team leadership. A team member can quietly speak into the ear of the lead if they feel they have new discernment.

28. Do not give out personal cell phone numbers. Provide the number of the church office or email address that can be forwarded to the team leader.

29. In special circumstances like a joint-church revival or conference, several ministry teams from different ekklesias have not received the same training sessions or reviewed policies. Prior information sent to the fellow churches will help to eliminate the wrong styles and methods. There is a vast difference between educating on demonology and hands-on training. Some may not even know how to listen to the Holy Spirit and follow with discernment.

30. New people who are learning must be observant in a team for a few months and closely supervised. Husband-wife teams are usually strong and will know how to move in unison. Teams that stay together will grow in unity.

31. Deliverance is messy, but easily contained. Right now, we see all levels of skill, some wrong teaching, a little of this and a lot of that, but all of it is going in the right direction since hearts are sincere and training sessions are held. It is amazing anyone wants to do this at all!

Post Deliverance

What do we do when the deliverance sessions are finished? Seekers still may need nurturing—real shepherding--including advising the Seeker of what is likely to happen when the demons were expelled. For instance, many sin habits will demand dedicated vigilance and resistance in order to master. When the spirits are dislodged; e.g., nicotine or addiction, there is a temptation to return with the sin to allow it back in. This is given to the Seeker.

You might feel comfortable in preparing a work sheet to address this common issue with scriptures to resist, and to encourage faithful freedom. You might want to include a telephone number for texting or email to obtain help. This can be handled by a dedicated team of intercessors or Spirit Warriors either those from the team or by other church ministry team members.

Historically, it was reported that some recent revivals shut down. People stopped attending. Upon reflection of "what happened," the assessment was made that when the pastoral leadership grew exhausted or prideful, hired bodyguards, left meetings early to avoid contact with members, took communion privately by excluding others, or generally kept themselves elevated in importance from church members they were called to serve, the Spirit was grieved. After all, it is always His revival.

Often, other factors were traced back to when the intercessor team was rebuffed. Perhaps they had a written word for leadership that would not even be accepted for evaluation but summarily ignored or dismissed.

Finally, in one case, church leadership disbanded the deliverance ministry because "it was messy and disruptive". Obviously, there cannot be a fiery message of the Lord from the platform and at the same time, a quenching of the Holy Spirit at the altar. He is everywhere in His Body working what He wants, how He wants, and with whom He wants. Give God room.

The book, *"Prayers That Rout Demons~ Prayers for Defeating Demons and Overthrowing the Power of Darkness,"* by John Eckhardt may be ordered as a great biblical reference tool to use during deliverance sessions. Another great resource is to research other deliverance warriors such as Greg Locke, Isaiah Saldivar, Vlad Savchuk, Bishop Alan Didio, Troy Brewer, Rick Renner, Jimmy Evans, and many others. They are trained or have trained others who become very experienced in deliverance. Look up their websites, podcasts, YouTube videos, and Internet connections to learn more.[3]

John Bevere has been a pivotal teacher in my walk from his early days in Orlando, Florida. He is the author of *"The Bait of Satan"* and many other books that reflect his uncompromising character and teaching.[4] We also recommend the newer works by Rabbi Jonathan Cahn on *The Return of the Gods* that are devastating the culture of Christian nations.

[1] Ephesians 4:17; Colossians 1:10-14; 1 Thessalonians 2:10-12

[2] Jesus spoke to the demon but He did not hold a conversation with them. Command their names and expel them by name.

[3] https://PastorVlad.org.

[4] Messenger International Ministries, John and Lisa Bevere.

| 15 |

Entering the Real Battlefield

*"If you know the enemy and you know yourself, you need
not fear the result of a hundred battles. If you know
yourself but not the enemy, for every victory gained,
you will also suffer a defeat.
If you know neither the enemy nor yourself,
you will succumb in every battle."*
~ Ancient Chinese Warrior Sun Tzu

The Discerning of Spirits

The gift of discernment of spirits[1] speaks on three levels when
it is in operation because some demons enjoy manifesting themselves
and will especially do so, when they are stirred up and addressed. The
Name of Jesus Christ is a powerful stir-up tool so, prepare yourself.

When we are invited on a spiritual adventure and accept, a road-
map to only that place will be given to us. As we look the map over, we
can see very clear markers to watch for and check off as passage points.
This trip of obedience can only be taken in the proper vehicle with
room for that one called.

There is no steering wheel or we would take over and get lost at any flashing, attractive highway detour. As we follow the map and get into narrower, off the highway paths covered in dusty gravel then thin grass, we will need the markers more than ever. But following on, we are most likely to arrive at the exact destination than somewhere ineffective.

When piercing the spiritual dimension by the Holy Spirit's gift of spiritual discernment, we are loaned the map to that destination in the unique dark kingdom to see within the Seeker. The roadmaps change as the journeys change and His gift of discernment is the flashlight to see what is hidden that no one can know. We must hold the flashlight in our spirits to hear what He is saying.

As one example of many, a young woman came for help. It was the first time I met her and one-on-one, we had a cup of hot chocolate and exchanged pleasantries. First, as she recounted her salvation experience, we settled into a trusting conversation in the living room. Let's call her Chrystal.

Soon she began pouring out her heart and with one ear I listened to some minor problems as I sought the Holy Spirit for discernment into the real core. After a few moments of conferring with the Holy Spirit, I interrupted her wandering tale, and began speaking to her about the flash of a vision the Holy One had just given. It was only a few seconds at most.

Looking into her sad eyes, I gently asked her this question, "Chrystal, what the Lord is showing me is an uncomfortable situation with a man holding a squirming child who is crying. Does this mean anything to you?"

Chrystal's brown eyes regarded me in wonder, tears welling up, and asked, "What did he look like?"

"I saw an older man with greying hair and full beard in a blue and red plaid shirt, smiling and coaxing her. That's all I saw in the spirit...but the little girl was anxious and helpless, trying to pull away from him."

"That's amazing." She began. "That was my grandfather who had sexually molested me regularly. It began when I was six years old and I've never been able to get over the betrayal and how unsafe I still feel around men. How did you possibly know that? I haven't told anyone, not even my parents."

"Well, I didn't know it but the Holy Spirit knows it and He wants you to be healed of that today. Are you ready to get rid of that shadow?" I waited for her to respond and she shook her head affirmatively, wiping her eyes.

"It means you must sincerely forgive him all his trespasses against you. And then you will have to trust your heavenly Father to He take those painful memory's away and replace them with what He has in mind for you, for your future."

Chrystal agreed to forgive her grandfather out loud who was long dead. Being deceased did not matter since this matter of dropping the grip on her mind was being commanded to the spirits of depression, secrecy, hurt, and shame. All the related tormenting demons were soon uncovered by the gift of discernment. The Holy Spirit extended deliverance to Chrystal and calm, peaceful healing in her soul.

You will find as you and your team wait on the Lord for Him to speak into the unique situations of each Seeker, that this is simply the way that especially secret demons can be exposed by the finger of God.

Jesus lived by communicating with the Father and receiving various powerful gifts specifically needed in each situation, whether for healing of physical ailments, redemption (for rich Nicodemus or a dying thief); full freedom, or feeding thousands, or rebuking the faithless. You, too, can walk in the Spirit by opening your spirit and believing His words to you.

There are other ways of discerning evil spirits that seem to be right out in front of your face and daring a confrontation. Tune in to the Lord and be alert to these possible expressions that show up in the soul and in the body. Next, we will address the body's signs first and then the soul's signs in a brief listing.

Manifesting in the Body

Sight. In the natural physical world, we can see, hear, smell, sense, and touch (skin sensation) the effects of the operations of spirits, both good spirits of others and evil spirits of others.[2] Testing evil spirits (by calling them to reveal themselves) shows their presence by their effect on a person. It can be by coughing, spitting, choking, writhing, blinking, yawning, crying, and the like.

They can take other forms which may be visible.[3] Evil spirits can indwell inanimate "familiar" objects decorated with welcoming zodiacal symbols, voodoo masks, Gautama Buddhas, and physical religious or secular idols.

Hearing. It is possible to hear the spirits using the vocal cords of Seekers when they cause them to cry, shout, shriek, laugh, mock, speak, groan, mutter, growl, whisper or blaspheme.[4] We have heard them sing vulgar show tunes with striptease music, and project a masculine voice from a woman's vocal cords. A frightened demon like self-pity, trembling fear, or even shyness may whimper, cloud up the Seeker's eyes with tears and pitifully beg to be left alone to stay behind. Do not pity them for one moment but expel them.

Touch. There are more instances of God's Spirit touching humans than evil spirits touching humans; however, it is possible to touch a person's skin and find it cold and clammy, especially the extremities where evil spirits linger. Seekers may complain of feeling 'spooky or weird,' their skin crawling, or hair standing on end. They will be cold and not hot, or feel air blown.[5]

Some Seekers have testimonies of having been beaten, sexually raped, pushed, or spat upon but these demonic antics are never tolerated during sessions because they don't get that far. Praise God, the Name of Jesus stops physical abuse or tearing by spirits during deliverance should it occur at all. Sometimes it can get away from you when they are thrown on the floor, so the team calmly picks them up and continues.

This is common in the spirit dimension. The bible records that the aroma of Christ as a sweet-smelling fragrance.[6] The very opposite comes from evil with the odor of death which is putrid, fetid, rancid, vile, and raises a stench in the room. Certain demons, and drugs and smoking are two, emit a terrible smell with bad breath, in vomiting, or through the skin. I have seen pale grey smoke come out of a Seeker's nose when the spirit of tobacco was identified. This is a common occurrence in deliverance and when confronting any of these manifestations command that spirit(s) to go m Jesus' Name without bodily attack or delay.

Taste. Seekers will sometimes have this sense especially with addictive substance spirits. Some go out by vomited or present weird tastes to the Seeker that need to be identified to be expelled. They are showing their presence.

Whole-body sensations feels the presence. Job experienced this under satanic attack (Job 4:5), when *"A spirit glided past me and the hair on my body stood on end."* Seekers may feel spirits leave suddenly by their hands and finger tips like arthritic or cancerous pain, or through their feet and toes from demons identified as dirty dancing, mischief, and ground demons.

Others cross over their lips in burps or skim across body skin. Some go through the loud passing of gas in a which as they exit. Please assure the Seeker that these are not embarrassing to the team and we are thankful to let them go in whatever manner possible.

Manifesting in the Soul

Spirits may manifest themselves in dreams or visions, nightmares, and trances. Familiar (family) spirits will sometimes make themselves known at seances.[7] This is often where Seekers began to open themselves to illicit supernatural revelations generated by the spirit world. Hearing the whisper or sometimes a shout of Satan or his demons is common because he loves to tell lies into people's minds. Some people will see them and report on what they are saying during deliverance.

When you have heard a murderer say he or she, "heard voices telling them to kill", believe it.

Primarily, all manner of Satan-implanted temptation comes to the mind first. It may or may not move into the natural senses as it is either given into or resisted. For instance, the seed of all sin begins by thinking on the temptation.

This stage may take years or just moments when the contemplation to sin goes into blossom by acting on the suggestion. temptation becomes sin acting on it. Nevertheless, the devil does not make a person sin. It is already natural for a sinner to sin: it is his nature and that will not change until he or she is born-again when sin becomes a choice, no longer a native instinct. He cleverly uses his wiles or clever methods to weaken and expose people to act antagonistic to God's will [8]whereby a choice to sin is then set up.

Surprisingly, it is not always the wicked devils who try to first gain entrance to the errant Christian or the worldly-wise. They can be bidden to reside when one opens himself or herself up to their spheres of work. Curious mind-sets (review Chapter 6), beg evil spirits to contact with them while seeking 'spiritual enlightenment' and is especially true of following high occultic experiences and vain philosophies.

Deceiving spirits appeal to the mind and often put in their appearance in humanistic, pseudo-medical, or psychological self-help books or teachings led by spiritualists in which clients are encouraged (and sometimes taught how) to contact their revealed spirit guide to hear directive voices, or get visions.

Recently at one of the annual international witches' conferences, seminars were held for them on *Learning Angelic Languages*. This is a counterfeit of God's gift of speaking in heavenly tongues[9] and entraps witches (who desperately need Christ) still deeper into Satanic mire when they perceive that they indeed have contacted something.

When Seekers tell the team what the demon is saying or will speak out its words in the deliverance session, prayer Spirit Warriors should deal with these evil forces harshly and tell them to be silent. It is suggested that you ask the Holy Spirit to reveal and expose them like this: "Holy Spirit in Juan, who is this demon speaking now?" Or, "Who is Juan seeing/hearing/feeling now?"

The Seeker will answer back from his or her spirit. Then confront it with: "Foul spirit of (whatever was named), I command you by the authority and Name of Jesus Christ to depart now. Come out of Juan!"

Then address the Seeker for confirmation of anything he or she experienced. "Juan, has the demon left you?" How do you feel? Juan will answer from his human spirit what he feels or experiences. Try the spirit again and confront it until it leaves.

When there is a blockage at this point, ask the Seeker to verbally reject and cast out of himself the spirit by name, in the Name of Jesus Christ. They must be very forceful at this point because the Seeker's declaration breaks the legal rights of the demonic to continue in him. Figuratively, the demon is forcefully evicted out of its "home" that is no longer available to it.

A prayer can be addressed to the Holy Spirit for His confirmation or for more discernment. "Holy Spirit, please tell Juan what the legal right is that has allowed Satan to remain so he can be healed." Or, "Holy Spirit, please tell us if there are any other open doors that remain in Juan. What are they?" A request for confirmation from the Holy Spirit might be, "Holy Spirit, is Juan free of all demonic influences in his body and soul?" Listen for the answer. Wait for the answer. Then finish with the session or pursue the enemy further with Juan's permission to continue.

It is biblical to understand that a demon who has cursed a person can have that same curse brought down on it. "You foul demon who caused the curse of witchcraft in this family, may it be returned to you now in the Name of Jesus Christ. The curse of God comes against you now. You go out of Juan now, and go to your punishment. You go. Go tell your master how you failed him."

Your **Weapons Permit** is valid nationally, internationally, and in the heavenlies! Study out Psalm 149:5-9, Psalm 91, 2 Corinthians 10:6, and Matthew 12:29. The Psalms are liberally sprinkled with warfare passages(psalms 91) and the classic list is in Ephesians 6:13-18.

Finally, be sure that Satan's method is to kill all the children of promise as soon in their lives as possible. His purpose is not to only maim, deceive into sin, but TO KILL and deliver us surely by the path to Destruction where Apollyon-Abaddon is in power. They don't get out of that pit. The righteous pious Christian must never give up on life because of so-called incurable illnesses (a physician's opinion), or at the onset of old age, or because of persecution and intolerable living conditions.

Battalions of Spirit Powers

You might ask, "What are some common demon groupies?" Which ones stick together? Demons are as powerful in acting within a person as they are believed to be powerful. What we mean by that is that demons are quite weak and helpless when confronted by the authority of the Word of God, with the worship of God, and with the power of the Name and Blood of Jesus. These wicked little guys will turn tail and run when exposed and expelled. Deliverance is nothing like what the sensational and worldly-popular movies image. Why? because God's children are protected by His blood and we possess greater power.

Satan is not God: he is not omnipresent, omniscient, nor munificent (generous). When left to develop on their own to facilitate rebellion, demons seem to find united strength in clutches of groups. Many come into the person together and need to go out together. There is often a strongman or leader demon who holds the groups together and will sacrifice the weaker demons (when confronted to vacate) in order to maintain their own territory, position, and power.

Evil spirits have differing levels of status within their group. They have different levels of strength to act out because they have either been allowed partial or full rein in a human, have been co-dependents or worshipped as indispensable (i.e., self-pity, addiction, I am in charge), or their presence is sourced by the host for personal notoriety and shared supernatural power.

A demon's status (how many levels is it below the Strongman?) consists of the value it is to the Strongman. Demons are used and abused. It might have the sheer opinion that to remain with the group is safe and becomes more comfortable as the human host continues in his or her besetting sins and willful habits. I have heard a weaker demon whimper and bed when it is given up (to be expelled) in order to hide behind stronger ones who wanted to stay.

Correspondingly, the opposite can be true. Spirits can be expelled quite easily in the atmosphere of worship when the human host gives praises to God surrounded by worshiping, overcoming Christians in agreement. The moving of the gifts of the Holy Spirit can become quite uncomfortable for any number of reasons, but it is exhilarating to those who are free to worship and love.

Sin must never be given permission to dig itself into the areas of spirit, soul, or body by any of us. Some deliverance manifestations can be as mild as a yawn in one believer—even when she or he is praying deliverance for another—or as violent as uncontrollable shaking and screaming. The apostle John instructs all believers to run a test on themselves and on other spirits in this passage:[10]

"Dear friends, do not believe every spirit, but TEST THE SPIRITS to see whether they are from God, because many false prophets have gone out into the world. This is how you can recognize the Spirit of God: Every spirit that acknowledges that Jesus Christ has come in the flesh is from God, but every spirit that does not acknowledge Jesus, is not from God. This is the spirit of the antichrist, which you have heard is coming and even now is already in the world. You, dear children, are from God and have overcome them, because the one who is in you (Jesus Christ) is greater than the one (devil, other humans) who is in the world."

For the following groupings, I have pointed out some of chief strongmen by naming their clans. From experience, demon families tend to change around and abide with those whom they are most comfortable and least likely to be discovered with. They are in terror themselves to be wandering alone again when an unsaved host dies, or when the Spirit of Jesus wins.

As you read the lists and those of you with experience will, no doubt, come across different groupings with different strongmen in charge. This listing is only given for informational purposes and is strictly subject to the Holy Spirit in you! Try the spirits.

Demons have different names in other cultures and I have found from sessions in South America, that even without knowing the local language of Spanish, spirits can be expelled in your own language. This will be apart from the understanding of the Seeker having a different language than the Spirit Warrior, because angel spirits (good and bad) know all languages—their own heavenly one, and our human ones.

In this situation, the gift of Diversities of Tongues is often very helpful, causing great consternation in the demonic realms when they hear prayers go up in the Name and Blood of Jesus Christ. This is especially very powerful in all languages—praises to our God, not to theirs! Yes, we intend to upset them.

As prayer Spirit Warriors, please search' the cleanliness of your own spirit to be sure that within, the Lord is the center of the intentions of your heart in this ministry. Pray about looking for opportunities for ministry to stand in the gap and help to set up a team in your fellowship. Success will be what God determines and you may be called to be a part of that success.

Studying the Appendices at the end of the book will give richer and deeper understanding of just what the Spirit of God in you is fighting against to free His children through you.

Consider providing, if possible and with the permission of your spiritual elders, a copy of this exorcism manual to be read by all Seekers before your team attempts ministry. I believe it will save much teaching time for you and ready them to receive from the Lord in the specific areas needing that divine touch of the Master.

As your sister in Christ, I would personally appreciate you writing to us with your experiences, reactions, and victories at the email address: SpiritWarriors@windstream.net. May our Father God love, guide, and keep you strong as you work and serve in His kingdom.

No matter how much we learn or experience, we will come to a place where there seems to be no answers. Come of the disciples returned to Jesus saying they could not deliver certain ones. He answered them[11] one time with, *"This kind does not go out except by prayer and fasting."* There are several questions that may be asked regarding Jesus' answer.

What kind (name) of demon?

Who does the prayer and fasting?

What hindered expelling this demon that blocked the exorcists?

The next chapter attempts to answer some of the more common reasons why certain Seekers do not get relief from their demonic entanglements. Read on.

[1] 1 Corinthians 12:10.

[2] 1 John 4:1; 1 Thessalonians 5:21; 2 Corinthians 13:5. We are never to test the Spirit of the Lord, Acts 5:9; 15:10.

[3] Revelation 16:13; Genesis 18:1-2; Luke 24:36-37.

[4] Luke 8:28-30; Mark 1:23-24; Acts 19:15; and 2 Kings 7:6.

[5] Judges 6:21; 1 Kings 19:5-7.

[6] 2 Corinthians 2:14-16.

[7] Matthew 1:20; 2:12-19; Genesis 31:11.

[8] Romans 1:20-32.

[9] Acts 2:4; 10:44-48; 19:1-7; 1 Corinthians 12:10, 28-31; 13:1-3, 14:2-22, 26-32 all describe the supernatural utterance in languages not known to the speaker.

[10] 1 John 4:1-3.

[11] Matthew 17:14-21.

| 16 |

Trouble Shooting

"...Jesus Himself fasted, He was not fasting
to repent or bring His desires under control; of course,
but to demonstrate His absolute dependence
upon His Father." Peter C. Moore, Trinity Seminary

Dealing with Roadblocks in Deliverance

A word must be said regarding the occasional occurrence of a Seeker who refuses to give up, renounce, or repent of some sin. What does the Spirit Warrior do in this case? First, you must be sure you are speaking to the Seeker and not to any demon.

When you address the Seeker by his or her name you will get an answer from them. If you are unsure, it is indeed him, demand in the Name of Jesus that he looks into your eyes and answer you until you are sure you are speaking with him. Then ask him to cooperate by repenting and renouncing that distinct spirit who refuses to go.

Normally the Seeker desires to be rid of all evil entities. They were the ones who initiated action from the church or Spirit Warrior by requesting help. Pre-session questioning should have revealed what they perceived as basic difficulties. However, if during deliverance there is a refusal to repent or renounce sin in one specific area (e.g., homosexuality) the deliverance session must stop. Do not work further in that or any area. Withholding forgiveness is another stopper. Gently terminate that willingness to rebellion and unbelief that holds back their own healing.

Spirit Warriors may create stop-stills. Be on guard that deliverance is not rushed into without observing the preliminary steps outlined. Those who are disobedient to God's voice when a word of knowledge is given, or who do not bind the spirits in the person or fail to spiritually seal the room (against other demons coming to their comrades' rescue), leaves outside doors open to continue the session beyond necessity.

Another way to encounter a solid wall is when Spirit Warriors themselves are not clean vessels thereby lending support and reinforcement to unclean spirits in the Seeker. Preparatory intercession for the Seeker must be given and the prayer team must work in unity. Jesus Himself stated that a period of prayer and fasting is sometimes needed to cast them out.

When there is an obvious stop-still, relate this to the one you are praying for and be sensitive in closing the session. Bind all spirits' activity from harming him or her. Make future arrangements to continue. Fasting and prayer are in order. Deeper teaching and counseling are needed until they can be rescheduled from those so gifted.

One singular incident that stopped us came while we were praying with a woman who went through the whole deliverance process until we came to the spirit of suicide. Right then, she stated that she had nothing to live for and adamantly expressed her plans to take pills and starve herself to death to "teach her ex-husband a lesson". When coached, she refused to repent of these death wishes and forgive him!

It was obvious she needed intensive counseling and teaching given by a spiritual director before we could step in. Since deliverance could not proceed, we immediately closed the session over her loud, argumentative protests. Later, she made a renewed commitment to Christ beginning with repentance and forgiving the ex-husband and lovingly helped through some rough spots by the body of Christ over a period of weeks before deliverance was again *requested by her* and given with success.

You may encounter the death spirit. In people with this, there is a deep, internal conviction—especially in death and life choices—that is made to either embrace life or embrace death. Those who want life show it by taking care of their bodies, putting on seat belts, watching their weight and what they ingest, and by immersing themselves in positive, healthy activities and friendships.

People who choose life, choose to fight inertia, resist early death and all manner of illnesses from the common cold to raging cancers will seek God's help and deliverance, when they sense spiritual danger or overwhelming conditions.

People who embrace death will resign themselves when confronted with a deadly cancer diagnosis. They view it as a "noble way to go" or a good reason to just give up on living. Often, they fulfill their physician's time frame by dying right on schedule ("You've got six months to live" they declare over you).

Other internal choices for death over life are seen in continuing a stress filled lifestyle, seeking "death-defying" adventures, adopting and continuing addictive and negative habits, or passively giving in to depression or the deliberate prolonging of illness.

Be aware that Satan's method is to kill all the children of promise. His task is not to maim *but to kill* and deliver us surely into his pits. The righteous pious Christian must never give up life because of "incurable illnesses," the onset of old age, or intolerable living conditions.

We must be absolutely convinced our lifework is completed and God is calling us home. Our prime example is Jesus Christ. Did Calvary's cross kill Jesus? Not in at all! He gave His spirit back to God when He said "Into Your hands I commend my spirit" Why? because He knew His human lifework had been completed.[1]

Yes, His whole purpose in coming to earth was to die for humankind's sin: but not until He determined by the counsel of His Father the exact second. And He did not hand His spirit to Satan, He gently handed it to His Father.

Take a breath. It is probable during very heavy deliverance to get only so far when the Seeker will need to rest and take time to digest what has happened to him or her. Time to walk out the deliverance already received strengthens new insights received during the session. Resting between times should include Bible study.

Deliverance is a ministry that prayer Spirit Warriors do not "do" to someone, but with them because Seekers must be 100% involved and committed to ridding themselves of demonic spirits. Without a doubt, God will give Spirit Warriors a word of wisdom during a session (ask Him) as to why it may be time to stop or perhaps why a particular demon won't come out right then. It is up to the Spirit Warrior to be sensitive to what the Lord is doing and humbly obey. This is love. And love does not rush God's process.

Relief Heals Rejected Seekers

It might help to first look at all the following verses God gave for you and them, to understand how unique each of us are. You are special![2] And if everybody DID walk away, we would be in the majority standing with our Lord alone. He understands.[3]

Because our inner being is supremely important to God, all physical disabilities we may have, are invisible to Him. God cannot reject His own creation but loves to take each of us just as we are. Even the self-pride of extreme beauty or handsomeness as the world defines it, will disable many from seeking a closeness with God. Believe God that you are physically acceptable. Thank Him for your body and praise Him that He has allowed you to live and serve Him in extremely unique ways!

Rejection is a two-edged sword because the one suffering from being rejected often turns back and rejects others from a self-defense posture. Both the reaction of being rejected and the action of rejecting others, must be confessed, and repented of. This is the time to get free by confessing out loud your forgiveness even if some of those who have rejected you or whom you have rejected, are deceased like parents, an old employer or teacher, ex-spouse(s), or children.

Their names will come to mind so go ahead and forgive them from your heart as a decision of your will. You will find this to be very cleansing to the soul that will lose all those tight bands that have held you back from experiencing life with joy. This takes work on your Seeker's part so be patient and wait until the names come to them. Remember, this is their basis of deliverance by determining to be free today.

Spirit Warriors: please take time and care with this area of having the Seeker forgive everyone by name (first name only is sufficient) because it is integral to completing the basics toward full liberation. In one person we worked with, it took the better part of three hours to get through forgiveness alone because the hurts were so deep. But how quickly the time went in actual deliverance after these roots were gently dug up by the hand of the Seeker that was guided by the Holy Spirit!

Be encouraged to ask the Lord to open your eyes and ears by becoming aware—instantly—to any depressive spirit that wishes to gain entrance. When you hear or detect your spirit begin to sag, fight it right where it raises its head. Have the Seeker read this and forcefully instruct it with conviction as a commander:

NO! You foul demon of _____:
You cannot find a home in me!
God is my strength and shield against you,
My present help in this time of trouble.
I choose joy, not Death.
Right now, by the name of Jesus Christ,
I renounce you, and I declare
That I am not your home! BE GONE.

Be vigilant.
Be persistent.
You have *already* overcome.

"Except by Prayer and Fasting"

During Christ's ministry years, the disciples became experienced in deliverance. Seventy were sent out before Calvary and Christ's sacrifice. Even so, He did give His authority to them to cast out demons in His name and His close disciples and for the most part, found out it worked. Nonetheless, they came to a dead end with one little boy who was diagnosed as an epileptic who suffered severely. In fact, he often fell into the fire his mother cooked on and fell into water sources to drown.

The devil was very much after killing this child. His dad brought him to Jesus for healing and that was what his faith was expecting. Here is the narrative from Mark 9:29 and Matthew 17:14-21:

> "So, I brought him to Your disciples, but they could not cure him. Then Jesus answered and said, 'O faithless and perverse generation, how long shall I be with you? How long shall I bear with you? Bring him here to Me." And Jesus rebuked the demon, and it came out of him; and the child was cured from that very hour. Then the disciples came to Jesus privately and said, "Why could we not cast it out?"
>
> So, Jesus said to them, 'Because of your unbelief; for assuredly, I saw to you, if you have faith as a mustard seed, you will say to this mountain, 'Move from here to there," and it will move; and nothing will be impossible for you. However, this kind does not go out except by prayer and fasting."

There are several clues to the answer of their question. First, Jesus rebuked[4] the disciples pointing out their faithlessness and perverseness. This was embarrassing to Jesus.

Second, He rebuked the demon and it left immediately. It knew its master. This cured the child of the epilepsy (a central nervous system neurological disorder that occurs when the normal electrical impulses are disrupted in the brain); the disease causes repeated seizures or unusual sensations and behaviors.

There is a definite linkage between disease and demon possession. This is good to know. The power of deliverance, healing, and salvation are the same (*sozo*). Expect this dynamic to be activated when you pray in any of those areas. So, the third thing Jesus taught gave the key to why they could not heal or deliver the boy: *"Because of your unbelief."*

Even a tiny measure of faith in God's ability to cure, deliver, and save would have been sufficient to move a gigantic mountain of problems. The healing should have been easy. Certainly not impossible. These men had experience that the name of Jesus worked. What happened here?

Third, even a mustard seed size of faith in God would not have moved this demon out for he was well entrenched in the intimacy of the deep brain physiology. Jesus gave the key: *"However, this kind does not go out except by prayer and fasting."*

Whose prayer and fasting were required? The young patient himself was wounded and sick. Perhaps the parents needed to extend themselves further than bringing the boy to Jesus although this was an act of faith.

Or, is it more likely by recalling Jesus' rebuke of their faithlessness, that disciples as Spirit Warriors, should be fasting beforehand and praying during the session for direct guidance from the Holy Spirit to see how to proceed during every deliverance encounter? Is salvation needed? Healing? Freedom of spirit? A strong lesson from the Master we can heed and learn from.

Unforgiveness Stops Deliverance

Here we understand that the Seeker can stop their own deliverance although they seem to express their need for a release from the torment, the sleepless nights, the aches and pains of early aging, and sincerity to see the Holy Spirit work. But He will not proceed further than saving their soul where we begin every session. This by itself is a miracle.

But, proceeding further to discover the core of their real problem and receive the Lord's deliverance will be stopped if the Seeker has any unforgiveness for another person(s). Sometimes they will be angry at God Himself "for letting it happen", whatever the sin against them is.

This topic is reiterated because it doesn't matter how much the Spirit Warriors, intercessors, Seekers, and others have prayed and fasted for victory. Unforgiveness cannot be overcome only by confession of the harbored sin (bitterness) against the Lord. Repentance must be petitioned.

We found that the sin against them must be recognized as hindering them. The person(s) may be long dead, out of their lives, or even forgotten by name. Ask if they are willing to forgive anyway. Encourage the Seeker in gaining a big victory right here.

The Spirit who needs their forgiveness and write the names down as they are revealed. The Seeker needs to pray aloud, calling all the names and expressing forgiveness. This does not mean they must contact them in any way, but it moves the deliverance session along to digging out the root problems.

[1] Luke 23:46; John 19:29-30; Matthew 27:50

[2] Psalm 100:3; 139:13-14 and 27:10. Genesis 1:31; Isaiah 44:24; 43:7; Isaiah 49:1, 5; Jeremiah 1:5; Exodus 4:11

[3] Ephesians 1:6; Is 53:3; Luke 4:18; Isaiah 61:1; Jeremiah 30:17

[4] Merriam-Webster.com. To rebuke someone is to express sharp disapproval, correction, or criticism because of their behavior; a sharp reprimand. 1 Corinthians 4:21.

READING 1 - WE ARE SPIRIT WARRIORS

"I am a soldier. I fight where I am told, and I win where I fight." ~ General George S. Patton

Our battle gear is assigned to the recruit at the point of salvation when we relinquish our methods and rationales to join His. Spirit Warriors are first responders. We get a Commander-in-Chief, His Secretary of State (The Holy Spirit), encrypted battle codes (Holy Bible), a set of keys to release prisoners and bind evil, a direct communications line to heaven, maps to the gates of Hell shrouded in darkness that requires night vision binoculars to discern the *who, what, when, how,* and *why* of every situation.

And we have a battalion of servant angels, the faith to believe the Commander, and enough trust to move forward under fire in protective custody, shoulder to shoulder with a new tribe of the like-minded to tell of our forays, to laugh with at the ironies, and help one another as a unit to achieve our destinies.

The Warrior's first initiation is learning how to lead those locked in disbelief, to a saving relationship with our Commander Jesus and do that consistently. This immediately expands our spiritual family as they get their own gear and functionally to join His kingdom work through careful discipleship and loving fellowship.

Winning souls is a first victory into the miraculous world we are supernaturally equipped to live in, because all that is necessary on our side is the boldness to simply share our own recruitment testimony.

Promotion comes by leaps of faith with a willing heart volunteering for hazardous duty, variously known as the Normal Christian Cross Life. We receive our second initiation by believing, asking for, and receiving the baptism power of the Holy Spirit designed for our supernatural service assignments.

The Spirit presents us with this boot camp level of faith: it is the personal gift of speaking in heavenly languages. It is the exact gift the first Jerusalem believers received as evidenced with His visitation of wind and flames of fire in the room where they waited.[1] Tongues began spontaneously from joy as one of the vocal prayer ministries, and later they learned were to be used in public gatherings, known as ekklesias, within strict rules of interpretation for understanding.

Many in our generation choose to stay outside the supernatural sphere at this stage because they count that one gift as foolish, thinking it is below their (self-righteous) pride. Maybe that is the point? Surely, they reason, there is something more spectacular than unknown gibberish that doesn't need my humility to get it?

Nope.

This is the right start to an ever-increasing humble journey all the way to the finish line. And believe me, your soul will need a prayer language the devil cannot understand or attack.

The Holy Spirit is also the quartermaster. *He is* all the resources, gear, gifts, power, weapons, orders, and doses of comfort when the blows pound us down and healing is required. Spirit Warriors accept the fact that the Holy Spirit only responds to our faith towards Him: unbelief turns a very dead ear. Those who move into His realm will be empowered for supernatural service assignments for He dwells in the supernatural.

Those who refute and refuse the supernatural side of God are known as cessation (ceasing belief of the supernatural manifestations of God for today), proclaiming erroneously that the healing, deliverance, and miracle gifts[2] were for the original apostles and have ceased in our end time. They display an ignorance of documented history sine those gifts flowed well in the Third Century church and currently where there is belief for them.

Some heretics (professing believers who part from the pure word of God's bible), go so far as to postulate their own opinion that there are no current leadership offices for prophets and apostles. This is rather personally selective for they do subscribe to pastors, teachers, and evangelists listed in the same verses of scripture![3]

Wow and wow again.

They separate their own misunderstood offices, right out of the bible. Are these Jesus-given offices too God-like, beyond our natural realm, and beyond human reach? But that is the whole point of being God.

Sure, people would like to have the miracle gifts first, but it does not go that way. Soldiers can't be afraid of the weaponry they are given or that rise against them, but use it to advantage. As Spirit Warriors, the footing of walk-by-sight, is left in the past as the parachute cords of trust pinch the thighs and crush the chest with assurance that provision is at hand. Gravity prevails.

Faith with trust in the Unseen Hand triumphs and thus begins the flights of intimacy that only faith-walkers practice. As we get to understand God's Handbook Codes (Bible), we grow in our faith and trust that qualifies us for higher duties, all by suspending our soul's will and entering His will.

Here is where *Snipers* qualify, the exorcists. They are not an elite class, but it is a courageous class, having just discovered we have all been given specialized tools of the miraculous: casting out demons, healing the sick, feeding multitudes, raising the dead—whether in spirit or body—by making disciples stronger than yourself.

These are the Spirit Warriors: listening to the Holy Spirit on one side and expelling demonic spirits by pulling down their strongholds on the other. Idols must be routed and displaced then replaced with God's truth.

Principalities must be subdued over world regions, laying waste to Satan's weak kingdom structure that retreats at the very name of Jesus and the assault by His fully armed warriors. Satan and his agents can do no more than obey his Creator and those of us who wield the sword of the Spirit and brandish the Commander's Name backed by His blood authority. We are the winners.

Once we fully realize the spiritual kingdoms that are really ruling world events and manipulating people to their will, we can engage with confidence. What has always been a mystery to me is the reticence of many proclaiming their Christianity, but not functioning in it and by His gifts, to get the job done in His way. Excuses of unbelief are hauled out, polished off, and brandished as "bible knowledge", denying the very words they quote.

As if, God is a change agent running scared of the disastrous turns of world events in the ongoing clash of all the kingdoms, both in the spirit and natural worlds, which act on behalf of their own command-ers. These draw back from God's WORDS that clearly outline the rules of combat.

They, through unbelief in the weaponry, or the commission, or the sheer heroism needed to leap into the dark of the battle line, are self-disqualified and settle into their ample bible knowledge, weak insti-tutions, and cowardly traditions. They recruit the timid, those easily dazzled by their specialized bible interpretations, and are swayed into the pagan cultures of which Paul stated:

> "Now the just shall live by faith, but if anyone draws back, my soul has no pleasure in him. But we are not of those who draw back to perdition, but of those who believe to the saving of the soul." [4]

We must understand and embrace our Father who only lives in the MIRACLE. He has this superior nature and no other. We humans are in a lesser dimension, limited to the dirt of the solid, the material, the visible, and tactile unless He takes us higher.

But still, the eternal beckons in no uncertain, but in sure terms: you were born exactly how you are, exactly for this time, and exactly for these advanced culturally darkened circumstances within the terror-filled hours we face. The year of 2020 is only the prelude to global chaos that will usher in the super-man Antichrist, to supply the satanic will.

Think of the First Century ekklesia that had life circumstances far worse, building on a crusted Pharisaical Judaism Jesus spoke against constantly. The Old Covenant was closing when angels filled the skies as He showed Himself in Bethlehem.

There was nowhere for the Ekklesia to go but to build the most unpopular new concept on a resurrected God, Jesus Christ, without precedent or pattern. They were the stones fitted together, relying on their personal contact with the Rabbi King, immersed in the baptism of the Holy Spirit, and walking in unity with each other. Imagine a time period when there was not one born-again, Spirit-filled Christian excepting the 120 from the upper room whom people thought to be drunkards?

In the first quarter of the 21st Century, we bump elbows (because of the false social distancing theory that prevents virus implantation), with many who say they walk with Christ but because of their disbelief in the tongues of fire or any other number of issues, engage in striking and sniping fellow soldiers in the hottest lines of battle over their chosen doctrinal fragments.

These perpetually lust for Eden—long sealed up—and to walk in climate-controlled past glories linked to entitlement fantasies. Vanity. Yes, the now remnant has few companions to rejoice with over victory exploits into the dark lands because so few venture there on commission. Welcome to the war!

This Spirit Warrior Guide focuses on kingdom privileges of redemption, exorcism, and miracles. It informs and prepares the activated for engagement in the dark lands of unwilling slaves or willing captives, that our King gave His unmatched, divine life's blood for. We go in because the unsaved are important to Him and someone came in for our rescue, too.

Succinctly put, a Spirit Warrior is a born-again, Christ-follower, baptized by and in the Holy Spirit and sealed by Him, commissioned, anointed, and led by His voice and through the black smoldering edges of disease, damnation, demonization, and ignorance—to pluck the lost and clueless out of repression and place them into the arms of the Father.

These we call the evangelists, soul winners, workers of miracles, exorcists, prophets speaking words of exhortation, comfort, and edification; the new ekklesia builder apostles.[5] They are the pastors who nourish, and teachers who cultivate into maturity and produce spiritual reproduction. When we have the seal of the Holy Spirit, He dwells within us. That means, we have access to all His gifts by His permission, to be used as our faith level embraces and masters new growth challenges.

The Kingdom is an orchestra that relies on each musician to play his and her instruments. Should you not believe for the sounding of the prophetic trumpets, you will never hear the full orchestration in its glory as Father provided for and intends. When you are the trumpet and must face persecution from the more acceptable, popular, or believable instruments, you must, none the less, sound yourself when called to do so.

For we are instruments unto Father, not unto each other. Never fear, all the trumpets will fellowship together and have tales of wonder, and how their sounding increased God's glory. Faith.

The Conductor who distributes His own instruments, expects you to learn, love, and sound out. Each instrument is a gift that is deployed for one particular use at a time.[6] The Conductor knows when each should enter the musical score and for how long, how loud, or softly, beautifully, and flawlessly sound out in order to fully enhance the whole presentation. This concerted faith exults the Father.

You may not like the shrill sound of the piccolo (e.g., the gift of tongues[7]), but that does not preclude the Conductor from using many piccolos to get just the right sharpness against the soft cello tones of reason. Piccolo haters and mockers lose the unique unassailable victory of its voice in God's concert for overcoming a passionless life.

> **Never be a Holy Spirit gift-hater**[8] for that is how one hates Him whose stunning Personality is disclosed and shared supernaturally to heal, save, and fill the earth with Joy. Lovers of Holy Spirit gifts are those alone who will serve the King as Spirit Warriors because those are the weapons of our warfare.

The sincere goal for writing this book was to present the powerful place of the Godhead as the Mover and Director in the affairs of human and spirit realms. May you confidently accept your commission and prepare for the journey of your lifetime!

[1] Acts 2:1-4; speaking in tongues of men and angels.

[2] 1 Corinthians 14:1-19 gives balance to the use of tongues.

[3] 1 Corinthians 7:17;1 Corinthians 12:27-30.

[4] Hebrews 10:38-39.

[5] 1 Corinthians 7:17; 1 Corinthians 12:27-30.

[6] 1 Corinthians 12, 14; Romans 12.

[7] Acts 2:1-4; speaking in tongues of men and angels and 1 Corinthians 14:1-19, gives balance to the use of tongues.

[8] Hebrews 10:37-39.

READING 2 - WHY THE HURRY TO HEAVEN?

"...strengthening the souls of the disciples,
exhorting them to continue in the faith, and saying,
'We must through many tribulations
enter the Kingdom of God." ~ Acts 14:22

The book of Acts remains open, alive, and vibrating with grace as ongoing generation after multiple generations have reproduced colleague believers called to Kingdom living in dangerous perilous times in remote places. We are at the end of that.

With tongue in cheek, I must say that we are truly sorry that Dr. Luke, its historical writer in just a few years after Christ's resurrection, did not live long enough to record all the rest of what the Holy Spirit would be doing through sequential centuries like ours. But we do have Christian history that bears witness to the Holy Spirit's ongoing miraculous works.

Comprehending the fact of God's unchanging operational processes is clearly demonstrated in Acts during the new Ekklesia's first gathering. This is still significant for us today. The introduction of the awesome Holy Spirit of God disclosed that He was no longer to look on from the outside, but came in this astounding way to dwell within each Body member. The Holy One started speaking out right away in His heavenly language that no one could learn!

Do you want the Holy Spirit to speak in His own tongue to you? Do you want to hear God's voice individually, personally, and intentionally? People are afraid of His near presence; worse, they think it is all about them. Embarrassment rises from standing apart from the herd. But this is precisely what begins the story of just how and by whom the Kingdom is to operate.

You read the ekklesia letters written by Peter, Paul, John, Timothy, and to Titus to clearly see that these biblical methods are not followed today in many Christian denominations.[1] By discounting and eventually not believing in the Holy Spirit's ongoing ways of operation has hobbled the power of the Ekklesia, led to its division, exploitation, persecution, and current apathetic love for cultural comforts so prevalent in the electronic 21st Century.

The *Sozo Gospel* epoch of saving, healing, delivering; of the miracles, signs, and wonders[2] like raising the dead and feeding thousands from a mere handful of food--plus God-given dreams and visions, all began when Jesus Christ sent the Holy Spirit Replacement as He *"sat down at the right hand of the throne of God."*[3]

With extreme concern, The Head of the Body left kingdom work assignments to we believers then and now for over 2,000 years. What mercy! The full gospel signs and wonders characterized the veracity that Jesus Christ's Presence was still at hand and was not anything like the promised hopes that pre-Calvary saints waited for and found in Christ.[4]

With this commission will be casualties at the hands of desperate power hungry and evil beings. We see it in Seal Number Five of Revelation 6 that reflects this truth presently. The current Christian martyrdom rate in the world is staggering. Check through these websites to get a picture of the tribulation going on globally with Islamism leading the killing. This is but a sampling so look for more. Theses links may no longer be functional, taken down, or erased.

- **Open Doors.** An average of 11 Christians killed daily for their faith. ttps://www.opendoorsusa.org/christian-persecution/stories/11-christians-killed-every-day-for-their-decision-to-follow-jesus/
- **The Voice of the Martyrs.** https://www.persecution.com/
- Nearly 1 million Christians reportedly martyred for their faith in last the decade. https://www.foxnews.com/world/nearly-1-million-christians-reportedly-martyred-for-their-faith-in-last-decade.
- **Independent News.** Center of Global Christianity Report on Boko Haram in Nigeria and Al-Shabaab in East Africa. Check out this site: https://www.independent.co.uk/news/christians-killed-martyred-900000-last-decade-africa-boko-haram-al-shabaab-study-of-global-a7526226.html
- **August 17, 2021,** it is reported that because of the fateful, poorly planned Biden Administration withdrawal from Afghanistan, over 200 Christian missionaries were hunted, some raped and all were beheaded. Looks like the Fifth Seal of Revelation 6 was just cracked open.

> The importance of intentionally living this short earth-journey is to remain focused on loving Yahweh God[5] *"...with all your heart, with all your soul, and with all your mind. This is the first and great commandment. And the second is like it: You shall love your neighbor as yourself."* That is how we finish well.[6] Make up your mind that you are here in the field of battle in all ways because we are not fitted for Earth, but heaven.

If you are a warrior for the Gospel, you have intentionally dressed out for persecution and tribulation episodes. Likewise, if you are determined to remain on The Home Front in the rocking chair of blind ease, you don't get warrior armor, or risk anything of importance, or leave the comfort zone of impiety, or represent Jesus Christ as an ambassador in a foreign clime-- be it political, racial, cultural, or dangerous. This person just passes time by hiding his other gift in their death shroud.[7]

This life has nothing to do with searching for and believing in, an escape hatch fabricated to avoid the persecution and tribulation of our times that Jesus Himself prophesied for those who overcome the worlds of man and spirits.

The rapture theory is not biblically provable and a handicap that disables full expression of being "all in" with Jesus Christ. Discard it. If it is true, greet it when it comes (as it will in natural death anyway). But, if it is a faulty doctrine, live as though it will never happen and is not a deciding factor in your obedient service. We do look for Christ's second coming.[8]

The Popular Secret Rapture Theory

Why the hurry to leave the assignments that can only be accomplished on earth? These exploits of obedience earn the treasures of reward that faithful stewards of His calling and gifts deserve. It will be quite a ceremony in the throne room of Paradise, including a personal introduction to our Father by His Son Jesus who dedicated Himself to grooming and training us, His Bride. Will we have something to present to Jesus or have we spent anxious moments of tribulation just waiting for a quick and untimely exit?

The Acts of the Holy Spirit have not stopped contrary to denominations of Christians who have endured unsound doctrine on the Second Coming of Christ as introduced mainly by John Nelson Darby (1800 -1882). Nor have any supernatural miraculous possibilities contained in the records of the New Testament stopped. Either all the truth outlined in the New Testament has been valid from Jesus' ministry through Pentecost when the authority was given the Ekklesia, up to Christ's second return, or we must be honest enough to also chuck out all the Epistles,

The Book of the Revelation of Jesus Christ as recorded by John, and all the supernatural and future events recorded to come. Many have done so by taking a snippet of Scripture here or a snippet there by misunderstood and rejected passages.

Interestingly, not one Church father nor biblical scholar going back to the era of Acts, had ever heard of a "secret rapture" -- the theological fabrication of Darby's of the 1800s. This error was compounded by the further teachings of C. I. Schofield (1843-1921). Thus, the "secret rapture theory" Darby invented on false conjecture in 1830, was incorporated in conjunction with Cyrus I. Schofield's bible translation notes on what he labeled as Dispensation/Pre-millennial.

Thus, began the rise of false belief that the supernatural gifts and intentions of the Holy Spirit have been dismissed and ceased after the 28 chapters of Acts were penned, however contrary to supernatural events and revivals initiated by the Holy Spirit in intervening centuries.

People not personally in touch with the Holy Spirit in an intimate, daily way, could imagine that He was no longer alive or actively involved with life on Earth. The proliferation of the false philosophical drivel of 'God is dead,' comes from either practicing their self-made human religions and/or, by ignoring and grieving the Holy Spirit's intrusions into their lives by simple unbelief in it.

Rather than clip out of the bible all the supernatural activities of God after Acts were recorded then label them as 'ceasing to exist' or, 'only meant for that time,' or, piecing and inventing ever new and corrupted versions and commentary notes for the Word of God,[9] we believe the full gospel (*sozo*) includes all the supernatural phenomena as the core genius of God!

We like to call what Mr. Schofield named, *The Church Age*, for what it really is: *The Full Acts of the Church* because this 2,000+ -year era witnesses the continuing behavior of obedient believers under the guidance and power of the Holy Spirit. From the activities of the First Century Church up to this moment in history as you are reading this-- and until His second appearance when we are taken off the planet in fact--we believers all over the world have been vigorously using the gifts and callings of the Holy Spirit in building His Kingdom. What other way is there, but God's way?

After much independent biblical study, we feel that what most people think of as, "the rapture" now is truly the Second Coming[10] of Christ.[11] With that catching away within visible sight of Him, His children are protected from God's final Wrath[12] to be enacted only in the latter part of the (Great) Tribulation, directed against the unsaved in the seven vial judgments.[13]

We are surely exempt from God's wrath meant for those unbelievers in Messiah Christ who will be fighting it out in the Valley of Armageddon, Israel, in those days. However, the Church will have been in the birth pangs that is the uncomfortable stage of the seven Seals and seven Trumpets before Great Tribulation marked by God's wrath in seven bowls of consequences only on the unsaved who worship the Antichrist, the False Prophet, and Satan who is chained up 1,000 years. Those are the recipients of the Great Tribulation.

Now we arrive in this 21st Century of approximately 2,000 years after Pentecost, to these last days. The Ekklesia was in its *GESTATIONAL* (pregnancy) period where great works of the Holy One were manifested and believers martyred for even bowing their heads in Christian prayer in hostile Europe. Some lost their heads or were licked up in flames of hatred for producing and printing common language bible translations, rescued from the dichotomy of Latin that Catholic tyranny locked up.

This period began morphing into the *BIRTH PANGS* of the last days through Laodicean sterility, mass media manipulation, erroneous bible commentaries, false teachings through birth pangs, labor, delivery of the kingdom.

The way saints today will miss experiencing the wrath of God is to naturally die and instantly[14] (so to speak, raptured upon death!) they will arrive into the Presence of the Lord Jesus Christ as is clearly written. Apostle Paul explained how that worked out to assure and comfort the relatives of those "who have fallen asleep".[15]

There is also a third and final return of Jesus Christ as recorded in Revelation 19:11-21. This appearance is quite distinctive from the first and second[16] appearances. It happens after the most intense portion of the Tribulation when the wrath of God's cup is overflowing and dealt with on earth. We, who are alive at that time along with those who have beforehand died in faith (already with God in heaven as a cloud of witnesses), return together on those beautiful white horses in righteous sparkling white robes, to rescue Israel out of complete destruction.

NOTE. This will be Christ's last coming, most probably after the marriage supper of the Lamb--, when He comes to remain for the next 1,000 years.[17] The story is poured out by John in the last two chapters of Revelation. The Body of Christ is there, as well as, all the army of heaven.

This third event is distinct from the other two advents because Jesus is clothed in a white robe dipped into and saturated by crimson red blood. He has been the sacrifice! From the description of His clothing of the Second Coming,[18] His (post-resurrection) robe is white and shining, no stains. The bloody robe of His final third appearance indicates that He wears His own atoning blood, not the blood of those with whom he fights in the final war since that had not happened yet at this point.

No, Christ's powerful, healing, and miraculous blood is a badge of victory, honor and divinity displayed proudly without a drop of it on those accompanying Him. He paid for redemption all by Himself.

In His own way, Christ continually assists us who follow Him, by utilizing the power of His Holy Spirit Whom He left on assignment to carry on His will through His children. Our part is to believe and act on all directions of the Lord.

This Reading is just something to consider and study on your own. It has no impact on salvation that cannot be lost or stolen, no matter how much of the Scripture we understand or don't understand or get it wrong. Study for yourselves until you have peace if this is important to you.

[1] Acts 20:17; 1 Timothy 5:17; Titus 1:5; Hebrews 11:2; James 5:14; 1 Peter 5:1 along with the instructions to the Corinthians.

[2] Acts 16:25-26 records the supernatural intervention of the Lord by earthquake.

[3] Hebrews 12:1-2.

[4] Hebrews 11:39-40; Hebrews 12:25-29.

[5] Matthew 22:34-40.

[6] John 14:12-14.

[7] Matthew 25:25. The whole parable begins at Matthew 25:14-30 and has to do with the relationship of servant to master. Apparently, this person did not respect his master as the lord of his life efforts.

[8] Revelation 14:14-16.

[9] Hebrews 4:11-13.

[10] The First Coming of Jesus Christ was His appearance as a baby first notated in the Book of Luke, Chapter 2.

[11] 1 Thessalonians 4:13-18.

[12] 1 Thessalonians 1:10.

[13] Revelation 14:14-16 explains the Second Coming of Jesus Christ Who personally separates the wheat (His children) from the tares (Satan's children) to rescue us from the Great Tribulation portion of God's wrath which no believer will endure. Now, of the Second Coming and when the division is made in verses 17-20, angels are utilized to place all unbelievers in the "great wine press of the wrath of God"; meaning, further time on earth (only a very few years) remain to work out the final time of grace. Grace, because although difficult, people will have this time to repent and cling to God.

[14] Philippians 1:21-26. Paul says that when he departs life on earth he is "with Christ". No years of moldering in the graveyard waiting for the Second Coming. No! Immediately alive and in person with Jesus Christ. The body returns to dust. The soul and spirit return to Christ instantly. Those who die in Christ leave the Land of the Dead (earth) to be promoted to the Land of the Living (heaven).

[15] 1 Thessalonians 4:13-18 is all in the context of answering the questions about what happens to all those who died already, waiting for Jesus' return? Be comforted, because we who are alive will be, "caught up together with them (those who have already died in Christ) in the clouds. They are already in the clouds waiting on us to be gathered to them! Hebrews 12:1 speaks of the Cloud of Witnesses as an incentive for us to, "...lay aside every weight, and the sin which so easily ensnares us, and let us run with endurance the race that is set before us." They have run their race and conquered all the challenges, pitfalls, bouts of doubt turned to faith, assaults of the enemies, endured the persecutions and advanced the kingdom. They are awaiting we who remain alive at His coming.

[16] 1 Corinthians 15:12-23; verses 2428 speak of Christ "*delivers the kingdom to God the Father when He puts an end to all rule and all authority and power.*" Continuing with verses 29-33 affirms the reasons Paul continues to live for Christ and why we should as well. This is based on the resurrection of the dead (body) when one dies as being dead in the world but immediately alive (caught up) to Christ.

[17] Revelation 19:7-9.

[18] Revelation 14:14-16.

READING 3 - CHRIST'S COMMISSION FOR CORRIE TEN BOON

Sandbagging

"All warfare is based on deception.
Appear weak when you are strong, and
strong when you are weak." ~ Sun Tzu

We are very familiar with Christ's great commissioning of His disciples as they went into battles and learned their warrior spirit. Mark outlines it best because it also describes how this life journey with Christ, would appear to the lost. There had to be brilliant flashes of supernatural touches from Him that assured this was not just another humanly fabricated religious system.

We don't get to choose the century, years, month, day, or hour to be born. We are not consulted about the nation, parents, social conditions of the time, safety issues, food abundance, wealth level, or whether there is a war or pandemic raging outside the birth room. We are never given the luxury of a preferred gender, skin tone, health level, DNA heritage assured in strength or longevity, or a thousand and one other possibilities at birth. Not our choice.

We do realize that every one of those decisions made by our loving Father is critical to reaching the potentiality of destiny with exactly the precise combination to achieve it. We reach our own first, close at hand. Going out further, it becomes more challenging and interesting to cross cultures and boundaries that must be crossed to reach the captives on the other side. Years after this encounter, I visited the little watch shop her family kept in Harlem. Walked up the very narrow stairs to the hiding place for many Jews on their way to life, not death.

Corrie ten Boon, a Dutch spinster found her family in the center of danger as they followed Jesus Christ. Boundaries were drawn, nationalities mixed, oppressors in charge, and a job to be done but it took incarceration in her case. I shook hands and hugged this formidable, sturdy Dutchwoman when she was invited to speak at our Spirit-filled Episcopal Church of the Good Shepherd in Maitland, Florida. I recall it was early 1986 when she humbly walked to the sacred desk. She was striking in holiness.

Corrie was an elderly woman filled with the strength of the Holy Spirit and authority. I observed her carefully and listened intently as she told the story of her encounter with the cruel, sociopath German tormentor who had been instrumental in the brutal death of her sister Betsy and 80% of the women under his supervision in the camp.

"How could I forgive him, Lord?" was a battle she fought for many years when chancing on him one morning in a church where she was speaking. Listen to Corrie's story taken from her personal journal.

Corrie ten Boon's Journey

My sister Betsy and I were in the Nazi concentration camp at Ravensbruck because we committed the crime of loving Jews. Several hundred of us from Holland, France, Russia, Poland, and Belgium were herded into a room built for 200. As far as I knew, Betsy and I were the only two representatives of Heaven in that room. We may have been the Lord's only representatives in that place of hatred, yet because of our presence there, things changed. *Jesus said, 'In the world you shall have tribulation; but be of good cheer, I have overcome the world.'*[1]

We, too, are to be over comers bringing the light of Jesus into a world filled with darkness and hate. Sometimes I get frightened as I read the

Bible, and as I look in this world and see all the tribulation and persecution promised by the Bible coming true.

Now I can tell you, though, if you too are afraid, that I have just read the last pages. I can now come to shouting 'Hallelujah! Hallelujah'[2] for I have found where it is written that Jesus said, *'He that overcomes shall inherit all things; and I will be His God, and he shall be My son.'*[3]

This is the future and hope of this world. Not that the world will survive--but that we shall be over comers amid a dying world. Betsy and I, in the concentration camp, prayed that God would heal Betsy who was so weak and sick.

Yes, the Lord will heal me,' Betsy said with confidence. She died the next day and I could not understand it. They laid her thin body on the concrete floor along with all the other corpses of the women who died that day. It was hard for me to understand, to believe that God had a purpose for all that. Yet, because of Betsy's death, today I am traveling all over the world telling people about Jesus.

There are some among us teaching there will be no tribulation, that the Christians will be able to escape all this. These are the false teachers that Jesus was warning us to expect in the latter days. Most of them have little knowledge of what is already going on across the world. I have been in countries where the saints are already suffering terrible persecution. In China, the Christians were told, 'Don't worry, before the tribulation comes you will be translated--raptured.'

Then came a terrible persecution. Millions of Christians were tortured to death. Later I heard a bishop from China say, sadly, 'We have failed. We should have made the people strong for persecution, rather than telling them Jesus would come first. Tell the people how to be strong in times of persecution, how to stand when the tribulation comes, to stand and not faint.'

I feel I have a divine mandate to go and tell the people of this world that it is possible to be strong in the Lord Jesus Christ. We are in training for the tribulation, but more than 60% of the Body of Christ across the world has already entered the tribulation.

There is no way to escape it. We are next. Since I have already gone through prison for Jesus' sake, and since I met the bishop of China, now every time I read a good Bible text I think, 'Hey, I can use that in the time of tribulation.' Then I write it down and learn it by heart.

In America, the churches sing, *'Let the congregation escape tribulation';* but in China and Africa, the tribulation has already arrived. This last year alone (1973) more than 200,000 Christians were martyred in Africa. Now things like that never get into the newspapers because they cause bad political relations. But I know. I have been there.

Several years ago, I was in Africa in a nation where a new government had come into power. The first night I was there some of the Christians were commanded to come to the police station to register. When they arrived, they were arrested and that same night they were executed. The next day the same thing happened with other Christians.

The third day it was the same. All the Christians in the district were being systematically murdered. The fourth day, I was to speak in a little church. The people came, but they were filled with fear and tension. All during the service they were looking at each other, their eyes asking, *'Will this one I am sitting beside be the next one killed? Will I be the next one?'*

How can we get ready for persecution? First, we need to feed on the Word of God, digest it, and make it a part of our being. This will mean disciplined Bible study each day as we not only memorized long passages of scripture, but put the principles to work in our lives. Next, we need to develop a personal relationship with Jesus Christ. Not just the Jesus of yesterday, the Jesus of history, but the life-changing Jesus of today who is still alive and sitting at the right hand of God.

We must continually be anointed by the Holy Spirit to do His work. This is not an optional command of the bible; it is critically necessary. Those early disciples could never have stood up under the persecution of the Jews and Romans had they not waited for Pentecost. Each of us needs our own personal Pentecost, the baptism of the Holy Spirit. We will never be able to stand in the tribulation without it.

Later that week, half the congregation of that church was executed. I heard later that the other half were killed some months ago. But I must tell you something, I was so happy that the Lord used me to encourage these people, for unlike many of their leaders, I had the word of God. I had been to the bible and discovered that Jesus said He had not only overcome the world, but to all those who remained faithful to the end,[4] He would give a crown of life.

This article was a direct testimony by Cornelia Arnolda Johanna 'Corrie' ten Boon, Harlem, Netherlands. She lived for God from April 15, 1892 to April 15, 1983.

[1] John 16:33.
[2] 1 Peter 4:14-15.
[3] Revelation 21:7.
[4] Revelation 3:11; Job 13:15; 2 Timothy 4:8; & James 1:12.

READING 4 - PROTOTYPE FOR DYNAMIC AWAKENING

"The Christian faith has not been tried and found wanting.
It has been found difficult and left untried."

G. K. Chesterton

Where are the Prophets of God?

Prophet Kim Clement[1] stated just three days before the fateful crashes[2] into The Twin Towers in New York City, the horrendous slide of fire into our Pentagon,[3] and the heroic takeover by patriotic passengers of United Airlines Flight 93,[4] that the opening of the very end times of the church period had nodded its head. And indeed, it kicked off the Arab Spring uprisings in the Middle East of 2011.

Now, over twenty years later during that most fateful year of 2020 when global tilts were felt, ancient prophets had described the beginning birth pangs that would pressure the whole world. We've watched the streets of the United States, Europe, Asia, Hong Kong, Indonesia, Australia, Central and South America—literally worldwide nations—bow under the false flag of Coronavirus-19 hyped as 'an extremely deadly pandemic'. Its planned advent swiped a dragon's claw at shaky governments and closed Laodicean churches.

Evil forces, both human and spirit, were quick to seize the sudden opening of this scale, causing deep oppression with national and business associations leveled to such a degree by the spirit of fear, that elected politicians discovered how to take freedoms as a tradeoff for their weak promises. They made unrealistic promises of health protection through providing free to the public, experimental and deadly vaccines, paper mask mandates, social distancing, and isolation policies that contradicted our Constitution.

Fear-mongering, combined with opportunity for huge profits, shut down economies, banking centers, routine and critical health services, public games, restaurants, and halted education causing a rise in population movement and anxiety. These faulty measures brought on food and comestible shortages black marketing.

This mild influenza strain categorized in the corona species with the common cold and standard flu, having a kill rate of less than 2% in those contracting it. And there were readily available safe medications to curb and stop it yet some manufacturing facilities were stopped in order to push people toward vaccinations instead. So why all the fear-mongering?

Out of this blanketed stratosphere of the fear of possible death, the very citadels of hope lost courage. Churches and ministries folded up by the thousands with the thought that some should never reopen and many did not. Pastors and church boards simply declared a shutdown for ten or more months into the future, well outside a flu season and contagion. Yet underground ekklesias of the world kept right on going. They've seen far worse persecution that a scare.

If this is all it takes to voluntarily cease corporate worship for our most powerful and watchful God, what are we really looking at? Hiding out? Getting secular subsidies? Or, do we get a choice of an opportunity that can go either way: helpless inertia and defeat or advancing the Kingdom of Jesus Christ in crises?

When Jesus shared with Peter the terrible things that would soon be happening to Him and the suffering caused by His own tribe Israel, *"...the elders, chief priests, and scribes—and be KILLED and raised the third day,"*[5] Peter reacted fiercely. He apparently didn't hear the hope of, *"...be raised the third day"*. His human instincts, young physical strength, anger at the very concept of harming his best, gifted friend, produced a rebuke for Jesus to be quiet and not say such things!

Little did Peter understand but that Satan was behind that rebuke against Jesus. We have two motives here: Peter for good and Satan for harm. Satan believed Jesus' words immediately! He was slated to die soon. Good. How far could he push Peter to back away from his own salvation? Satan indeed knew that the sacrifice of Christ Messiah would take away all the authority he tricked out of Adam on earth, so long ago. He would lose his keys to his own kingdom of evil power and be at the behest of these filthy, mere mortals. Unthinkable!

Satan stirred up Peter's flesh to act out of his self-concerns. Peter's motivations were love as he knew how to provide it. Not understanding the next thing Jesus would say to his anger-riddled face, days later Peter would profoundly question his own love for Jesus.

But we understand your heart, Peter. And we see how the devil can take a sincere and pure motive of friendship love as you knew it to push and crush the Receiver of those words. Satan hung around Jesus and the disciples, waiting for any slimy chance he could get to destroy The Plan. And this was it. He manipulated Peter's misdirected love to bring a stinging rebuke and argument against Christ's God-ordained destiny of redeeming all those who would have faith in Him to join His kingdom and leave his own.

After Jesus named the true enemies of the gospel, here now, a close friend Peter is siding with their demonic aspirations to kill Jesus. But we know that is what they do best. Here follows a clever repartee from Jesus who speaks to Peter's face while He speaks to Satan directly behind that face.[6]

> *"But He turned and said to Peter, 'Get behind Me, Satan!*
> *You are an offense to Me for you are not mindful of the things of God, but the things of men.'"*

Satan was playing in Peter's head. So Jesus rebuked Satan for using Peter's sincere but childlike, ignorant heart, to get at Him. Of course, Satan is not mindful of God's plans, ways of doing all things well, or the saving of mankind. His motivations are well known: he's a killer! Jesus forcefully uncovered Satan and faced off for the battle ahead. Peter was just in the middle. Don't you feel that way sometimes?

Peter is caught up in something way above his head. He had no clue of what just happened in the saturated spirit world all around him. Jesus told Satan to"...*get behind Me Satan* (not behind Peter). *You* (Satan) *are an offense to Me* (not to Peter's naive motivations), *for you are not mindful of the things of God,* (Me, Jesus) *but the things of men"* (men like Peter).

Jesus was telling Satan to 'eat My dust as I make My way to Jerusalem to fulfill Father's orders'. Snakes eat dust. In essence Jesus is declaring: 'Peter is not a worthy opponent for you right now but one day he will be so powerful in the baptism of My Holy Spirit—in healing the sick, bringing the good news of salvation to thousands AND, casting out your puny Hench-demons—you will be no match for him! So, lay off.'

Jesus' sentiment continues in my mind...'just wait behind Me, fella. Soon, you'll give up the keys of death and the very gates of Hell and your illegal hold over humanity will be broken by My warriors. Remember? I saw you fall from heaven when we forced you out, and I see you, Satan, falling into the Lake of Fire ahead. Meanwhile, My Spirit Warriors are coming after you including Peter, with all I've given them to displace, reject, and destroy your evil works. They will remove millions of captives from your boundaries. I've just said to Peter, not only My future at Calvary, but your future after the Resurrection and Pentecost.

Before this tirade, Jesus had previously entrusted the keys to the kingdom of heaven and the power of binding and releasing earth's lock-ups.[7] Christ's fiery declaration in the spirit world reached the ears of

Satan: the challenge of limitation of powers and those being destroyed by all the Peters to come.

We know the rest of the story. The end of this incident for Peter was the repair Jesus had to make after he suffered the severely misunderstood criticism he took personally. Peter simply gave up after Calvary and went back to fishing, something he could understand. Hadn't he tried to save Jesus?

Jesus made certain to repair the breach in Peter's soul (he had the keys, after all) by making deep penetrating into the spirit questionings: *"Do you love Me?"*[8] each time covering Peter's three denials to Christ that said, "I don't love You. I don't even know You."

Jesus was not seeking adoration. He never looked for that at any time. We love Him willingly or self-volition. No, He was providing warfare weaponry with the goal accomplish by Himself with the giving of the most strategic keys in the war of the ages. In the context of the CORE and PURPOSE of dual kingdom combat, human souls are what needs to be released on earth from Satanic grasping which simultaneously BINDS his authority, power grabs, and default destination of destruction eternally for those souls.

There is a resounding binding of Satan's works while releasing the locks on heaven's gates by salvation's identity: the born-again spirit. There is an echo here from earth to heaven's chambers and back again as locks click and doors unhinge.

Simply put, when the spirit is born-again in the sinner, wherever he or she was locked up to eternal death then released (loosed), a recording is made in heaven. A recorded victory of Spirit Warriors who mostly function as evangelists first. That makes all believers Spirit Warriors able to facilitate that translation from dark to light by sowing the Word of God.

We cannot win souls. Jesus Christ rescues souls and opens spirits by His Holy Spirit Who is at work when His words are spoken by His servants to sinners. The invitation to salvation is presented in real time on earth but all results are His glory and His doing.

We are the witnesses.

[1] www.HouseOfDestiny.org; search YouTube.com for his messages.

[2] Boeing 767 carrying 81 passengers and 11 crew, Flight 11.

[3] Boeing 757 hijacked by five Saudi men affiliated with al-Qaeda on the morning of September 11, 2011 deliberately crashed into the Pentagon in Arlington County, VA killing all 64 aboard including 6 crew and themselves and another 125 inside the Pentagon.

[4] United Airlines Flight 93 was a domestic passenger flight hijacked by four al-Qaeda terrorists, as part of the September 11, 2001 attacks. Landed in Somerset County, PA. All 44 people on board were killed including the four hijackers.

[5] Matthew 16:21-23.

[6] Matthew 16:24-25.

[7] Matthew 16:13-19.

[8] Matthew 26:34-35 (*"And so said all the disciples,"* not just Peter); John 21:12-17.

READING 5 - THE PRINCIPLES OF
BINDING & LOOSING

"Blessed are you Simon Bar-Jonah...I will give you the keys
of the kingdom of heaven, and whatever
you bind on earth will be bound in heaven, and
whatever you loose on earth will be loosed in heaven."
Matthew 16: 17,19

PRINCIPLE #1 For Unsaved Sinners

There are two passages that record Jesus' teaching on binding and loosing. One is quoted above and the other one is found in Matthew 18:18. Both are within the context of dealing with a sinning brother or sister in the ekklesia. Surprised? Neither passage mentions the devil or evil spirits getting themselves bound on earth and sent to hell or anywhere else.

For a fact, it is impossible for humans to physically restrain or command demons to go to a location of final judgment (Hell, Hades, the Abyss, Bottomless Pit, Gehenna, or Lake of Fire)[1] before they are finally judged by Jesus Christ. Remember what Legion and all the demons begged Jesus for when He healed and delivered the demoniac in the country of Gadarenes?[2]

The wretched man was running for Jesus from afar and began to worship Him. He wanted to say, "Save me," but from his throat, from that man's own voice box, came the thundering voice of Legion, the

Strongman who held chains on his soul, speaking to Jesus whom He knew well from eons past. He even invoked God's name as protection:

> "What have I to do with You, Jesus, Son of the Most High God? I implore You by God that You do not torment me." For He (Jesus) said to him, "Come out of the man, unclean spirit!"
>
> Then He quietly asked him, 'What is your name?' And he answered, saying, "My name is Legion; for we are many." And "...also begged Him earnestly that He would not send them out of the country. Now a large herd of swine was feeding there near the mountains. So, all the demons begged Him, saying 'Send us to the swine, that we may enter them.'...at once He gave him permission.
>
> Then the unclean spirits went out and entered the swine (there were about 2,000); and the herd ran violently down the steep place into the sea, and drowned in the sea."

Jesus did not come 'to torment' them because it was before their time of final judgment. They were doing what demons do. Rather, He gave permission to find a new home with a nearby herd of swine that Jews could not touch. Ironically, they were so violent with fear when they entered the swine, that they stampeded at the intrusion, falling to their deaths over the cliffs with Legion with all his gang, still without a home. Now, people needed to run!

So, what does Jesus mean in these teachings of binding and loosing on earth?

The context of the whole passage begins at Matthew 16:13-23, when Peter is given the keys to Christ's kingdom because of his declaration that identified Jesus correctly as the divine Son of God by the prompting of *"My Father in Heaven"*. Jesus responded further, *"...and on this rock (of Peter's declaration), I will build My Church (Ekklesia in the original) and the gates of Hell shall not prevail against it"* (the Ekklesia).

So powerful are *"the keys of the kingdom of heaven"* that *"the gates of Hell shall not prevail against it."* We realize here that Hell has open gates (portals) and as Christ's servant-soldiers attack those dark gates (of unbelief), that they must give way: they will not, and cannot, prevail against an assault by Holy Spirit inflamed believers on mission. Those who are assaulting the gates of Hell are Spirit Warriors and front line evangelists. By God's word, the captured are rescued before they enter the door named Death. There are no locks on Hell's gates for they are wide open all the time.

In an opposite way, the kingdom of heaven has gates with locks that must match the keys Peter were given to open. There is no casual getting into the kingdom of heaven, for the gates (portals) are locked and uniquely opened only by using the same confession as Peter's: *"You are the Christ, the Son of the living God."* This is a person's affirmation of personal belief by faith[3] and Christ becomes Savior to us, born-again.

Since the gates of Hell shall not prevail against the onslaught of the Ekklesia, there must be the confrontation, the fight against the unmovable fortress named HELL. The only way the kingdom of heaven, as represented in global localities and centuries of inroad Christianity, is through the preaching of the gospel of life.

The lifeline must be thrown out right at the gates of Hell. They don't know that Christ died for the benefit of the whole world of sinners but continue to move in the dark toward destruction. Some are running there; others are simply sliding in as old age encroaches after few or many warnings of danger and solution.

The Ekklesia is separate from the kingdom of heaven. It is placed within the core of the Kingdom that will continue after His return until the final battle. The Holy Spirit is not removed from Earth at the Second Coming. There is still much work to complete when the seven Bowl Judgments are poured out. People will be saved, not abandoned.

Localized ekklesias have been loyal to Jesus for centuries. They continued to believe the bible's simple message and its manner of achievement has always been relevant for them. Nothing in the bible passed out of service in the first century, simply because later groups did not accept them.

We have a living, supernatural God that has not changed battle plans, equipping gear, and a directed communication system to the troops. Those who are willing to do His will on earth, are expected to behave as those same principles are followed in heaven. For the millions of times that the Lord's Prayer has been made, why has it not been believed as evidenced by action on it?[4]

Why, indeed.

Overall, the combination of all Holy Spirit-directed victories builds and expand Christ's kingdom in every place. He gave to Peter, as the first one to declare his faith in Christ as Messiah—not as rabbi, teacher, prophet, son of Joseph, a carpenter, a miracle man—or in any other functions the unsaved call Jesus: HE IS THE CHRIST OF GOD. This key opens the prophetic promise of victory over the very fortress of Hell, at its entrance gates, opened wide at the end of a broad boulevard.

That means to us who follow as Peter did, with our own faith declarations in Messiah, holds the promise to be ours. We get keys, too. All the demon soldiers that guard Hell's gates as butlers, will shove defeated sinners into death's door making it impossible for one more opportunity for eternal life. Their victories cannot not hold fast when a sinner comes to Christ and is instantly translated from that kingdom into His kingdom of Light by Truth. It is a defeat racked up for the devil and a victory counted for our side. Yes, score is being kept in big books.

As Spirit Warriors realize we can take the walls of darkness down, the more exposure is accomplished. This knowledge floods into personal victories for Seekers, too. For example, when a Seeker, tormented with let's say homosexual issues (complex, deceptive lies fortified by stolen pleasures), deliverance comes all at once in exorcism.

The open gate of the homosexual path to Hell is closed and unavailable when exposed for what it is. No more detention for them as the brilliant light and beauty of Christ's freedom becomes real by faith as the final gasps of horror are made by fleeing demons.

The entire bundle of Satan's agenda has been loosed, opened, released, stolen. This is the first key, but He gave us at least two keys, maybe more we haven't discovered yet, as a second set of two are mentioned here. It is the two-fold prophetic word given by permission only for the Church. Besides the overwhelming victories against enemies in spirit warfare and defeating Hell's gates, Jesus gave each of us a second SET of Kingdom keys. One will close up (bind) and one will open up (loose) the gates of heaven.

Heaven's gates are *"...narrow and difficult is the way which leads to life and FEW find it."*[5] Its gates are never open but always locked to unauthorized entry. *"You must be born-again".* It takes keys of faith for us, but there must be a Master Key that opens all of heaven.[6] This had to be paid for and was, only by the life blood shed by Christ and His subsequent resurrection to secure keys for us. Put all the keys together and Hell cannot prevail. But we must know about them and use them.

Now, to get to our title passage of Matthew 16:18-19 that describes the authority of the Master's keys that are given ONLY to those born-again and called, like Peter, who require them in kingdom responsibilities; in the comings and goings, the loosing and binding. Let's look at that verse again with a bit of amplification:

> *"And I will give you the keys of the kingdom of heaven, and whatever you BIND on earth will be bound in heaven* (at the same time, equally), *and whatever you LOOSE on earth will be loosed* (at the same time, equally) *in heaven"* (by concord, verification, sealed).

The context here is establishing Christ's Ekklesia powers on earth to batter down Hell's easy, almost-conquests. When we get a full understanding of the assignment to release the gospel in its *sozo* fullness, the binding up of death along with its permanent consequences, happens. Demons are not bound to places: but they can be bound from their activities in God's territories.

They will become permanently defeated (captured and bound) and off limits to those sinners who cry to Jesus for help, salvation, deliverance, peace, healing, and freedom from death's torments. Spirit

Warriors are on these front lines of desperation for believers just as evangelists are for unbelievers.

When demons are exorcised from one person's body, they roam around for centuries looking for a *'clean and swept house'* to begin their torments over again. Demons are active, doing what demons do on earth until they are bound by God's final judgment and that will happen after the tribulation era and Millennial reign of Christ with His saints.[7]

The works of all fallen angels, demons, principalities, dominion holders, The Old Dragon, Satan, Apollyon-Abaddon and his dark cadre, the human Antichrist beast, all false prophets, the Harlot Babylon, and the many fraudulent counterfeits of history will be facing God's final judgment courtroom as 'the unlisted' in the Lamb's Book of Life. Their names are in the other books, the black books, that end in the eternal lake of fire. All be vacated and judged by us as witnesses in that courtroom, included the ones we expelled multiple times.

To summarize, each of us were born into a raging war of great magnitude that began in Eden.[8] Other millions do not survive being birthed. Those that do, wander around in ignorance of not much more than survival mode, figuring out life unless a Christian-someone tells them the truth of the gospel and presence of the war, and is believed.

The division on earth is not ethnic, national, political, religious, the haves and have-nots, or any such humanly devised fabrications. The division on earth is in the spiritual dimension: either born-again (alive) or not born-again (dead).

We start out as needy babies, *"for all have sinned and come short of the glory of God,"*[9] automatically born as part of the dark kingdom as opposed to being born in God's family. Thank you, Adam and Eve! But someone with their keys to the kingdom of heaven, unlocks the gospel of Jesus Christ, and our belief is kindled, faith bursts out, and the dead human spirit is ignited by God's Spirit that begets us as a living spirit-being.

Instantly, we exit the kingdom of darkness with its wide ways to destruction because we have been loosed from its attraction. The narrow way becomes brilliant with God's glory, and open communication with Him is the new normal Christian life!

Gradually by faith, we grow that spirit up, taking back our rightful place from the domination of the soul life that led us down many dangerous and crooked paths. The Holy Spirit implanted a set of keys to the kingdom of heaven in each saved and Spirit-sealed saint. We don't know that and some never look for Him enough in nature, or His bible guide to Life on Earth, to find out. Mentoring disciples to Jesus Christ by mature saints speeds the sanctification process. That's boot camp. Get involved.

Remember, we are in an unseen battlefield now. Bombs of destruction come close when a family member is ensnared in addiction, sins of the flesh, love of the world, or abortion as a personal comfort solution. We witness the carnage of the devil in broken people all around the world who have either relinquished their minds to him or have gotten their sound mind from Jesus Christ in faith (Chapter 6). It's a choice even after salvation.

From ground zero of salvation, we are equipped for the adventure of the Great Commission with soldier status. Yahweh provides us with fighting gear,[10] His powerful gifts,[11] unique calls to action, and the keys of binding the dark side's effectiveness that release captives into Life.

When we spiritually bind by verbal rebukes, restrictions against further harm, and citing the blood of Jesus' sacrifice, Satan's works within them is stopped then. Jesus says "...and whatever you bind on earth will be bound in heaven." There is agreement and backup in heaven by the Recorders of Life. The unexplored "whatever" category is what we figure out through the Holy Spirit as we travel time on our journey.

Faith expands.

We love to worship Him, feel His anointing, be led by His voice, be immersed in His love and get blessings to succeed in sharing His message, teaching the weak, and getting new assignments for the battle zone. So, on this side, we have fun and purpose with going on rescue missions and using our gear.

What we spiritually loose and release from Satan's grip that has held the wandering, deluded, and weakened believers and the unsaved stuck in place by his little demon sprites, will be recorded in heaven on their books. God's saving gospel combined with bringing healing and miracles as *'signs following'* us, and the frontal assault on battle lines using exorcism, brings a corresponding accord in heaven to affirm the victories. They rejoice, too.

New beginnings for Seekers and fresh warriors are reconciled to Father, on our side. The score is updated moment by moment.

PRINCIPLE #2 For Saved Believers

There is another context besides soul-saving as recorded in this Matthew passage found in chapter 18:18. This binding and loosing principle deals with a sinning brother or sister in Christ, not with the unsaved. These are the ones in a local ekklesia fellowship who swallowed Satan's lie, sinned against themselves, and trespassed God's Lordship. They are at the prayer room finding themselves as the center of Ekklesia discipline before the elders.

Here we see a method of cleansing the fellowship of the rotted apple, so to speak. This does not happen in seeker-friendly, religiously comfortable, and Laodicean churches because corrupting sin is not monitored or disciplined. People move on to more comfortable surroundings to hide out.

Binding Satan's authority comes after binding one's sin that has captured them. Authority over us relates to forgiveness.[12] This is on two levels. Either God's forgiveness of our trespasses at salvation or our forgiving of other's sins against us in the fellowship.

This is a critical point in the deliverance minister and ministry. When forgiveness is withheld (a) by God because there is no faith to believe Him and repent or, (b) by a person because of their hardness of heart. That last position is deadly for deliverance.

This is a real barrier behind which tormenting spirits hide behind should the elders exhaust all efforts at reconciling to God or man, are *"...given over to the tormentors"*[13] You will never lose salvation, but you will not enjoy the Holy Spirit Who is distanced by your unforgiving arrogance.

The forgiveness of others directly relates to having answered prayer. Jesus was teaching on this issue that would nullify the keys He gave us, so we must give this for Seekers who want deliverance for themselves, but want no deliverance for those they won't forgive. Peter is again our spokesman for all the disciples.

> *"Lord, how often shall my brother sin against me, and I forgive him? Up to seven times?"*
>
> I can just see the smirk on Peter's face.
>
> *Jesus said to him, "I do not say to you 'up to seven times, but up to seven times seventy."*

The point Jesus was making that even 490 times is a large number of undetermined opportunities to forgive someone. Imagine having a fellow brother or sister in your life that trespasses that much against you/ This could only refer to a long-term relationship by blood or marriage as a relationship that is unavoidable for years.

So, are we being told that there may be difficult, obnoxious, un-relenting trespasses made against you in your lifetime to constantly forgive, so you remain clear before the Father and have your prayers answered? We must love by forgiveness that much? Well, now.

Breakage needs repair, not discard, not divorce.

We are committed to praying for the growth of that trespasser—right in our circle—as they are becoming molded into the image of Jesus Christ. The forgiveness test is long term.[14] It apparently benefits the 'victims' more than the trespassers. Jesus is not speaking of physical abuse or violence in the home or church which has other ramifications. He told us to forgive (dismiss, loose, let go) any offenses against our sensibilities and standards that will become bitterness and an open path from torment.

Following Christ is not for wimps![15] Look at the consequences in the Seeker asking for understanding and wounding done against them by trespassers, and some with very, very serious sins, impacting them in childhood, in marriages, by accidents, or wrong choices. Still, we forgive.

Suffering it out means an intentional application of God's love to them. This is the weapon to overcoming the evil toward you and releasing the evil influencers in them causing the pain.

[1] Revelation 20:14. This whole passage relates to the Great White Throne Judgment of people not written in the Lamb's Book of Life. It does show when Death and Hell will be terminated into the lake of fire burning forever. 1 Corinthians 6:3 says that we will judge (evil) angels; 2 Peter 2:4-11. Mark 1:23-26 is another unclean spirit Jesus speaks to.

[2] Mark 5:1-20.

[3] Romans 10:8-12 is God's plan of salvation that is key to His gates of heaven.

[4] Matthew 6:5-15. Why make this petition when it is not believed or carried out?

[5] Matthew 7:13-14. Wide are Hell's gates to destruction. Heaven's are narrow and difficult to find because the human spirit must come to life by faith.

[6] Revelation 21:12.

[7] Revelation 20:11-15.

[8] Genesis 3 is rich. Observe closely.

[9] **Plan of Salvation:** Romans 3:23; Romans 6:23; Romans 5:12, Romans 5:8, Romans 10:9-10, and John 3:16-17. The Gospel in a nut-shell: 1 Corinthians 15:1-4.

[10] Ephesians 6:10-18.

[11] **Gifts of the Father** (Rom. 12:3-8; Acts 4:36; Heb. 10:25; 2 Cor. 8:2; 9:11-13; 2 Cor. 1:12; 8:2; 9:11, 13).

Gifts of the Holy Spirit (1 Cor. 12:8-10, 28; 1 Cor. 12:7, 14:31; Mark 16:17; Acts 2:4, 10:44-48; 19:1-7; 1 Cor. 12:10, 28-31; 13:1-3, 14:2-32).

Gifts of the Son Jesus (Ephesians 4:11, also 12 Cor. 12:28; Rom. 1:16; Isaiah 6:1-13; 2 Cor. 5:14-20.

Special Graces for service: Hospitality (1 Peter 4:10-11; Matt. 25:35-40).

Celibacy (Matt. 19:10; 1 Cor. 7:7-9, 27; 1 Tim. 4:3; Rev. 14:4.

Martyrdom (1 Pet. 4:12-13, Acts 7:59-60; 2 Tim. 4:6-8. ~ Paul Walker, *New Spirit Filled Life Bible* notes on pages 1849-1858.

[12] John 20:22-23.

[13] Matthew 18:21-31.

[14] Matthew 18:32-35.

[15] Matthew 10:38; 27:32; 1 Corinthians 1:17; Galatians 6:12.

READING 6 - BE DEMON GANG
SPECIFIC: THE LIST

"Quietude, which some men cannot abide
because it reveals their inward poverty,
is as a palace of cedar to the wise,
for along its hallowed courts the
King in His beauty deigns to walk."
~ Charles H. Spurgeon, 1834-1892

Identify Demon Gangs

A word of explanation is in order before reading the various demon *gangs*, as Dr. Derek Prince called them. Be very careful to understand what some of the names on these lists mean. Because some acts or attitudes are named here does not necessarily indicate they are sinful or demonic.

Take for example the term 'debate'. In the case of one having an overpowering tenacity for debate (aggressive argumentativeness), it rises as a possessing force within them; it is enslavement and must be released.

To another person, 'debate' may be a practical way to air facts and opinion or take a scriptural stand in a secular classroom. When it is bible doctrine, it is called an apologetic. Therefore, debate is neither sinful nor demonic but a tool of formal speech.

In a deliverance session, each area must be prayerfully questioned. The Seeker will bear witness to Truth in their spirits whenever the

Word of Knowledge goes forth putting a finger on a besetting sin of theirs. It is helpful for Spirit Warriors to be familiar with the various families to try the spirits for ridding the whole nest at once.

In all cases, the Holy Spirit is your guide and will reveal Himself by His gifts to the praying team. It is also likely that several sessions might be needed by a Seeker over a period of months or years—as he or she is ready to relinquish control and allow God access to heal.

* * *

GANG OF FEAR. All common fears: fear of reproof, trepidation, the fears of animals, germs, viruses, people, heights, loneliness, spiders/insects/reptiles, darkness, death, the unforeseen future, failure, rejection, suffering, pain, the unknown, being robbed, accusations, disapproval, judgment, condemnation, religious figures, public places, small places, blindness, sex, intimacy, poverty, wealth, snakes, demons, madness, and all kinds of fears: whatever a demon can convince a person to be in fear of no matter how small or great.

This is a huge Principality over global affairs to remove freedom from individuals and nations in order to concentrate controlling power to the few. When people are afraid for survival, this spirit overwhelms faith. Other members in this gang may be: insecurity, doubting, unbelief, fear of fears, nervousness, pills, shyness, perpetual timidity, inward anger, passivity, imagined allergies, mind control, a blank mind, or pattern of lifelong unemployment, caused by habitual generational poverty enforced by entitlement fantasies and laziness.[1]

GANG OF LIARS. Lying, perjury, deceit, deception, pretense, exaggeration, pride, falsehood, play-acting the truth, false accusations, faking it; fraud; hypocrisy, wee liar, cute or white lies, black lies, cunning, affectation, fakery, con-man, unreality, insincerity, sophistication, double-crossing, daydreamer, fantasy, theatrics, jaunty spirit, aggrandizement, changed my mind, unfaithfulness, transvestite, homosexual, transgender, confusion, selfishness, broken vows, criminal, thief, sarcasm, cynicism, hopelessness, unbelief, adultery, fornication, slander, gossip, the independent spirit. There is an 'Ananias spirit' which promises God something, then withholds it by lying to the Holy Spirit. It can operate in conjunction with a 'Sapphira spirit' where another person covers or lies as an accessory to the first one's fabrication.[2]

GANG OF PRIDE. Lucifer spirit, pride, 'I am god,' man-divine, vanity, ego, covetousness, greed, arrogance, Antichrist, boastfulness, conceit, pride of body: anorexia, bulimia, muscle man, Mr. Atlas, body fixation, scarification as decoration. There is pride of life, haughtiness, false pride, spiritual pride, pride of competition, vain glory, snobbishness, uppity spirit, elitism, indignation, mockery, superiority, inferiority, extravagance, waste, indulgence, miserliness is false pride; fame, pride of intellect, religious pride (my nation/skin color/denomination is...), bigotry.

Leviathan (king of the children of pride-Job 41:1); top dog, top gun, spiritual eyes blinded, closed spirit, domination, possessiveness, materialism, enlightened, Jezebel spirit, intolerance, loudness to dominate or punish, divorce, rejection, physical and verbal abuse ('I am older, wiser, stronger, better') materialist (I own the most and the best); perfectionism (all or nothing thinking), narcissism, and the Diotrephes spirit ('I am in charge').

GANG OF BONDAGE. Cravings for addictive substances such as marijuana, heroin, narcotics, wild herbs, and mushrooms that are hallucinogenic, prescription drugs that are security-addictive; liquors, wines, alcohol, compulsive caffeine, chocolate, sugar, substance sniffing or vaping, and fetishes. Compatible members in the Bondage gang could include Legion, gluttony, intemperance, self-indulgence, slavery to work, sex, pornography; bondage to religion, racism, a Ku Klux Klan spirit, and anti-Semite.

Political compulsion, Occult masters, submission, sacrifice, self-appointed martyrdom, male or female dominance, liar, heavy metal blasphemous rock music, magic, subliminal suggestion, hypnosis, trance, visualization, gambling, lotto, lottery, bingo, all games of chance for gain; precognition, ESP, handwriting analysis; Ouija, spirit of poverty, ancestor worship, idolatry, and masking.

GANG OF REBELLION. Hostility; malice, hatred, temper, strife, rage, anger, envy, jealousy, mischievous spirit, spite, leprechaun, disputer, backbiting, bitterness, argument, aggression, unreasonable, despising, derision, purposed opposition, division, vengeance, sadism, quarreling, lust, unforgiveness, retaliation, cruelty, meanness, bully, impudence, contention, disobedience, bickering, frustration, slanderer, arson, crime against nature, crime against humanity; vindictive, inhospitable, agitator, nervousness without cause; harsh, cruel, disloyal, treason, insubordination, incivility and mob rule.

Others may include enmity, murder, abortion, suicide, infanticide, genocide, animal murder (killing animals for fun, not for food or safety); bribery, torture, hurtful, mean spirit, bully, slanderer, gossiper, selfish, defile the environment, nonconformity, blasphemy, belittling, raider, destroyer, accuser, pitilessness, stoic, tension, indifference, silence as punishment, hedonism, bully mouth, defiant attitude, independence, unbelief, trouble-maker, gang banger, enforcer, 'I will,' love-killer, Communist, Nazism, traitor, dictator, tyrant, evil discrimination, polygamy (Sister Wives situations), and Absalom spirit (father or mother-hater).

GANG OF THE PSYCHE (Mental /Soul). These attack the soul with schizophrenia, multi-personality, double-mindedness, mental disorders, illness, psychology, vain imaginations, seared conscience, mania, mental weakness, madness, crazy, insanity, derangement, anxiety, intellectualism, doubt, unbelief, paranoia, practical (not medical) retardation, indiscriminate, imbecility, senility, hallucination, tension, worry wart, frustration, divider, incoherent, forgetful (on purpose is a type of lying); nervousness, headache, migraine, dread, nervous habits, restlessness, insomnia, apprehension, stress, gloom, depression, despair, despondency, discouragement, defeatism, defector, complainer, power-monger, and death wish.

Others may include hopelessness, disgust, suicide, morbidity, burden, heaviness, barking, uncanny laughter, skepticism, mind roving, dissatisfaction, control by dreams, cowardice, rash, glum, improvidence, twitching, fidgeting, misery, ignorance, hesitation, pessimism, instability, despondence, melancholy, neglectfulness, loss of memory, faltering, faint-hearted, wavering, overbearing competitiveness, driving spirits; heartache, rationalization, pressure, unnatural grief, sorrowful, depression, oppression, chronic fatigue, unbridled talkativeness, mind control; sectarianism and false religion, delusion, deception, irrationality, panic attacks, argumentative debate to dominate, idolatry, and Legion.

GANG OF PERVERSION (Abnormal to God's Laws). Most of these are compulsions from a power demon that forces a person to do what they do not want to do: lust, vice, lust of the eye, illicit sexual desire, perversity, blasphemy, filthiness, unclean, abusive, passion, ravishment, sex against animals, rape, sodomy, wild affections, anal sex, forced sex, impurity, fornication, rape, adultery, lasciviousness, root of sexual impurity, carnality, dirty dancing, incest (Moab spirit), harlotry, idolatry, provocativeness, filthy thoughts, sodomy, whoredoms, prostitution of body or business; child molestation, pedophilia, sex trafficking, seduction, foulness, vulgarity, defilement, filthy conversation and unclean jesting.

Then there are vices that can be attached to like sexual indulgence, homosexuality, lesbianism, immorality, fantasy lust by sexting, telephone sex, and video sex; all pornography, genital and breast exposure, naked flashing, frigidity, impotence, unfaithfulness, unholiness, fallacious, cunnilingus, degradation, debasement, deprivation, and bestiality.

Auxiliary demons that attach to perversion may identify as love gods/goddesses, Baal, Astarte, Ashtoreth, fertility worship, depravity, inordinate affection for animals, phallic or sexual symbols, nudity, immodesty, Legion, sadism, masochism, sadomasochism, fear of sex, hatred of sex, reprobates, compulsive, tempter, flirt, root of perversion, enticement, Venus, Eros, fetish, torture, unusual crimes against nature, liar, obscenity, playboy, gigolo, stud, playgirl-sexual mistress, and all Sexually Transmitted Disease (STD), and venereal disease (VD).

GANG OF INFIRMITIES (Weaknesses). Blind, deaf, and dumb spirits; convulsion, cancers, fevers, allergies, and pride of allergies;

curse; tumor, epilepsy, narcolepsy, pain, weakness, sickness, infirmity, infection, bronchitis, swelling, cold, pleurisy, heart trouble, death, pneumonia, virus, diabetes, asthma, arthritis, AIDS, and HIV.[3]

Others that may attach to this Strongman are weaknesses in the body and brain areas: Alzheimer's, dementia, crippling, self-pity, worry, attention-stealer, manipulator, fake immaturity, alcoholic, fetus worship, fetus murder, idolatry, rebellion, unbelief, death wish, arthritis (often comes with critical spirit), hate, suicide, euthanasia, reproductive or impotency.

GANG OF RELIGIOUS SPIRITS (Idolatry). Witchcraft, spirit of Baal, Molech, spiritualist, fortune teller, Ouija Board with familiar spirits, psychic readings, voodoo, tea leaf, hand, and cranium reading; numerology, medium-channeled with its familiar spirits, enchantment, wizard, hypnotism, palm reading, table tilting, crystal ball, anything occult, crystals, water witching, warlock, handwriting analysis, automatic writing, horoscope, astrology, pendulum, black and white magic, charms, conjuration, incantation, fetishes, religiousness, ritualism, formalism, legalism, and necromancy

All false religions and cults such as Islam, Moonies, Hari Krishna, Jehovah's Witnesses, Christian Science, Urantia, Rosicrucian, Theosophy, Subuddhi, Unity, Mormonism, Bahaism, Unitarianism, Buddhism, Tao, Hinduism, New Age, One World Unity, Atheism, Mary-Mother of God worship, and Agnosticism.

Religious spirits come in with the false doctrinal materials including the Book of Mormon, Satanic or New Age bibles, dominion theology, devilish piety, anti-Christian propaganda, worldliness, Satan worship, fetish idolatry, false sacrifice, false science, blind obedience, willful disobedience, penance, apostasy, heresy, delusion, false burden, persecution, seance, spirit guides, false compassion, false ministry, darkness, clairvoyant, Jezebel, worship of religious figures (living or dead) or religious icons, saint worship, and idols. Assata, Eckankar (soul travel) remote viewing, Pharisaic spirit, Tarot readings, Faro, bondage, metaphysics, death, and hell worship.

Other possibilities of demon entry doors include: imaginary friends, doctor worship, Goddess Rah, Mark of the Beast, religious symbols Inverted Pentagram, the antichrist symbol of 666, upside-down crosses, broken crosses (e.g., Nazi cross), peace symbols, the hex, unicorn, all-seeing eye (dot in the middle of the forehead), occultic and celestial symbols, satanic-worship symbols, racism and reverse racism, the False Prophet, false religion, false teachers, false apostles, UFO fixation, Philistine spirit, clergy-worship, and an Alexander spirit that undermines authentic spiritual leadership in the ekklesia.

GANG OF SELF-CENTEREDNESS. These hyphenated words each begin with 'self-' and show the direction of centering in the soul area instead of living out of the spirit. We have encountered self-pity, self-will, self-consciousness, self-conceit, self-righteousness, self-content, self-sufficiency, self-justification, self-deception, self-rejection, self-delusion, self-seduction, self-hatred, self-centeredness, self-condemnation, self-indulgence self-adoration, and self-protector. This list can be almost endless because it depends on the priority and idolatry in a life.

Selfishness is any emotion or trait that centers on or around the self-life, guilt(s), hypocrisy, inferiority, shame, slackness, false security, superiority, false peace, grumbling, complaining, fault-finding, neglect, judging, criticism, no self-worth, suspicion, distrust, martyrdom, passivity, escapism, fantasy, withdrawal, stoicism, lethargy, slumbering spirit, inaction, possessiveness, control, shyness, jealousy, and a hasty spirit (me too, me first, me only).

GANG OF WORLDLINESS (Carnality). Love of the world, foolishness, inconsistency, laziness, greed, false success, love of money, generational curse of habitual welfare support, cowardice, insufficiency, wrong diligence, pickpocket, untruthfulness, curse of God, ungodliness, career god, unscrupulous, indolence, dishonesty, pouting, dishonor, vacillation, taking advantage, prosperity idol, 'I deserve' spirit; impulsive, envy, jealousy, covetousness.

Worldliness can ride on procrastination, perfectionism, critical spirit, comparing with man, lust for business, clothes horse, trendsetter, obsession of electronic and mechanical vehicles, vain philosophies, over-education, pride, murder of reputation, bankruptcy, frivolous legal suit, warmonger, merciless, cheater, superficial, know-it-all, mockery, show-off, worldly-wise; the serpent, pride, vain ambition, party spirit, haughty, commercialism, prostitution, politicking for spiritual favor, wastefulness, decadent lifestyle and using money to control.

GANG OF PRINCIPALITIES (Princes of Human-Governed Areas). One World Order, globalism, Islam, Vashti, Jezebel, Herod, Babylon, Leviathan, Behemoth, Apollyon (rules the bottomless pit), Chongo, Gog of Magog, Sodom, Gomorrah, Laban, Jubal, Haman, Antichrist, anti-Semitic, world pride, Santana, Caesars, Greek mythical warring gods (Apollos, Mars, Jupiter, Saturn, Pluto, Hermes); Chaos, Cush, Molek, Moab, Beelzebub, Lord of the Flies, Dagon, The Beast, Powers of the Air, king-of-the-mountain, and False Prophet.

There are power level demons ruling over families, cities, nations, regions, oceans, and continents. The Spirit of Devils and the Red Dragon[4] Legion, Baal, Ashtoreth, Angel of Light, and the Rulers, Authorities and Powers of the dark or netherworld.[5]

This is certainly not an exhaustive list of principalities and powers. Prayer intercessors have stood for their cities and nations to uncover all principalities having power and authority over their geographic areas because the Lord reveals it to them as resistance.

[1] Proverbs 19:15; Ecclesiastes 10:18.

[2] Acts 5:1-11. These spirits are very common in courts of law.

[3] Babies can be born with the HIV virus and many, if not most, can be healed of this disease and grow out of it. Ask when the Seeker contracted the disease.

[4] Revelation 12; 16:14.

[5] Ephesians 6:12.

READING 7 - POLITICAL CORRECTNESS

"But words are things, and a small drop of ink, falling
like dew upon a thought, produces that
which makes thousands, perhaps million, think."
Lord Byron, 1788-1824

Shaking!

A massive amount of nation-shaking began in late 2019 when a military bio-terrorism laboratory weapon in the form of humanly concocted killer viruses, was released from Wuhan, China, that began the worldwide vibrating and setting the spirit of Fear to laughing uproariously.

The Antichrist was out and about somewhere in the shadows.

Their bio-weapon was almost harmless up to 98% who would not die of it because cures were readily available if not blocked. It was not quite as lethal as even the standard viral influenza, its close relative. Standard flu also belongs to the 26 corona-species of viruses including the common cold, HIV, SARS, some cancers, plus other strains. Of course this information was not released for over two years by independent microbiologists.

With time of onset into January 2021, research done by board certified virologists and authentic medical experts, we finally learned that the faulty PCR testing kit was unable to distinguish between various corona virus species as SARS-2/Corona-19, the 'Delta Variant' and common cold. It was reported that people who tested positive but were "without symptoms" probably got that result because they had had a cold or the standard flu within the corona species, at some point in life but did not have the novel, lab-produced China influenza right then.

This was the implementation of deception perpetrated out of greed and twisted ideology of a logical fallacy. The 'plan-demic' as many labeled it, was super-charged by millions of media misinformation downloads on the public that Big Pharma supplied along with the documented lies coming from the Center for Disease Control, an in-dependent for-profit corporation.

Add to that motivation the incentive to float patents on the virulent mixture, with the government paid out monetary benefits for report-ing "positive test results" alarmingly high in hospitals, pharmacies that were paid off so customers could get it free, and miscellaneous jabbers with their own motivations.

It seems the real weapon was never the virus, but would prove to be the Chinese fabricated, unapproved or peer-reviewed, or laboratory tested, mislabeled *vaccine* that is better described as a genetic medical experiment (rDNA). Horrifying to learn was the analysis of the liquid of fragments of human pre-born, aborted fetal tissue, various hard poisons, graphene oxide, and more, with the programmed ability to replicate itself within the body to self-destruct its own immune system by a spike protein.[1]

This was popularly called "the Jab" by medically astute people who would not erroneously continue the lie as "a *vaccine*". It is not a proper vaccine like others before it, and deceived the masses into believing it would either prevent or ameliorate covid symptoms. Still more horren-dous is the specter of the boosters upon boosters pushed to maintain The Lie and cause irreparable, permanent injuries, sterilization in some cases, blood clots, heart damage, neurological disabilities, and death in thousands of cases around the world.

What proved categorically terrifying was to witness the global impact that the spirit of fear generated through worldwide misinfor-mation, controlled Internet networking, and the shutdown of the commercial and social worlds all because of a fear over the possibility of contracting this influence with a death rate of under two percent because of its falsely hyped lethality.[2] The spirit of fear put the submissive mask of paper on millions that was useless but signaled the compliance with The Lie.

Looking at history, the demonic spirits of fear and violence were rampant in the whole earth in Noah's days too. Despite preaching the truth for one hundred years, redemption from destruction came too late because of a lack of faith ruling the earth. That was the first and only time in history when the whole world was shaken and shut down altogether until now, in our days. And, here we are again as Jesus said it would come in the last days.[3]

Take note that a *novel militarized bio-weapon* was used to shut down whole nations, bankrupt them, destroy the middle class's wealth, by eventually forcing the use of completely ineffective facial masking paper and fabric that could not possibly stop a micro virus; basically, they were out to depopulate the world. Social distancing was invented out of thin air, as if an invisible wind-driven microbe, could stop every six feet where the next person stood and not enter the unmasked eyes but would enter only the unmasked nose and mouth. Social distancing serves for Artificial Intelligence (AI) to track only if people are at least six feet apart.

So, common sense and real logic eventually asks, *"Why is the determination of this new world order to force-treat healthy people of a very curable flu with a bogus shot?"*

Here we see the clash of the kingdom of Christ against the kingdom of Satan. For one proof, these false mandates compelled arbitrary church and business closings, stopped food production, denied children schooling (the death rate was less than .06% in children under 18 who contracted it), closed international air travel, covered fraud in the United States' 2020 elections, and forced useless lock downs in homes to fuel the fear of death even more persistently. Constant boosting of these falsehoods made by prolonged media deception (billions of death-at-the-door notifications), further enforced the massive deception by rogue political and economic misinformation until the truth emerged a year or so later.

By summer of 2021, various governments including France, Germany, Canada, Israel, and the United States (the list grows) are forcing a New World Order goal of 100% vaccination, implementing door-to-door confrontations with free jabs. We believe taking the jab is NOT the mark of the beast but could be the precursor to the mark of the beast when the Bill Gate's patented technology of Luciferase ink was granted to create an invisible tattoo that can be read data (health, banking, GPS) in a person's body. On July 11th, 2021, it was internationally announced by the United Nations, the Roman Catholic pope, and many nations and organizations signing on, that this was the first day of the New World Order.

> Would this be the crises of the Second Seal that Christ opened in Revelation 6:4 as the fiery red horse of *"people killing people"* rides into our end times history for the first time?

Where was the Laodicean church in 2020 America, when The United States Constitutional First Amendment of the inalienable rights to speech, worship, and assembly were over-ridden because of a projected, unsubstantiated health threat? Our Christian brother and Justice to the U.S. Supreme Court, Clarence Thomas, assured the nation that our Constitutional rights could not be affected or annulled by anything.

Most churches, in fear and ignorance, voluntarily shut themselves down at illegal political orders, put on facial coverings that effectively stopped preaching, communication and signal submission, voluntarily quitting to sing in worship, make verbal prayers, assemble anywhere, anytime, with anyone? They offered up their influence rather than pushing back tyranny. Many church buildings closed in fear, some permanently, until The Constitution was invoked by a very few courageous Christian attorney warriors whose efforts stopped the overriding liberal governmental nonsense and people arose in the capitols and the streets.

This shameful period will be recorded as the most bizarrely perpetrated hoax on the world, of all centuries. It opened the gate to a Principality of Fear that panicked the world as the Spirit of Amalek destroyed the most vulnerable. Friend, be aware that much evil like this is on the horizon as we clearly read in the opening of the seven Seals, Trumpets, and Vials of *The Revelation*. More, yes, much more to come. That's one reason Spirit Warriors must be emboldened to oppose fear and bring healing to the wounded.

And it causes pause for wonder that, if a mild influenza like Corona-19 can create such chaos, shutdown of freedoms, and unnecessary death as suicides sky rocketed during shutdowns as did domestic abuse and child respiratory illnesses from masking. What will the weapons of the Dragon create next? Will we give up our hard-won liberties for some vague, untested experimental promise of health security? There is no such thing.

Will you take a bogus vaccine[4] filled with aborted human fetal tissue, graphene oxide (90% plus ingredient), mixed with other lethal poisons capable of permanently changing the human DNA forever? Will we take the endless boosters alleging protection from other, fabricated diseases like Delta+, in a panic mode of disinformation? There will be no end to what can be invented and legalized or mandated by the evil side if no resistance is felt by them to desist and back off. This verse bears repeating:

> *"Therefore, SUBMIT TO GOD, RESIST THE DEVIL and he will FLEE from you."*[5]

Why have some church leaders led their fellow believers to distance in pews and pace themselves in aisles, and cower in identified corners marked with measured spots of tape based on nothing at all but political opinion? Why have church members allowed it? Does no one know the word of God or, in our case, the United States Constitution that backs up the Word of God?

Truth is here if you look for it: an almost equal amount of standard virus influenza occurred in this same time period of masking, distancing, home isolation, and non working hours yet prevented nothing. It came as usual in its season.

Their constructed draconian measures were never used in years past to prevent the flu, and it didn't do so in any way this time, as typical reporting data proved. Those were simply behavior control measures obeyed out of fear and not trust in God for keeping and healing them.

More importantly, do we trust the voice of the Holy One who gives discernment into the wiles of the devil and wishes of power-grasping wealthy influential elites, as we stand watch on the walls of the Kingdom of Christ?

> Will you stand watch to:
> *"Give the more earnest heed to the things we have heard, lest we drift away?"*[6]

This book is about Kingdom living with the offense and defense of it. Granted, a Christian believer can go AWOL for short periods or become deserters by intention, leaving the Kingdom by their sin choices. However, while they are standing outside of God's intentions for them, they will become aware that the weaponry of Ephesians 6 is reserved only for those sent by the Holy One into the chaos of the conflicting kingdoms banging on our Kingdom walls in need of rescue. It will not apply to them.

We've looked around the world and seen the shaking with fear, the raising of fists and bricks, the fires and looting started (hardly a protest), to taunt us with obscene panic legislation through congenital lying (in the political and media kingdoms), as millions dumbly retain "social distance", hoping it will all work out in the end.

Do you feel them encroaching our Kingdom walls to make a crevice in our covenant with God to destroy what Christ is to us and promises as unshakable in us? And, we who are the wall watchers, do hear and see it all to warn in alternative media outlets, in church halls where allowed, and among friends to disseminate Truth that sets free.

Spirit Warrior teams are assembled by courageous churches to do the battle as pocket squads who enlighten and rescue those who have been captured and held tightly go free. You meet them at your altars when a call is made for salvation, healing, problems in life, or deliverance. Of the most pitifully needy, are the children abused by sex and slave traffickers with nowhere to hide and no way to escape. These are picked off by the spirit of Amalek[7] working in traffickers across the world and in your city, too.

All sorts of captives need rescuing which Jesus Christ spoke about and authorized to His willing disciples to do in His name. Let's get awake, spiritually, and physically prepared, forewarned, equipped, and organized to do damage to all that conflicts with His will on earth. Millions are waiting to just be saved from the hell on earth they are living in right now.

Welcome to The Solution.

[1] Dr. Sherri Tenpenny

[2] Dr. Lee Merritt, Dr. Judy Mikovits, Dr. Jerry Tennant, Dr. David Martin, and many other doctors and virologists reveal the experimental genetic engineering (a.k.a., "vaccine") ingredients. Please do your research into valid science and not media misinformation feeds.

[3] Matthew 24:37

[4] James 4:6-10

[5] Hebrews 2:1-4

[6] Numbers 24:20; Deuteronomy 25:17-19. The Amalekites as a nation were destroyed but their demons were released and are roaming the earth today selecting victims who are the most tired, weary, and struggling in life.

APPENDIX A - THE DECLARATION OF FAITH

*"...if you **confess with your mouth** the Lord Jesus and **believe** in your heart that God has raised Him from the dead, **you will be saved.** For with the heart, one believes unto righteousness and with the mouth confession is made unto salvation." ~ Romans 10:9*

Dear Lord Jesus,

I am Your child and fully trust You for my salvation from death and its consequences. Thank you for dying for my sins and bringing me into Your family.

I agree with the Father, that You gave me eternal life and this life is in You who came in the flesh, died, and rose from death in victory.

I confess that Jesus Christ is my God and the only begotten Son of God and I give ALL my allegiance, my life, and my love to You Lord Jesus, with my body, soul, and spirit.

I ask You now to be the only lord of my life and repent of every instance of disobeying You and going my own way. Forgive my pride.

I forgive all people who have offended me. Please forgive me of the trespasses I have made against You and others, and deliver me from evil.

Because of this confession of my faith, I now take every part of my soul, body, spirit, authority, and destiny that I allowed Satan and evil spirits to take advantage of.

By the testament of the blood of Jesus Christ, I declare that evil has no place in or around me and command it to depart.

For it is in your Honorable Name, Lord Jesus, and with these witnesses, and by my position as your child, I thank You Jesus.

Amen and again I say, Amen.

APPENDIX B - CONFESSION OF TRIUMPH

"He who overcomes shall inherit all things,
and I will be his God and he shall be My son." ~ Revelation 21:7

The Confession of Triumph (victory) *is* compiled with directed scriptures that can and will renew your mind and assist in conforming you to the image of Jesus Christ. There is power in the confession of the mouth that goes into the human spirit, out to the Heavenly Father, and to all principalities and powers that can hear and realize that the confessor means commitment to Almighty God. This is a verbalized threat to their position.

As a preliminary to deliverance, the prayer team and Seeker may read this together as an affirmation of their spiritual positions. It is best to Read Aloud with Conviction.

For post-deliverance follow-up, the Seeker will find this confession very strengthening in devotional times and at any time of stress and attack. There is no special feature about this confession other than repeating the Word of God to your spirit. It is not a substitute for prayer or Bible reading. Think of it as an aid to focus on the promises of God to you as His beloved child.

My Confession of Triumph

HOLY, HOLY, HOLY IS THE LORD GOD ALMIGHTY:
WHO WAS, AND IS,
AND IS TO COME.[1]

You are worthy, our Lord and God, to receive glory and honor and power for you created all things, and by your will they were created and have their being.[2] Worthy is the Lamb who was slain to receive power and wealth and wisdom and strength and honor and glory and praise![3]

I CONFESS and BELIEVE that Jesus is the Christ and that I am born of God. I love you God, my Father, and want to obey and carry out Your commands.[4] This, my faith, has overcome the world. My righteousness comes from God through my faith in the blood of Jesus Christ.

Therefore, I no longer have any condemnation or guilt because I am in Christ Jesus and the Spirit of Life has set me free from the law of sin and death.[6]

I have the Word of God in me because I have confessed my sins and have been purified from all unrighteousness.[7] I came to Jesus because the Father enabled me to come and I speak the Words of Life because they are the Words of Christ which are Spirit and Life.[8]

I have taken off my old self with its practices and have put on the new self which is being renewed in knowledge to the image of its Creator. Therefore, I am a new person: holy, dearly loved, clothed with compassion, kindness, humility, gentleness, and patience. I have the Peace of Christ ruling in my heart.[9]

Jesus Christ came by water and by blood and His Spirit testifies to this truth, for these three agree and I testify that I have eternal life because Life is in the Son and I have the Son.[10]

I have followed Christ in water baptism according to His example and have been baptized in the Holy Spirit. I came to Jesus Christ because I was thirsty and I drank [11] Since I have believed in Him as the scripture has said, streams of living water flow from within me.[12] I have received the baptism of the Holy Spirit with fire and am made complete. [13]

I ACCEPT and BELIEVE that You, O Lord, will fulfill Your purpose for me; that Your love endures forever...for You have searched and known me even when I sit and when I rise. You, God, perceive my thoughts and are familiar with all my ways. You hem me in from behind and before and have laid Your hand of blessing on me [14]

Now the Spirit witnesses with my spirit that I am His child heir, and joint-heir with Christ because I do share in His sufferings.[15] I can do everything through Him who gives me strength[16]

I CLAIM TO BE FILLED BY THE HOLY SPIRIT with the knowledge of His will through the gifting of spiritual wisdom and understanding[17]

I do, right now, offer my body as a living sacrifice to God which is holy and pleasing to Him. It is my spiritual act of worship. I choose not to be conformed to the pattern of the world but to be transformed by the renewing of my mind.[18]

Now my God has rescued me from the dominion of darkness and brought me into the kingdom of the Son He loves.[19] My mind is set on the right, the lovely, the admirable: on all that is excellent and praiseworthy. I choose to think about these things.[20]

I HAVE THE MIND OF CHRIST.[21] I am paying attention to the words the Lord is telling me by keeping them in my heart for they are Life and health to my whole body. Above all else, I am guarding my heart for it is the wellspring of my life.[22]

I have called on the Name of the Lord so there is deliverance for me. I am among the survivors and He has called me.[23] I am close to the Lord for He is close to the brokenhearted and saves those crushed in spirit. I have been delivered out of ALL my troubles.[24]

I know that in all things God works for my good because I love Him and am called to accomplish His purposes. Therefore, God is for me and who can be against me? None! for Christ intercedes on my behalf.

Who shall separate me from the love of Christ? Not trouble, hardship, persecution, famine, nakedness, danger, or the sword because...

I AM MORE THAN A CONQUEROR through Him who loves me.[25] The Lord is my Shepherd so I will fear no evil when He prepares a table of blessing for me before my enemies! Goodness and love follow me all the days of my life and I choose to dwell in God's presence forever.[26] For You are my hiding place; You will protect me from trouble and surround me with songs of deliverance.[27]

I SUBMIT MYSELF TO YOU, Father. I actively resist the Devil and all his hordes and he—even now—flees from me![28] Jesus Christ has given me authority to trample on snakes, scorpions, and to overcome all the power of the enemy.

NOTHING WILL HARM ME. I do not rejoice because spirits must submit to me, but I rejoice that my name is written in heaven.[29]

I intend to be strong in the Lord and in His mighty power. Therefore, by an act of my will I put on the full armor of God so I can take my stand against the devil's schemes. For this reason, my struggle is not against flesh and blood but against all rulers, authorities, and powers of this dark world and against all the spiritual forces of evil in heavenly realms.

I AM STANDING MY GROUND and when I am through with this battle on earth and everything else, I INTEND TO REMAIN STANDING.[30]

Right now, I am putting on the belt of truth, buckled around my waist; the breastplate of righteousness over my heart; my feet fitted out with the readiness that comes from having the Gospel of Peace within.

In addition to all this, I take up the shield of faith with which I can extinguish ALL the flaming arrows of the evil one. I take my helmet of Salvation and the sword of the Spirit which is God's Word. I will pray in the Spirit on all occasions, keeping alert for God has rescued me from this present evil age.[31]

I TAKE THE AUTHORITY of the Christ within me and bind on earth all the powers and principalities of darkness, Satan, demons, devils, evil spirits, carnal spirits, curses, and occult forces in the Name of and by the Blood of Jesus Christ.

Your promise is that those things are now bound in heaven. Likewise, I now take authority to accept the power of the Holy Spirit in me and over my family, releasing everything that Satan had bound so I may live in the very blessings of my Father. Be done now, in Jesus' Name[32]

I acknowledge and confess that I am from God and have overcome every spirit that denies Christ has come in the flesh. I have overcome the spirit of Antichrist because the One who is in me is far greater than the one who is in the world.[33]

I CONFESS by an act of my will that I am born of God and will not continue to sin because I choose not to sin. God keeps me safe from the evil one who cannot harm me. Even if the whole world is under the control of the evil one, Jesus Christ is True God and Eternal Life and will return for me at the appointed time.[34]

As acts of the Renewed Mind within me, I WILL be joyful always, to pray continually, and to give thanks in all circumstances for now this is God's will for me.

I CHOOSE to not put out the Holy Spirit's fire or to treat prophecies with contempt. I will test everything; hold on to the good and avoid every kind of evil so that the God of peace may sanctify me through and through in my whole spirit, soul, and body to be kept blameless until Christ's return.[35]

And just as I received Christ Jesus as my Savior, Deliverer, Healer, and Friend, I will continue to live in Him, rooted to the depths of my being and built to the heights of my potential.[36] O Lord, I am confident that You have shown me a most excellent way to behave, and I embrace LOVE.[37]

I ACTIVELY PLUCK the FRUIT Of The HOLY SPIRIT so that the very character of God may be grown in my inner spirit. I appropriate Love as Joy, Peace, Patience, Kindness, Goodness, Faithfulness, Gentleness, and Self-control, choosing to live by the Spirit and keep in step with Him [38] I will bear fruit in every good work.[39]

By an act of my will, I am rejoicing now and will rejoice in all things. I want my gentleness to be evident to all because the Lord is near at hand.

I WILL NOT TO BE ANXIOUS about anything but in everything by prayer and petition, with thanksgiving, present my requests to God. By this means the peace of God will transcend my human understanding and will guard my spirit and mind in Christ Jesus.[40]

Thank you, my precious heavenly Father, that I am a chosen person, a holy nation, a child belonging to You so that I might declare the praises of Christ who called me out of darkness into His wonderful light.[41]

MY HOPE IS GOD, that in that day, You will spread your tent over me and never again will I hunger. Never again will I thirst. The sun will not beat upon me nor any scorching heat for the Lamb at the center of the throne will be my Shepherd and You will lead me to springs of living water; and God will wipe away every tear from my eyes.[42]

Amen, praise and glory and wisdom and thanks and honor and power and strength be to our god forever and ever.

Amen and again I say, AMEN![43]

KEYS To The CONFESSION Of TRIUMPH

Every sentence in the Confession of Triumph (victory) is bible-referenced. You are concurring with God's word as truth for you. Reading it brings you into agreement with the Lord Jesus Christ in the themes listed with their scripture citations.

The Confession of Salvation

1. Revelation 4:8
2. Revelation 4:11
3. Revelation 5:12
4. 1 John 5:1-6 9
5. Romans 3:22-25
6. Romans 8:1-2
7. 1 John 1:9
8. John 6:63-65
9. Colossians 32:10

The Confession of Water Baptism

10. 1 John 5:7-12 11
11. Acts 10:47

The Confession of Holy Spirit Baptism

12. John 7:37-39
13. Matthew 3:11

The Confession of Assurance of Salvation

14. Psalm 138:8-139:1-5
15. Romans 8:16-17
16. Philippians 4:13
17. Colossians 1:9-11

The Confession of Deliverance, Healing and Health

18. Romans 12:1-2
19. Colossians 1:13
20. Philippians 4:7-8
21. 1 Corinthians 2:16

22. Proverbs 4:7-8
23. Joel 2:32
24. Psalm 34:16-17
25. Romans 8:28-38
26. Psalm 23
27. Psalm 32:8

The Confession of Authority for Spiritual Warfare

28. James 4:7
29. Luke 10:19-20
30. Ephesians 6:11-17, 31
31. Galatians 1:4

The Confession of Power to Bind Evil

32. Matthew 18:18-33
33. 1 John 4:4

The Confession of Walking Worthy and in Blessing

34. 1 John 5:18-20, 36
35. 1 Thessalonians 5:16-25
36. Colossians 2:6-8

The Confession of Having the Fruit of the Spirit

37. 1 Corinthians 12:31-13:13
38. Colossians 1:10-11
39. Galatians 5:22
40. Philippians 4:4-7

The Confession of Thanksgiving and Praise

41. 1 Peter 2:9-10
42. Revelation 7:15-17
43. Revelation 7:12

APPENDIX C - GLOSSARY OF TERMS

Abortion—The willful taking of a human life in utero during the nine-month period of pregnancy. It is a human life sacrifice to the devil before the idol of "self". God is the Master of Life which is extremely sacred. Miscarriages are natural as God-allowed expulsions and are not to be confused with willful, malicious abortion (Psalm 139:13).

Absalom Spirit—Conspiracy to steal royal or governmental power and authority by malcontent deceit; usually from an insider position (Absalom, 2 Samuel 15).

Abyss—Conceived of as the subterranean abode of demonic hordes (Rev. 20:1; Luke 8:31). The Greek word means very deep, a bored hole, and in the New Testament only, "the bottomless pit". In the Hebrew language it is Sheol for the primordial dungeon (Gen. 1:2, and 7:11; Proverbs 8:28). It is a place set apart by God for confinement of this Principality in regions below the earth, on the level of Satan as a Principality in the regions of air and land when human exist. By Revelation 20, Abaddon in Hebrew and Apollyon in Greek is the king of the bottomless pit (Rev. 9:1-11), not Satan who will be bound and chained there 1000 years under Apollyon's authority.

Adrenochrome—is a natural compound found in the adrenal glands that spike during moments of fear or terror and is incredibly addictive. It is said to be harvested by killing children after taking their raised adrenochrome level of blood used in satanic rituals and for maintaining a youthful body.

Aesculapius—The Greece-Roman god of medicine. It has been a serpent symbol of medicine for hundreds of centuries.

Ahriman—A hostile spirit: Ahura Maula's antagonist who is a spirit of darkness and evil in Zoroastrianism.

Amalek spirit—Taken from the curse God put on the Amalekite nation in Deuteronomy where they did not honor Israel but took out the old, infirm, stragglers, livestock handlers with sheep and goats as they left the Red Sea and Egypt behind. As these evil spirits were disembodied, they like all spirits, search for a new house; tormentors of those who are weak, down, depressed, or sickly.

Amulet. An ornament or charm supposedly charged with magical powers and used to ward off spells, disease, and bad luck.

Ancient One. A name sometimes given to an officiating priestess at a Black Satanic Mass.

Anorexia Athletica. Compulsive exercise and compulsive weight loss starvation combined.

Anorexia Nervosa. This is an eating *disorder* (indicates that the normal function of the mind and/or body is impaired) characterized by compulsive, chronic self-starvation with a refusal to maintain a body weight within 15% of a person's normal weight. Condition may be from a distorted body image, irrational fear of weight, or obsessive-compulsive (scrupulosity) mindset of obeying some religious ideation.

Apep. This is an Egyptian term that is the same as the Greek name for the ancient Egyptian enemy of Ra (Sun god). Apep, the 'Uncreator'; a serpent dwelling in the middle dual earth of total darkness (bottomless pit). It is believed to try to swallow Ra and steal the rising of the sun each day. Apep is held at bay (never conquering light) by Set, the ancient Egyptian god of chaos.

Apophis. The descriptive name given by NASA to Asteroid-99942 as the god of chaos. Astrophysicists have ruled out a strike to earth on April 13, 2029, or in 2036, or 2068 being too far outside the earth's orbit for the next 100 years. However, the Third Trumpet judgment could be an asteroid strike (Revelation 8:10-11) named by God as *Wormwood.*

Apophis. Second definition. A giant serpent demon worshipped in Egyptian mythology. Its demonic influence has characteristics with contrasting qualities that make it difficult for people to understand another person (or the gospel) and can lead to friction in the personal life. The root is **apophasis**—denial, repudiation, to deny, be away from or be off topic. It is a popular strategic manipulation creating misinformation (chaos); an abuse of language to cause a lie (fallacy) look like truth. Metaphorically, the darkness serpent trying to eat Ra (light) and rob it of rising each day.

Arcana. A secret process or formula; the 22 Tarot pictorial cards make up the major Arcana and 56 (or 52) cards divided into four suits are the minor Arcana. See Tarot and Tarok.

Artemis—Greek for Roman goddess *Diana-Cybele,* the mother goddess of fertility worshipped in Asia Minor as the "many-breasted, Men from heaven" (Acts 19:24-25, an Ephesian deity).

Ashtoreth. Goddess of love, fertility, and war. Often paired with a male deity like *Baal.* Female deities such as *Ashtoreth* (consort of *Baal)* and *Asherah* (consort of *EL,* the chief god of the Canaanite pantheon). *Ashtoreth* was associated with the evening star and was the beautiful goddess of war and fertility. She was worshipped as *Ishtar* in Babylonia and as *Astarte* in Aram (Arabia). To the Greeks, she was *Aphrodite,* and to the Romans, *Venus.* Worship of the *Ashtoreth* involved extremely lascivious practices (1 Kings 14:24; 2 Kings 23:7).

Astral Projection. Symbolized by a witch on a broom; the demonic empowering through a person's spirit to project his or her soul away and apart from their body (out-of-body experiences, soul flying) to another location where they can see, hear, touch, and smell. It is ungodly and a part of the fallen nature that is used by Satan and in witchcraft.

Augury. The divination from omens or portents predicting things to come to pass from chance events as the fall of lots or dice.

Avatar. A concept in Hinduism within Hinduism that in Sanskrit literally means 'descent'. It signifies the material appearance or incarnation of a deity on earth; to make one's appearance. Software is developed create one's own avatar (lookalike) or cartoon figures, r used to play games.[1] Avatars are idols and strictly forbidden for Christ followers to create, use, tattoo on the body, view movies/videos; use to consult with demonic avatar images, using Bitsrips,™ Bitmoji™ or emoji or other apps, created for self-representation. These apps are harmful, able to collect users' information and data. We are made in God's image alone.

Baal. A word meaning "lord". Baal, the god worshiped by the Canaanites and Phoenicians, was variously known to them as the son of *Dagon* and the son of *El*. In Aram (Syria), he was called *Hadad* and in Babylonia, *Adad*. Believed to give fertility to the womb and life-giving rain to the soil, he is pictured as standing on a bull, popular symbol of fertility and strength (1 Kings 12:28). The storm cloud was his chariot, thunder his voice, and lightning his spear and arrows. The worship of Baal involved sacred prostitution and sometimes child sacrifice (Jeremiah 19:5).

Bacchus. The Greek god of fermented drink or wine (*Dionysus*); excess revelry, orgies, addiction; the glorification of drunkenness and the "party spirit".

Baculum. A witch's wand, staff, or broomstick.

Balaam Spirit. Balaam was a corrupt teacher and false prophet who deceived God's people into compromise with worldliness. Balaam advised the Midianite women how to lead the Israelites away from God (Numbers 25:1-2, 31:16, Jude 11) into sin.

Black Magic. Greek word is *magéia;* sorcery. Destructive magic (supernatural powers) used for harm, deceit, and destruction; Satanists used black magic rites to cast incantations and curses (Rev 21:8; 22:15).

Black Mass. A travesty of the Christian mass (the Eucharist or Lord's supper) by which Satanists blaspheme God and ridicule Christianity; possible human sacrifice, the drinking
of human or animal blood and other abominable practices.

Blessing. The favor of God, fruitfulness, prosperity, right relationship with God. NOTE: only God can bless: Satan and his agents cannot bless. Humans can bring and be a blessing to themselves, to other humans, to creation, and to God.

Bottomless Pit. In Hebrew, the word for bottomless pit is Sheol (most likely grave). Unlike hell that has gates and a broad pathway leading to it (Matthew 7:13), Sheol is the body's final resting place. Also, a prison, dungeon, dry fountain/cistern, pit in the earth, or well bore. Also, a trap of destruction—corruption, ditch, grave. The king of the bottomless pit is a powerful fallen angel named Abaddon (OT Hebrew) and Apollyon (NT Greek) of Revelation 9:1-2, 11:7. It is only found in Revelation.

Bulimia. Greek "great hunger". A psychological eating disorder characterized by repeated or sporadic binge and purge episodes; over time, some bulimics ruminate (unforced regurgitation, chewing, and re-swallowing food) food. Bingeing is an un-restrained consumption of large amounts of food in any setting in a short amount of time. Purging may be done by the intentional vomiting of food or by using laxatives and urinary diuretics.

Cantrip. A spell cast by a witch; a witch's charm against others to their harm.

Channeling. A New Age term for demon possession where a consenting human allows his or her own spirit and voice to be used as the "channel" for an evil spirit's manifestation. Some channelers have familiar spirits with names like Lazarus, Seth; Saint Germain, Mafu, "Jesus", Abraham Lincoln, or Ramtha; they charge fees to allow the spirits to make appearances or teachings and are used as a mouthpiece for New Age literature coming straight from the mind of Satan in the form of "bibles" and "prophecies". This is an international phenomenon and popular with some movie stars and world leaders.

Charm. Chanted or spoken words used to invoke a spell; a specific object said to have supernatural powers.

Clair-audience. The power or faculty of hearing something audible not present to the ear but regarded as having objective reality.

Clairvoyant. A person who uses clairvoyance which is the power or faculty of discerning objects not present to the senses; ability to perceive matters beyond the range of ordinary human perception.

Compulsion. The state of forcing oneself or being forced to behave in a prescribed way, as the compulsive washing of hands; rituals, excessive cleaning, compulsive eating, or fasting food. These actions may be thought to ward off super-stitious substances (germs); using objects or behaviors in religious ways as chants or tokens that prevent bad things from happening.

Coven. A group of Satanists or witches and warlocks, usually numbering not more than 13 (six males, six females, one leader), which meets regularly to worship Satan and work evil spells.

Curse. A charm or spell designed to cause harm or be destructive cast by Satan's representatives such as witches, in rock music, some rap, etc.; by humans, God's agents, and prophets. God Himself can bring curses in certain circumstances (1 Samuel 19:9).

Demons or "Devils". To occultists: any non-human spirit. According to the Word of God, the Devil (there is only one) is a rebellious angel who forsook God, was thrown out of heaven and now roams the earth seeking entrance in or against humans, animals, or objects in order to molest, vex, harass, destroy, kill, and embolden breaches between humankind and God. Such demons could cause mental disorders (John 10:20), violent actions (Luke 8:26), bodily disease (Luke 13:11,16), and rebellion against God (Revelation 16:14). Their purpose is to kill and take people into Hell with them as they obey their lord and master, Satan.

Diotrephes Spirit. Arrogant, dictatorial spirit of a church leader who gossips and expels members out of the fellowship one way or another; dividing the sheep from leadership (3 John 9).

Divination. The practice to seek, foresee, or predict future events or discover hidden knowledge gained by the interpretation of omens and with the aid of super demonic powers; corrupt prophetic utterances; prognostication.

Divining Rod. A forked rod or stick believed to indicate the presence of water or minerals when it dips downward over a location as a result of spirit input.

Djinn. Also known as Al-jinn or the magic genii (in English "Genies") reside or are trapped inside magic bottles or lamps; jinn, jann, ginn, shayatin, or shaytan. In pre-Islamic folklore, this race of spirit beings is a variety of interfering spirits of high intelligence, able to rule over entire kingdoms, but unseen by humans; often thought to be either benevolent if let out of the lamp, or vengeful and demon-like upon release. They are not quite so evil as demons since they are unable to affect humans with god-Allah's will. Said to possess supernatural powers that must be conjured in special magical rites by a djinn Witcher to perform various good or vengeful services or deeds. In the Greek, they are the Daimones. Yes, they are demons.

Dragons. Dragons abound in the mythology of ancient peoples: *Leviathan* in Canaanite lore, *Set-Tython*, the red crocodile of Egypt. Metaphorically used to depict the enemies of God and of Israel (Rev. 12:3, Ps 74:14, Ezra 29:3).

Eckankar. An organization teaching that man can only reach an advanced spiritual state by communicating with "spiritual travelers" and other "highly developed persons in the other worlds" (these are actual demons). They use soul travel and out-of-body experiences in this religion.

Ekklesia and ekklesia. When Ekklesia is capitalized, it indicated the world-wide Church body. When not capitalized, it indicates local fellowships of believers organized to follow the New Testament model of governance with the offices of teacher, pastor, evangelist, prophet, and apostle, functioning as individual believers all using their gifts during the assembly. The modern model of one pastor in charge of a congregation is not biblically sound and never planned. Ekklesias have elders that oversee the congregation's needs.

Familiar (Family) Spirit. A demonic spirit who serves a witch or medium, or who inhabits animals; appears at seances and may act as an impersonating agent. Demons who are *familiar* means they are in affiliation. These lying spirits manifest experiential knowledge or lie to carry out tasks for mediums, witches, and Satan.

Free Masonry. A Satanic-Lucifer worshiping religion and secret society which Christians are forbidden to join. Their god is **Baphomet,** a fake deity allegedly worshiped by the Knights Templar that subsequently became incorporated into various occult and Western esoteric traditions. The name *Baphomet* appeared in trial transcripts for the Inquisition of the Knights Templar starting in 1307. It first came into popular English usage in the 19th century during debate and speculation on the reasons for the suppression of the Templar order. Baphomet is a symbol of balance in various occult and mystical traditions (including Free Masonry), the origin of which some occultists have attempted to link with Gnostic, Hermetic, Cabbalists, and Templars, although purported to be a deity or a demon. Since 1856, the name *Baphomet* has been associated with the '**Sabbatic Goat**' image composed of binary elements representing the 'symbolization of the equilibrium of opposites' of half-human and half-animal, male and female, good and evil represented by breasts and an erect penis (non-binary) with Masonic symbols and two goat horns. (Wikipedia).

Gargoyles. A hideous figure of a grotesque human or animal form used as practical or decorative features on buildings or furniture thought by pagans to ward off evil spirits; images of demons.

Gnome. An ageless, often deformed "fanciful" dwarfed figure who lives in the earth and guards precious, unmined ore or treasures; an elemental being in the theory of Paracelsus (1493-1541 AD) that inhabits the earth. Popular figures used in fairy tales and garden landscaping.

Gnostic. False prophets speaking under the influence of spirits alienated from God; they must be biblically tested (1 John 4:1-4). One of the most dangerous heresies of the first two centuries and rampant today, it teaches that the human spirit is entirely good and matter (body) is entirely evil; salvation to them is the escape from the body achieved not by faith in Christ but by special knowledge. An ascetic and licentious religion.

God. *Elohim Yahweh Jehovah* in Hebrew. He is one Holy God in three personality manifestations: as God the Father, God the Son-Jesus Christ, and God the Holy Spirit. His power is overall. He is Lord of lords, King, of all kings. These names reveal Who He is:

1. Jehovah-Tsidkenu - Jehovah Our Righteousness
2. Jehovah-Kadesh - Jehovah Who Sanctifies and Keeps
3. Jehovah-Shalom - Jehovah Is Peace
4. Jehovah-Shammah - Jehovah Is There; the ever-flowing, ever-present One

5. Jehovah-Rophe - Jehovah Heals and Delivers
6. Jehovah-Jireh - Jehovah's Provision Shall Be Seen
7. Jehovah-Nissi, - Jehovah My Banner (for battle)
8. Jehovah-Rohl - Jehovah My Shepherd

Grimoire. An ancient book of witchcraft spells that belongs to an individual or witch coven.

Groupie. A person, especially a young teen or woman who regularly follows a pop music group or other celebrity in the hope of meeting or getting close to them (Oxford Dictionary).

Heaven. Has 12 gates (portals) that are closed to the unredeemed. Heaven's gates are opened with the three free keys earned by the blood of Christ shed at Calvary, His being raised back to life, and the faith He provides for those who are by faith, "in Him". Christ symbolically gave to keys to His kingdom to Peter upon his confession that *Jesus was the Christ, the Son of the living God* on behalf of the Ekklesia (Matthew 16:16-18); the third heaven represents a permanent home for all who believe in the Messiah Jesus Christ and are born-again (Romans 10:8-13). God's throne is situated there (in Paradise), seated by the Father and Jesus Christ.

Hell. An under the earth (darkness) location of final judgment, with gates (portals) that are open all the time (Matthew 7:13). Jesus earned the keys back from Satan that Adam lost in the Garden of Eden by believing *The Lie.* At the final Great White Throne judgment of God after the Millennial reign of Christ with His saints, Hell and Death, known as the second death, are entirely thrown into the Lake of Fire that burns forever and ever (Revelation 20:11-15).

Holy Bible. The inerrant Word of God consisting of both the Old and New Testaments; to be believed, relied upon, and afforded a place of sacred respect in its often use. Jesus Christ stated, *'Blessed is he who keeps the words of the prophecy of this book"* and, *"Warn everyone who hears the words of the prophecy of this book: if anyone adds anything to them, God will add to him the plagues described in this book. And if anyone takes words away from this book of prophecy, God will take away from him his share in the tree of life and in the holy city, which are described in this book"* (Rev. 22.7). All other bibles are false.

Jesus Christ. The ONLY Lord Christ Messiah; the only begotten Son of the Father, Jehovah-God and partner with the Holy Trinity of Father, Son and Holy Spirit. He is divine God. He was conceived by the power of the Holy Spirit and became incarnate (a human being) from the Virgin Mary (a human, Jewish mother who was not, and is not divine). He lived on earth about 33 years and was always, and at all times, obedient to the Father. He suffered physical death on Calvary's Cross which was His perfect offering to God on behalf of all humanity's penalty of their sin nature, thus freeing humankind from the power of sin and death.

Resurrection. He ascended (rose alive) from the grave in resurrection power, opening the way for eternal life to those who receive Him and live for Him as their only Lord and Savior, enduring to the end. He is returning for His own at the appointed-of-God time (Rev. 14:14-16) in an open show of victory over all principalities, powers, kingdoms, and world systems. He is alive now and presently seated on the heavenly throne at the right hand of God the Father, interceding for the saints. There is no other way of salvation except through personal faith in Jesus Christ as Savior.

Jezebel Spirit. Wresting the authority of a headship from a lawful leader and using that illegally gotten authority for self-purposes. In the church, a male or female who seduces or manipulates a ministry away from the recognized leader. In politics, any hireling that controls the head of state through ill-gotten efforts.

Lady. To Satanists, the female leader of a coven.

Libertine. Partying, sexual orgies, addictive substances used, drunkenness, licentiousness, anything goes immorality; envy, argumentativeness, selfish ambitions, fits of rage, dissensions; vices which gratify the carnal nature, either mentally in libertine philosophies (politics), or in the body to bring unrestrained pleasure (Gal 5:16-21).

Legion—A Roman military legion was made up of 6,000 men. In Mark 5:9, the term suggests possession with many powers opposed to Jesus, and/or numerous demons residing within one person.

Levitation. The act or process of levitating by means held supernatural; to rise or float in the air in defiance of gravitation, usually done during a spiritualistic séance and sometimes in a magic act.

Ligature. A spell (curse) which prevents a person from doing something cast onto them by a witch, warlock, or coven.

Logical Fallacy (untruth). An intentional error in reasoning that renders an argument invalid by its rhetoric. All logical fallacies are non-sequitur; meaning, arguments made in which a conclusion does not follow logically from what preceded it as a preterite (apophasis) strategy that draws attention to a point by seeming to disregard it; e.g., "Abortion is nothing more than getting rid of a blob of tissue, but don't let me influence you."

Luciferase Enzyme. Luciferase is a generic term for the class of oxidative enzymes that produce bio-luminescence (glow) and is usually distinguished from a photo-protein; first used by Raphael Dubois who invented the words luciferin and luciferase, for the substrate and enzyme, respectively. It is an enzyme used for bio-luminescence by various organisms in nature, as the firefly and marine microorganisms. The scientist produces a construct in which the regulatory region of a target gene is fused with the DNA coding sequence for luciferase (Wikipedia). Bill Gates developed and patented this enzyme to be used as an internal body coding method (attaching to graphene oxide)[2] that will enable its reading of personal data; such as an indelible tattoo or marking that can be invisible or irreversible.

Lycanthropy. also known as "a wolf-man, wolf-woman, shape-shifter, were-wolf, or child of the moon is a human being that has the ability to transform into a large wolf at night (usually involuntarily and during a full moon) or on command." (Wikipedia) werewolf; a belief that one has taken on a wolf appearance or possibly another weir-animal, using witchcraft or demonic magic in order to bring physical harm.

Magic. Its root words are *magos* and *magus, mageno* meaning "sorcerer" (of Iranian origin). Used in the occult to influence and control people; the use of charms, spells, and curses believed to have supernatural powers over natural forces; extraordinary negative influence to bewitch and control; tricks of illusion and sleight of hand; enchantment.

Magister. The male leader of a witchcraft coven.

Magis. A male witch as a wizard, warlock, sorcerer, shaman; a conjurer who practices magic arts. Originally, one who performs feats of sleight of hand and illusion; magician, juggler.

Materialization. The physical manifestation of a spirit being; to cause to appear from the dead; to transition from spirit to material form: a vision, apparition, so called, "ghost".

Mantis. Greek root word meaning "diviner, prophet"; akin to be mad or manic; relating to the faculty of divination.

Mantra. "Sacred" counsel and formula from the mind: a mystical form for invocation or incantation (as in Hindu yoga and TM). A mantra is a personalized word-chant (each devotee has his or her own) and is used to put the mind into a blank state for receiving "wisdom". It is unholy to use mystical word(s) to invoke demon spirit guides. The repeated use of religious music/lyrics, smoke machines, and visuals to induce a trance-like state to get "into the spirit" is not God's Way. This was very common with snake handling religions. God never calls us to blank out the mind or lose self-control. Acceptable worship to Him is to worship in truth with the whole spirit, soul, and mind, voluntarily and in love.

Mask. Masque, Maschera; to cover or partially cover the face used for disguise. A figure of a grotesquely carved head or face mask used as adornment by shamans; a keystone that conceals, disguises, or forces silence. This is the pretense of being someone or something supernatural or mythological able to cover over, as sin. Face masks can be used by fear-mongers as a means of controlling people during perceived crises.

Masochism. Sexual perversion of gaining pleasure in physically abused, abusive, tortured, domineering, or being dominated by, the lust object.

Meditation. Godly use of meditation is a Christian's active, self-controlled, and conscious communication going God-ward from the human spirit: it is not possible in a passive trance state.

Ungodly meditation is the practice of relinquishing a mind (soul) to a demonic entity to achieve a bond with the Universal Mind. Common to all eastern religions and in psychology; thought to be a way to "draw on hidden powers from within".

Necromancy. To pray to or attempt to, conjure up the spirits of the dead for purposes of magically revealing the future or influencing the course of events; sorcery. This deception is made through seances, visualization, hypnotism, Yoga exercises and ungodly meditation to contact deceased relatives, famous figures, and even "Jesus". As lying spirits, demons will answer to any names to gain entrance into the seeker.

Necrophilia. An unusually erotic interest in, or stimulation by corpses, the dead, murder, or death; an obsession.

New Age Movement. Religion having four basic tenets: 1) God is all; all is God/ all true reality is divine, 2) Personal enlightenment is necessary since all people live in ignorance of their "divine" nature, 3) All enlightenment comes from the spirit world, altered states of consciousness and psychic powers, and 4) A united world is the solution to human problems by social, economic, religious, and political means. New Agers are dedicated to preparing their followers for a perfect "heaven on earth" by using occultic means.

New Age Symbols. *Pentagram* (five-pointed star), *Enneagram* (nine points within a circle), shapes of triangles, diamonds, circles, crescent moons, *swastikas*, and the *hexagram*. Other tenets are symbolized by suns, rainbows, the lotus, crystals, dragons, serpents, the yin/yang, unicorns, *Pegasus* (flying horse), centaurs, mermaids, Sign of 666, the all-seeing eye, *Egyptian ankh*; by magic wheels, the *mandala circle* for Satan, and by the *karmic wheel* representing birth, death, then reincarnation.

Nine degrees of Evil Spirits according to Heinrich Cornelius Agrippa: *Of Occult Philosophy, Book III, Part 2.*

1. **False gods**. Spirits who usurp the name of God, would be worshipped for gods, and require sacrifices and adoration (Matthew 4, whose prince is *Beelzebub*, an old god also *Lucifer's*
2. **Spirits of Lies.** The lying spirits in the mouth of prophets: *Acab*; of the *Serpent Pytho/Pythias.* Spirits that joined to the Oracles and deludes men by divination and predictions, so that he may deceive.
3. **Vessels of Iniquity** are also called vessels of wrath and death; inventors of evil things and all wicked arts such as Cards and Dice, malice, and deformity: *Belial.* Proceeds from them

4. **Revengers of Evil.** Their prince is Asmodeus, viz., causing judgment.

5. **Deluders** who imitate miracles, serve wicked conjurers and witches, and seduce the people by their miracles as the serpent seduced Eve; their Prince is *Satan* who in Revelation, that he seduced the whole world, doing great signs, and causing fire to descend from heaven in the sight of men...by reason of signs which are given him to do.

6. **Aerial Powers** offers themselves to thundering and lightnings, corrupting the air, causing pestilences and other evils; given them to hurt the Earth and Sea, holding the four winds from the four corners of the earth; their Prince is *Meririm/Meridian Devil*; a boiling spirit whom Paul in Ephesians called the Prince of the Power of this Air.

7. **Furies Possess** which are powers of evil, discords, war and devastation, whose prince in the Revelation is called *Apollyon* and *Abaddon*: that is, destroying and wasting.

8. **The Accusers, Inquisitors** whose Prince is *Astarte,* a searcher out; in Greek is called *Diabolos,* that is an accuser, or calumniator: accuser of the brethren, accusing night and day

9. **Tempters and Ensnares** are in last place, one of which is present with every man, which we therefore call the *evil Genius* and their Prince is *Mammon* interpreted covetousness.

Number of The Beast. 6-6-6 is man's number tripled (Revelation 13:18); the number taken by adherents of New Age philosophy from ancient Babylonia as the triple Aphrodite and by secularists and Satanists.

Numerology. Asian or religious study of the significance of numbers in a person's life/future, to a nation, or any other object in question with each number having a "certain power" relating to occultic connections.

Occult. From the Latin, *occultus,* meaning secret or hidden, to conceal; from hell: not revealed or easily detected or apprehended. The occult refers to secret or hidden knowledge available to Satanist initiates; it is hidden knowledge of the supernatural and deals in parapsychology and paranormal phenomena; involves the action or influence of (evil) unnatural agencies or some secret knowledge about them and is as old as Satan's activity on earth to produce his kingdom.

Oduifa Cult. Drawing from the Uruba people of West Africa is an occult, ancestor worship ping religion where the dead are inquired of to give guidance and provide unnatural powers. The two female founders of the Marxist group, Black Lives Matter (BLM), are reported to have called on the Oduifa spirits to assist their 'protester members' by witchcraft to drive their rebellious, violent acts to higher levels of success.

Omen. A prophetic sign; an occurrence or phenomenon believed to portend a future event; augury, evil divination.

Paradise. Found only in the New Testament three times. A park, orchard, garden (like Eden). It means a very happy, blessed place of the future for the saints. It has never been underground or near Hades (Luke 23:42; 2 Cor. 12:4, Rev. 2:7). The Paradise of God is around His throne, close to Him as a special location in heaven with the Tree of Life and the River of Life right where Jesus took the thief that day.

Parapsychology. Study concerned with the investigation of evidence for telepathy, clairvoyance, and psychokinesis.

Pergamum. Modern Pergamon, Turkey. The ancient capital of Asia, built on a cone-shaped hill rising 1,000 feet above the surrounding valley. Its name in Greek means, *citadel* and is the origin of our word parchment. Satan ruled from Pergamum when it was the official center of emperor worship in Asia (Rev. 2:12-13). Satan rules as the principality over the center of man's world power. Comparing to the modern era, places like New York (UN HQ), London, Beijing, The Vatican, Brussels (World Court/European Union HQ).

Philistine Spirit. OT Philistines are the forefathers of Islamic peoples. The spirit is a continual resistance to permanent control of the land (Israel) and possessions that God has reserved only for His purposes. Spiritual philistines are uncircumcised of heart: they will not be brought under God's authority. Philistines produce Goliaths that fail: God produces Davids with destiny.

Poltergeist. Greek *poltern* = to knock, and *Geist* =spirit or ghost. A noisy, low-level mischievous "ghost" held to be responsible for unexplained noises, tapping, footfalls, shoving, or knocks.

Powers. The devil has supernatural power expressed through psychics, shamans, and willing humans but does not have all the power! Christ followers have more supernatural power (indwelling Holy Spirit) and Christ's authority than demons, the devil, and the demon-possessed have. Spirit Warriors take away demonic power by exorcism.

Precognition. To know an event beforehand; clairvoyance relating to an event or state not yet experienced. A feeling, dream, or visualization that something is going to happen and come to pass. Precognition is Satan's counterfeit of the gift of the Word of Knowledge or a prophetic word from the Lord Holy Spirit.

Psychic. A medium, witch, magus. Greek root *psyche* is soul; knowledge lying outside the sphere of physical science that is immaterial, moral, or spiritual in origin or force. A person who is sensitive to nonphysical or supernatural forces of influence; a person operating under demonic influence out of their soul-state.

Psychology. The secular pseudoscience of the mind and study of human behavior with over 10,000 theories in play. It is involved with manipulating the mind, will, intellect, and emotions (soul) in proscribed manners of treatment, medication, and/or hospitalization. Psychology is worldly-wisdom that attempts to heal or re-arrange the soul outside of proper submission to the Spirit of God. Christians direct themselves to Jesus Christ and the Bible (not psychology) to solve problems from a renewed and re-born spirit.

Psychokinesis. Movement of physical objects by the mind without use of physical means; may be used in conjunction with precognition and telekinesis.

Psychometric. Divination of facts concerning an object or its owner through contact with, or proximity to, the object. Utilized by some criminal investigators to use mediums' occultic contact skills.

Remote Viewing. The practice of seeking impressions about a distant or unseen target, reportedly "sensing" with the mind; genuinely regarded as a pseudo-science. It is associated with GAIA worship, clairvoyance, and sometimes called 'anomalous cognition', or, 'second sight. The difference between natural psychic receptivity and remote viewing is that the latter is a trained skill that the average person can learn when open to it. Strictly, it is forbidden to Jews and Christians to project one's soul to receive demonic information, all without leaving your physical body or geographical location.

Renounce. To formally declare, reject, and abandon; to give up, refuse, or resign a position.

Rulers of Darkness. They only have power over the deeds of darkness. Apol-lyon rules the dark underground regions of the abyss and bottomless pit that never sees light. Demons lose their power of darkness (hideousness) when identified that brings light and understanding.

Sabbat. Occult quarterly or semi-quarterly meeting of witches and Satanists; not to be confused with Shabbat (Sabbath Day).

Sadism. Delight in cruelty; sexual perversion of bringing mental and/or physical pain to the love/lust object.

Satan. Hebrew word is *Satan*, translated directly. Rev. 20:1-3 reveals other names for him as "the dragon", "that ancient serpent", "the devil", "the Accuser," Lucifer and others that include Shiva, Satanas, and Sanat. Satan is the archenemy of God, God's nation Israel, and enemy of all Christ followers. Michael, an archangel of God and protector of Israel, defeated Satan in heavenly warfare (Daniel 12:1). Satan relinquished his powers of Death and Hell when Jesus Christ rose from the dead as conqueror. Now, he has the limited powers of thievery-deception, destruction, and threat of death to afflict evil on people or against nature. He has been since his creation by God, and now is, under complete and full control (Job 1:8-19, Heb 2:14). Christians have been given authority from Christ to resist and expel Satan as Spirit Warriors.

Satyr. Hebrew root word for Satan; it is depicted as a chimera with the lower half as a goat, and upper half as a human male having horns. Later, as a Sylvan deity in Greek mythology. Satyrs are fictionalized as being fond of revelry with lecherous, abnormal, and violent male sexual cravings. It is a New Age symbol for Satan depicted by a goat's head in an inverted pentagram or circle.

Seal. The demon's summoning signature or diagram.

Shabbat, Sabbath. The seventh day of the week.

SIX-SIX-SIX (666). The number of The Beast and identifying mark of the Antichrist that his followers take on or into their body. Can be traced to the ancient Babylonian religion which primarily worshipped a Mother Goddess (The Queen of Heaven of Rev 17). Satan's last days' revival of Babylonians control includes SIX as a number symbolizing the sacramental sexual ecstasy in which worshippers achieve union with the divine universe and with the Queen of Heaven (Ashtoreth, Anath, Asherah, the Great Whore, Babylon the Great, the Mother of Harlots); 666 is a Satanic unholy number representing the *Triple Aphrodite* in an unholy trinity as Mother-Father-Son. The number 69 (one upright 6, one upside-down six) is another obscene sexual symbol. This 666 numeric is a major sign of Free Masonry.

Spirit Cooking. This is a satanic ritual where pig's blood (possibly human blood), fresh breast milk, and fresh sperm are used to act as a medium trying to connect the evil spirits to the material world. This concoction is consumed by worshippers.

Spirit Spouse. A spirit spouse is a demonic spirit that marries a human's spirit and this is normally done in the dream through sexual molestation (intercourse). There can be male or female spirit spouses connected with frequent sex dreams; incubus, succubus, perverse spirits, sexual marine spirits, with evil partners (Yahoo! search).

Spirit Warrior. A born-again Christ-believing, and following Christian who is literally fulfilling the commission of Jesus Christ as stated in Mark 16:15-18.

Spiritualist. A male or female medium calling to Satan. Consulting a medium is judged as being one (Deut. 18:1041) and an abomination. Death by stoning was God's sentence against all mediums (Lev. 20:21) under the Old Covenant.

Sorcery. Greek for *Pharmakêia* (pharmacy); magic, usually of the black variety; behaving as a witch, sorcerer, or sorceress; the use of power gained from the assistance or control of evil spirits, especially used for divining.

Subliminal Mind Control. Latin for "below the threshold;" to produce a sensation or a perception existing or functioning outside the area of conscious awareness; to divert the conscious in another direction by a power outside the mind in order to control its thought patterns. This method is not to be used by Christians in any pretext.

Tarok. An ancient card game popular in Central Europe and played with a pack containing 40, 52 (standard modern deck), or 56 cards equivalent to present day playing cards plus the 22 Tarot cards used as trump cards.

Tarot Cards. Fortune telling cards used by spiritualists made up of a deck of 22 pictorial cards, each card representing certain portents or "fortunes".

Telekinesis. The apparent production of motion in objects as by a spiritualistic medium having no contact or other physical means; spoon bending, and so on.

Teraphim. Household gods; portable idols representing a desired trait like safety or protection (Gen 31:19). May be life size and resemble humans (1 Sam 19:13-17). Teraphim were consulted, prayed to, or spoken to. Demons inhabit the object and enslave the owner by dependence on belief of the object. A modern-day teraphim may be a small statue of "St. Christopher", believed to keep people safe while in travel.

Unicorn. A mythological, one-horned animal generally depicted with the body and head of a horse, the hind legs of a stag, the tail of a lion, with a single horn in the middle of the forehead; from ancient Babylonian love feasts, it is believed to be tamed by virgins.

Unisex Bible. Promoted by the National Council of Churches, liberal churchmen, New Age leaders, and radical feminist groups demanding the words "Lord" and "King" be replaced by "Sovereign" with the word "God" to be changed to "Our Father and Mother"; "Son" (Jesus the Christ) was replaced with "child". The feminine words of "she" and "her" were to be used to refer to God. These changes (Rev 22 sow Scriptural confusion, discord, and heresy in the Church and correlates with the Mystery Religious system of Babylon.

Upside-Down Cross. Often used as a mockery of the cross of Christ; sometimes shown with the extensions broken and facing downward (classic peace symbol). Another cross Satanists incorporate is an upside-down question mark-cross, questioning the deity of Jesus; Hitler's swastikas are bent crosses.

Visualization. To conjure up an image of a spirit for contact, e.g., a relative, famous person, historical figure. **Guided visualization** is used in modern psychology and in cultic gatherings where a leader gifted in this technique helps set the scene by having the patient or group blank out their minds and imagine exactly what they are being told as he/she speaks. A candle flame, crystal, or mandala is often used to focus one's eyes on as they listen (blank mind). Demonic spirits may or may not appear.

Voodoo. Of African and Caribbean origin *tutelary deity, demon*. An occult religion derived from African ancestor worship practiced chiefly by Haitians, characterized by propitiatory rites and communication by trance with animistic deities; one who deals in spells and necromancy; a sorcerer's spell.

Voodoo Hex. A jinxed, hexed object that is used as a charm. It combines magic, spiritualism, death curses, dolls, and the use of fetishes to intimidate, harm or kill the person of its object.

Vulgarity. Coarse, obscene words from a crudeness of spirit expressed in unrefined language; cursing (to damn) by using sexual, racial, or religious terms as swearing in God's name; negative terms to call others a jerk, stupid, ugly, moron, idiot, scumbag, fatso, nigger, white trash, and so forth. Demons are fond of vulgarity.

Warlock. Leading witch who can break faith (troth) with the Devil; to lie. A man practicing the black arts; sorcerer, conjurer.

Weird. Of or relating to or caused by witchcraft or the supernatural: magical, odd, fantastic, eerie, creepy, uncanny; ill fortune, fate, destiny; of a soothsayer. "Weird Sisters" were the fates of mythology carried forth in British myth.

White Magic. So called good magic supposedly beneficial as practiced by witches. No curse (magic) can bless.

Witch. Female medium who practices magic although some witches prefer to practice either white or black magic. Biblically, spiritualists contact the dead that is forbidden (1 Sam 28:6-20).

Wolf Spirit. Those already in or wanting to come into the church who appear as believers but are predators who maim sheep, ravage the flock of God, and destroy the work of God in a fellowship (Mk 7:15, Jn 10:12); undermines the shepherd to split a church and steal sheep (Acts 20:28-31).

World's Wisdom Spirit. It is recognized in people who feel they have the answers for life apart from using God's heavenly wisdom. This wisdom comes from advice columnists, self-help pop psychology, the Internet, and life coach experts. It is earthly, nonspiritual, soulish and of the devil, and does not bring peace (James 3:13-18) because it deals with stirring up the soul and can't touch the spirit.

Yoga. A Hindu theistic philosophy teaching the suppression of all activity of body, mind, and will in order that the self may apprehend its distinction from them and attain liberation; a system of exercises for attaining bodily or mental control with direct association to the demonic entities that each exercise represents.

Yogi. An adherent who practices yoga; a markedly reflective or mystical person who leads others into error; spirit guides.

Zodiac. An imaginary belt in the heavens 18° degrees wide that encompasses the apparent paths of all the principal planets except Pluto and has the ecliptic as its central line. It is divided into 12 constellations or signs, each one representing astrological purposes to extend 30° of longitude. So-called signs of the heavens in the Zodiac are Aris (tam), Taurus (bull), Gemini (twins), Cancer (crab), Leo (lion), Virgo (virgin), Libra (balance), Scorpio (scorpion), Sagittarius (archer), Capricorn (goat), Aquarius (water bearer), Pisces (fishes). Spiritualists use these signs in astrology to project divination and influences supposedly from the stars and planets, onto human affairs and terrestrial events. This is inspired of Hell and a way for some to make money on unsuspecting and gullible fools. It is strictly forbidden to the Christian.

Zombie. Niger-Congo origin; akin to the Kongo Nzambi god. The voodoo snake deity; the supernatural power that according to voodoo belief, may enter to reanimate a dead body; a will-less and speechless human in the West Indies capable only of automatic movement who is held to have died and been reanimated (the walking dead). It is often believed to have been a person drugged by the shaman into a catalepsy for the hours of interment. It is part of the cult *Zombie.*

OCCULT HIGH DAYS

Satan continues his attempts to pervert and convert the natural and God-ordered creation to serve his ends. He is the supreme counterfeiter of all that is true, striving to deviously garner as much honor, fame, attention, and adulation as possible by competing for Jesus Christ in human minds.

For this reason, he has given his children (Satanists and pagans) their own days of celebration in pale image of Christian days of worship. There are four major holidays that come from religions in which the moon or a moon goddess is worshiped as a major deity. Halloween, Candlemas, Beltane, and Lammas fall in this witchery category.

It is imperative that Christians and their children should have nothing to do with these unholy and demonic high worship days. Christians are to avoid and expose all appearances of evil, keeping unspotted from the world system which is Satan's kingdom in man's hands.

The four lesser high days of Yule, Vernal Equinox, Saint John's Eve, and Michaelmas are based on the natural solstices and equinoxes and are used in witchcraft and by other pagan groups.

Time was created when God placed the sun and moon in the sky in Genesis 1. The times of the seasons themselves are not occult in nature. Solstices are God's natural events of longest and shortest days of the year. Equinoxes are God's days in which night and day are the same length.

1. **Halloween**. October 31. Halloween is the end and beginning of the witches' year. It marks the beginning of the death and destruction associated with winter. At this time, the power of the underworld is unleashed and spirits are supposedly freed to roam about the earth. Occultists consider Halloween the best time to contact spirits and perform child sacrifices. So, Christian, why would you want your children or grandchildren out roaming around on Halloween for a handful of candy? Hallowe'en is the evening before All Hallows' Day (November 1st), better known as Christian All Saints' Day in orthodox religions. Christians never participate in Halloween in any way. It is idolatry.

2. **February 2.** Historically, Satanists will celebrate the lengthening of days and the approach of Spring. In Christianity, it is observed as a church festival in commemoration of the presentation of Christ in the temple for the Hebrew purification of the Virgin Mary after childbirth.

3. **Beltane.** April 30 also known as Walpurgis Night. Beltane roughly coincides with the time for planting crops. The Celts and some others offered human sacrifices at this time. Walpurgis Night is an occultic event for witches who ride to at an appointed rendezvous, having a nightmarish quality. The closest Christian tradition (from A.D. 777), is in celebration of a saint whose feast day falls on May 1st.

4. **Lammas.** July 31 occurs about when fruits and vegetables are ripening and the harvest season is beginning. On the next day, August 1, Christians brought loaves of bread from the first ripe grain, offering it to the church for consecration.

5. **Yule.** December 22. The winter solstice, or shortest day of the year, marks a special event for celebration to Satanists. In Christianity, December 24th is the nativity (human birth) of Jesus Christ. December 25th is Christmas Day, set aside for the united celebration of Christ's birth with church services celebrated with the Eucharist.

6. **Vernal Equinox.** March 21. Day and night are the same length, with days getting longer.

7. **Saint Johns' Eve.** June 22 is Midsummer. This is the summer solstice, or longest day of the year.

8. **Michaelmas.** September 22. The autumnal equinox when day and night are the same length and the days will be getting shorter. In Christianity, the nearest feast day is September 29th as a celebration to remember Saint Michael the Archangel who traditionally fought on behalf of Israel, God's chosen people.

---

[1] www.Merriam-webster.com. Avatar derives from a Sanskrit word meaning 'descent'; first appearing in English literature in the late 18th century as reincarnation by a descent of a deity to the earth.

[2] www.Stewpeters.tv (Red Voice Media) on the Rumble channel, posted July 29, 2021 with whistle blower former Pfizer employee Karen Kingston, who confirms poison (graphene oxide) in Covid 'vaccine' (made by Moderna and Pfizer pharmaceuticals), is a deadly bio-terrorism medium able to form connectivity between humans and electronic means.

APPENDIX D - SPIRIT STRONGHOLDS

The Dark Crafts Revealed

To be free from the connection with the occult, every known practice you have participated in must be repented of by name out loud. Along with this, verbally renounce all involvement your relatives practiced that left you connected.

By forsaking each one out loud, you are giving testimony against Satan so he has no further legitimate right to attach himself. The following lists are not exhaustive. Should you know of other occult practices you participated in, or literature you have read, joined closed groups, cults, or anything at all dealing in these strongholds, add them for both repentance and renunciation.

Some things included here may be unfamiliar but go ahead and renounce them anyway as you read. Take your time with this list and be thorough. Studying these areas to understand them (research work) does not bring on a soul connection. The harm is done when a person takes these areas as truth instead of Jesus Christ Who is Truth. In other words, they have become a form of idolatry.

Begin by a sincere prayer for God's forgiveness for all involvement you have ever had with the occult. A simple form for a prayer of forgiveness may be repeated:

> "Father God, in the name of Jesus Christ, I renounce and reject all of Satan's connection to, and power over me. Specifically, I repent of, and expose these occult areas: _____."

False Cults and Religious Organizations

Bahai, Unitarianism, The Way, Unity, Christian Science, Tao, Shintoism, Jainism, and the Upanishad's religions as ancient forms of Buddhism (a spiritual tradition based on human potential rather than an external divinity); Hinduism with their gods named Brahma, Vishnu, and Shiva. Ham Krishna; Hinduism with its Kundalini spirit as a divine-feminine energy or shakti. Yoga with its controlled exorcise practices, mind control that may lead to psychotic episodes, Meta Yoga and Para Yoga. Tai Chi, Confucianism and all Eastern religions and mysticism are devil-based and attempt to bring together the human mind and body into alignment with (Kundalini) demonic spirits.

Islamism and Islamic occultic books and doctrines of the Koran including the interfering Arabic Djinn spirit (also known as Al-Jin, genii, ginn, jann, jinn, shayatin, or shaytan) who does supernatural bidding when conjured.

Zoroastrianism, Rosicrucian (The Georgia Guide Stones), Jehovah Witnesses, Mormonism, Theosophical Society, Islamism, Armstrong Scientology (L. Ron Hubbard), Santeria, Sun Myung Moon, Divine Life Mission, The Love Family; secret societies of any kind including Eastern Star, Order of Masons, and Freemasonry Cabbalists, Mystery Religion and teachings, Alchemists, Pyramidology, Worldwide Church of God, The Church Universal and Triumphant, The People's Temple, Alamo Christian Foundation, Unification Church, Spiritualists Church, and Church of Religious Science; Children of God, Human Potential Movement, Sufi Healing Order, Manifested Sons of God, Order of the Owl, Ouija Foundation, Church of Satan, Wicca, Eckankar, Spiritualism, Magic arts and Occultism, the National Council of Churches and the World Council of Churches; the Esoteric Brotherhoods of Mysticism.

Mysticism is a spiritual belief stating that a connection can be obtained with God or to the spirits, through thought and meditation.[1] Denounce occult mysticism in all forms.

Contrast this with Christian Meditation which is practiced when we concentrate to read or hear the Holy Bible and deeply think on God for the spiritual connection with Yahweh God (Father) and Jesus Christ through His Holy Spirit. Meditation is the Old Testament and New Testament way of hearing from and listening to God.

New Age[2] *beliefs* are common among both religious and nonreligious Americans. ... But many Christians also hold what are sometimes characterized as "New Age" beliefs – including belief in reincarnation, astrology, psychics, and the presence of spiritual energy in physical objects like mountains, minerals, or trees. Fundamental ideas for the New Age movement (1970s) are to unite a body of diverse believers with two simple ideas.

First, it predicted that a New Age of heightened spiritual consciousness and international peace would arrive and bring an end to racism, poverty, sickness, hunger, and war. This audience is exploited by New Age Deepak Chopra and his Meta-Human (mind-body healing platform), in New Age Meditation Movements and soothing, mind-emptying music such as performed by Yanni, Enya, Kilarō, Vangelis, George Winston and many others labeled as New Age meditative music.

Others include the Mystery Babylon Religious System, New Group of World Servers, Tam Center, Planet 150 Stewards, Warriors of the Rainbow, Children of the Dawn, The Lucis Trust, occult Holistic Medicine, the Urantia Church, Institute for the Study of Conscious Evolution; The Planetary Commission for Global Healing and the Quartus Foundation for Spiritual Research (both headed by John Randolph Price); Lord Maitreya (New World "Messiah"), Mark Age, The Hierarchical Board, University of Life, The Plan, and all others you can think of.

Occult Philosophies

Shadow of the Demon Lord Rule books, The Trove, Spells, Reddit (games)--all works by Robert J. Schwalb Entertainment. All Cornelius Agrippa's works: *Demon of Magic* (languages for demons and angels) *King of the Dead.* Works by occultist Dion Fortune (1890-1946)[3] and many other Satanically inspired philosophers of evil. Theosophy, Aldkado, Pyramidology, Mind Sciences, Subud, Urantia, Metaphysics, Moral Rearmament, Religious Science, Spiritualism, Scientology, Silva Mind Control, Holistic Movement, Mind Dynamics, Judo, Karate, Kung Fu, Taekwondo, Anhedonia, E.S.T. (Erhard Seminars), ECaP (B.S. Siegel), LifeSpring, Sufism, Positive Mental Attitude PMA, Transcendental Meditation-TM, Subliminal Mind Control as self-help "positive suggestion" recordings, even so-called "Christian" tapes are produced; Extrasensory Perception-ESP, and Catastrophism. There are too many to mention and take newer names.

Ancient mythological societies (Baal, Ashtoreth, Teraphim, Egyptian, Greek, Roman, African, European, in the Americas, and all Oriental and Eastern deities). Aquarian, Anthropophytes, Pantheism, Animism, Karma, Reincarnation, the I Am Self-consciousness selfism that invokes the "self-powers within" in order to become a god; occultism as a prosperity or poverty gospel; GALA-planet "mother-earth" as a greater goddess to serve, and "For the Greater Good" which sacrifices the individualism God gave each human to enjoy Him.

Witchcraft, Satanism, And Spiritualism

Free Masonry, Numerology, Astrology, throwing money into a wishing well, consulting or praying to the dead or for the dead; sorcery (witch crafting), Shape-shifting, Lucifer worship, satanic holidays including Halloween, Black Mass, making curses by using grimoires (books of spells); levitation, interpreting omens, and materialization. Playing the Ouija game to contact the dead by use of spirit guides, black magic, white magic, native American family spirit guides and ghosts. Divination, Voodoo, Evil Eye, Tarot and Tarok Cards, Angel Cards, palm and head readings, automatic writing, fortune telling, astral projection, reading and believing in horoscope readings from birth date; use of precognition and false gods as friends or spirit spouses. Some participate and believe they have *spirit spouses* whom they meet on a regular basis. That is a term to dress up demonic-allowed sexual molestation.

The Root Man; acting as a medium or sorcerer; watching, attending, or participating in seances; tea leaf-, sand-, sticks-, stones-readings; use of a pendulum, love charms, crystals, or magic potions. Chanting Eastern meditations, yoga, mantras, guided visualization, attempts to, or the practice of, mental telepathy; the use of a divining rod, Indian rain dances, handwriting analyzed for the future, reading fortune cookies, magical healing, playing occult games, been hypnotized, or have hypnotized others; use of psychedelic drugs.

Any in person or televised visits to false god temples of worship sites (even as a tourist) or other witch covens, websites, and spiritualists' haunts like the Georgia Guide Stones monument to seek wisdom. Entry into cult homes, places of business, and treks to Stonehenge, Tibetan monks, Indian mantras, and the like to "search for truth". Forbidden are Druidism, shamanism, demonic Hollywood horror and science fiction, snuff films and videos, occult movies like The Walking Dead, Zombie cults, Vampire flicks, and many others.

The use of parapsychology, paranormal or poltergeist phenomena, involvement with necromancy, necrophilia, masquerades, psychokinesis, telekinesis (spoon bending), psychometric, clairvoyance, Clairaudience, secular psychology, Discarnate Intelligence, or attended seminars and public tours by "ghost guides" so popular at Halloween.

Portals are opened with the possession of occult symbols, masks, decorations, good luck charms and numbers, and objects of religious icons. Veneration to religiously assigned saints, using a rabbit's foot for luck, reading Chinese Zodiac symbols, images of dragons, unicorns, peace symbols, upside-down crosses, Satanic triangles, and pentagrams; icons of the yin-yang, sun and moon symbols, shaggy goats, ALL prayer beads, worry stones, familiar objects, and New Age symbols will bring their attached demons.

Occult Entertainment

This is a dated list. Research the current releases, but there are thousands more for sure. Disney Entertainment is rife with the occult and perversion, including Barbie Movies and opening Queer (their word) summer camps for children. Jeanne Dixson's books and articles; Napoleon Hill's books, *Think and Grow Rich, Success Through a Positive Mental Attitude, The Magic Power of Belief; I Ching*; Edgar Cayce materials; All Sybil Leek or other witch's literature; *Power of Positive Thought; The Shack, Jonathan Livingston Seagull, Magic of Thinking Big, I Can*; all books by A. Ford, *Psycho-Cybernetics* (Maxwell Maltz), *Love, Medicine & Miracles* (B.S. Siegel, MD), *Getting Well Again* (Simonton); *Dream Power* (Faraday). All material by Anton LeVey including the *Satanic Bible* and Free Masonry encyclopedias and doctrine books.

Publishers. Anything at all published by these astrological and psychic printers: Doorways to The Mind, Fate, & Horoscope Guide, Inner Light-Enlightenment in the New Age, Metapsychology-The Journal of Discarnate Intelligence, New Realities, Prediction-The Magazine for Astrology, and the Occult, The Unexplained-The Unknown Visited and Explained. Books by: Alice Bailey, Barry McWaters, John Randolph Price. The following are occultic books, comic books, TV shows, cartoons, movies, and toys reaching our children as exposed by Texe Marrs[4] from his excellent book, *Dark Secrets of the New Age*.

Books. All Harry Potter books by J. K. Rowling, MACOS (Man: A Course of Study) teaches children genocide, homosexuality, euthanasia; *The Dragons of North Chittenden* by Susan Fromberg Schaeffer, *The Dragon ABC Hunt* for three- to six-year-olds by Loreen Leedy; *Secret Spells and Curious Charms* by Monika Beisner, *King Stork* by Howard Pyle, *I Will Call It Georgie's Blues* by Suzanne Newton, *Water Music* by

Sarah Sargent, *Nelson Malone Meets the Man from Mush-nut* by Louise Hawes, *Dragon Dance* by John Christopher, *Elliott and Wm* by Carolyn Meyer, *The Littlest Witch* by Brandi Dougherty (pre-kindergarten), and *Buckland's Complete Book of Witchcraft.*[5] There are thousands you can research.

Television. Remember, TV is just to "tell-a-vision". Whose visions are being told in these programs? Most are focused to disprove God. Be alert to occult programs like *Thundercats* (full of sorcery images and the magical eye of Thundra (the Third Eye of Hindus and All-seeing eye of the Egyptian-Babylonian sun god, Horus). The main character talks to his dead father's spirit and his magic sword levitates; Yoga positions, handling serpents to test God; anything with demon gods portrayed.

The Smurfs were early TV New Age doctrine generators written by scriptwriters, directors, and producers to desensitize audiences to New Age occult symbolism, levitation, magical chants, and Satanic pentagram symbols. Papa Smurf used enchantment to ward off evil. *Rainbow Brite* is another New Age representation of man's bridge to godhood. *She-Ra, Princess of Power* is a fantasized story of *Mystery Babylon, Mother of Harlots* incarnate. *He-Man, Master of the Universe* is a supernatural man-deity (super-man) with occultic symbols and practices as pyramid and crystal power, serpents, the Satanic ram's head, skull, witches' charms, potions, and spells. Be on the lookout for much more along these lines, in cartoon and violent video game formats.

Movies. Disney Studios, Barbie and Little Mermaid movies, Science Fiction and Horror flicks most often uses supernatural effects, death themes, and demonic graphics; "E.T." and any other Spielberg productions that are occultic; classics like *Close Encounters of the Third Kind, the Star Wars* series, Ninja black warrior movies, *Dune, a* young man's initiation into godhood; *Raiders of the Lost Ark* and *Temple of Doom* movies exposed children to evil powers and then taught them to enter their exercises. Don't miss the LGBTQ+ productions too numerous to mention, including drag queens reading misinformation literature to children about the beauties of being gay.

Toys. A partial list includes witching toys, Ouija Boards, Angel Cards, Tarot and Tarok cards, pendulum readers, worry dolls, and figurines of licensed cartoon occult characters such as *She-Ra, He-man, Masters of the Universe, Skeletor*[6] *Power Lords Shaya, Queen of Power* extraterrestrial stories), the Harry Potter series; *Raygoth, Gapplog,* and *Crystlar* which all introduce children to a strange world where magic reigns following a cosmic demon war. Classic toys include *Dungeons and Dragons, Dragon Raid* and all demonically graphed skateboards, power dolls, and a multitude of toys. Look for T-shirts and clothing with small Satanic pentagrams and triangles, hexagrams, upside-down crosses, swastikas, lightning bolts, Nazi crosses, occultic symbols, skull and crossbones, and gothic decorations with the number 666.

There are many, many more materials to clean out of your home and off your family phones and Internet favorites lists. You will know which books, articles, and literature you have read that are occultic in nature that glorify Evil. Ask the Lord to reveal them to you even if you cannot remember the names of publications, books, articles, web sites, television presentations, pornographic scenes, or slash movies. Include them in your confession as *all general occultic influences* which you have ever attended, read, or indulged.

As time goes on, you will become aware of the occult in all possible products, artwork, and educational goods. Be prepared to discover and renounce all occultic participation no matter how fleeting or you think is trivial as an on-going cleansing of your life by the Holy Spirit. Seek the Lord for new things to be revealed and repented of. Carefully see what you and your children bring home from school and college—especially textbooks. It is plain to see that deliverance is the constant application of the cross-life in self-denial as is reliance on the Lord to block demon-attracting portals.

This cleansing will not be easy and may not be a quick work in your life because the world we must live in, is growing darker and darker by the thievery of godliness deposited by generations before us beginning with those pilgrims to our New World.

At times, false gods brought to us by false teachers and hireling pastors and instructors are the most difficult to discern because they are in *our house and in our mind*. These are wolves in sheep's clothing. Ask the Holy Spirit to expose them and speak up against these demonic agendas.

Watch and pray against them. Be open to God's Spirit in all things.

[1] Google Nov. 11, 2004.

[2] Wikipedia, October 1, 2018.

[3] Non-believer in Christ is Theresa Bane, a self-proclaimed, professional vampirologist and mythologist specializing in cross-cultural vampire studies and demonology wrote, *Encyclopedia of Demons in World Religions and Cultures* (2012).

[4] All Texe Marrs' books are recommended for further enlightenment. These occultic and New Age materials are found in school and public libraries or may be a part of some school curricula.

[5] There are literally thousands of books, toys, video games, witchcraft, and wizard guides. Just search the web to see if you have interacted with any and renounce "all occult literature".

[6] Closely examine instructions that come with herbal extracts, tinctures, incense and remedies that promise to alter consciousness. Look at games to see occultic connections. *God Box* guarantees a direct line to their "god".

www.ingramcontent.com/pod-product-compliance
Lightning Source LLC
Chambersburg PA
CBHW072052020426
42334CB00017B/1486